BABYLONIAN LIFE
AND HISTORY

Portion of a sculptured stele of Ur-Nammu, a king of the third Dynasty.
From "Ur of the Chaldees," about 2300 BC.
From a photograph taken by C. L. Woolley, Esq., M.A., Director of the Excavations
at Ur for the Trustees of the British Museum and the Trustees of the Museum
of the University of Pennsylvania at Philadelphia, the discoverer of the monument.
(Reproduced by the courtesy of the Trustees.)

BABYLONIAN LIFE AND HISTORY

—◈—

SIR E. A. WALLIS BUDGE, KT.
M.A., LITT.D. (CAMBRIDGE), M.A., D.LITT.
(OXFORD), D.LITT. (DURHAM), F.S.A.

SOMETIME KEEPER OF EGYPTIAN AND ASSYRIAN
ANTIQUITIES, BRITISH MUSEUM. CORRESPONDING
MEMBER OF THE ACADEMY OF SCIENCES, LISBON

With ten plates and twenty-two illustrations in the text

INTRODUCTION BY MAGNUS WIDELL

BARNES & NOBLE
NEW YORK

THE BARNES & NOBLE
LIBRARY OF ESSENTIAL READING

Introduction and Suggested Reading
© 2005 by Barnes & Noble, Inc.

Originally published in 1883, revised in 1925

This 2005 edition published by Barnes & Noble, Inc.

Barnes & Noble, Inc.
122 Fifth Avenue
New York, NY 10011

ISBN-13: 978-0-7607-6549-4

Printed and bound in the United States of America

5 7 9 10 8 6

Contents

LIST OF PLATES AND ILLUSTRATIONS   VII

INTRODUCTION   XI

PREFACE   XX

I. THE COUNTRY OF BABYLONIA AND THE EUPHRATES AND TIGRIS   1

II. BABYLONIAN CHRONOLOGY AND HISTORY   11

III. THE CITY OF BABYLON   49

IV. THE BABYLONIAN STORY OF THE CREATION   63

V. THE BABYLONIAN STORY OF THE FLOOD AS TOLD IN THE GILGAMISH EPIC   70

VI. BABYLONIAN RELIGIOUS BELIEFS   80

VII. THE CODE OF LAWS OF KHAMMURABI   96

VIII. BABYLONIAN RELIGIOUS AND MAGICAL LITERATURE, LEGENDS, ETC.   105

IX. THE KING OF BABYLONIA AND HIS PEOPLE AND THEIR LIVES   128

X. BABYLONIAN WRITING AND LEARNING   147

XI. BRITISH MUSEUM EXCAVATIONS IN BABYLONIA BY
    R. C. THOMPSON, H. R. HALL, AND C. L. WOOLLEY   175

XII. THE EXCAVATIONS AT KISH, NEAR BABYLON   203

APPENDIX   211

ENDNOTES   221

INDEX   225

SUGGESTED READING   245

LIST OF PLATES AND ILLUSTRATIONS

PLATES

PORTION OF THE GREAT STELE OF UR-NAMMU,
KING OF UR ABOUT 2300 BC   FRONTISPIECE

LIST OF ELEVEN TEMPLE ESTATES COMPILED
FOR BURSIN, KING OF UR ABOUT 2230 BC   25

THE SUN-GOD TABLET MADE FOR
NABÛ-APALIDDINA, KING OF BABYLON
ABOUT 870 BC   37

BRICK STAMPED WITH THE NAME AND
TITLES OF NEBUCHADNEZZAR II, KING
OF BABYLON, 604–561 BC   39

BAKED CLAY CYLINDER OF NABONIDUS,
KING OF BABYLON 555–538 BC,
MENTIONING NARAM-SIN   46

PORTION OF A BAKED CLAY TABLET
INSCRIBED WITH A VERSION OF THE LEGEND
OF THE FIGHT BETWEEN MARDUK AND
TIÂMAT (BÉL AND THE DRAGON)   68

PORTION OF A BAKED CLAY TABLET INSCRIBED
WITH A VERSION OF THE BABYLONIAN ACCOUNT
OF THE DELUGE   75

CLAY MODEL OF A SHEEP'S LIVER, INSCRIBED
WITH OMENS   120

BOUNDARY STONE INSCRIBED WITH THE CHARTER
OF PRIVILEGES GRANTED TO RITTI MARDUK BY
NEBUCHADNEZZAR I ABOUT 1140 BC   127

BABYLONIAN SYLLABARY WRITTEN 455 BC   161

ILLUSTRATIONS IN THE TEXT

MAP SHOWING THE POSITIONS OF THE CHIEF
CITY-STATES IN LOWER MESOPOTAMIA   8

INSCRIPTION IN "LINE" BABYLONIAN ON A STONE
GATE-SOCKET OF ENANNADU, PATESI OF LAGASH
ABOUT 3000 BC   14

INSCRIPTION ON A MACE-HEAD DEDICATED TO
THE SUN-GOD OF SIPPAR BY SARGON, KING OF
AGADE ABOUT 2700 BC   17

INSCRIPTION ON A MACE-HEAD OF MANISHTUSU,
KING OF KISH ABOUT 2572 BC   19

INSCRIPTION ON A CYLINDER-SEAL CONTAINING AN
ADDRESS TO UR-NAMMU, KING OF UR ABOUT
2300 BC, BY KHASHKHAMER, VICEROY OF
THE CITY OF ISHKUM-SIN   22

INSCRIPTION ON A CYLINDER-SEAL CONTAINING A
PRAYER TO THE GOD SHIDLAM-TA-UDDUA BY
KILULLA-GUZALAL FOR THE LIFE OF DUNGI (SHULGI),
KING OF UR 2276 BC   24

PORTION OF AN INSCRIPTION OF KHAMMURABI,
KING OF BABYLON 1955–1913 BC, RECORDING
THE BUILDING OF A TEMPLE TO ISHTAR IN THE
CITY OF KHALLAB   26

LETTER FROM KHAMMURABI TO SIN-IDINNAM   29

MAP OF THE RUINS OF BABYLON   50

THE DRAGON OF BABYLON   51

EXTRACT FROM THE INTRODUCTION TO KHAMMURABI'S
CODE OF LAWS   98

PORTION OF TEXT WRITTEN IN "LINE" BABYLONIAN   151

EXTRACT FROM A SIGN-LIST SHOWING THE PICTORIAL
ORIGINALS OF CERTAIN CUNEIFORM CHARACTERS   152

INSCRIPTION FROM A BRICK OF UR-NAMMU   153

INSCRIPTION FROM A BRICK OF UR-NAMMU   154

INSCRIPTION FROM A BRICK OF ENANNADUMA   155

BABYLONIAN MAP OF THE WORLD, MADE TO SHOW
THE COUNTRIES IN WHICH SARGON OF AGADE
CARRIED ON WARS   171

INSCRIPTION FROM A BRICK OF NUR-IMMER,
KING OF LARSA ABOUT 2027 BC   178

THE BULL OF HEAVEN   184

INSCRIPTION OF A-AN-NI-PAD-DA, KING OF UR   185

SCENES FROM THE "MILKING PANEL" AT
TALL AL-'UBÊD   190–191

THE CULTIVATION OF WHEAT IN THE TUAT   199

INTRODUCTION

IN E. A. WALLIS BUDGE'S CLASSIC WORK, *BABYLONIAN LIFE AND HISTORY*, published in 1925, the reader will find everything from Babylonian vampires to the practice of "baby farming" in Mesopotamia, the ancient land between the two rivers Euphrates and Tigris. Budge brings to his readers the most famous Mesopotamian myths and legends, such as mankind's first recorded story of the Creation, the Babylonian story of the Great Flood, and the adventures of the world's first epic hero, Gilgamesh. *Babylonian Life and History* provides an introduction to the religious, political, and intellectual foundations of ancient Babylonia. It brings to life the sometimes-grisly laws of the Old-Babylonian king Hammurabi, and we learn of even older laws, reforms, and ancient "tax cuts" by the Sumerian governor Urukagina. The book also includes a survey of some of the most important contemporary excavations of Mesopotamia conducted primarily by the British Museum. An earlier edition of the book was originally published in 1884 as part of the *By-Paths of Bible Knowledge* series for the Religious Tract Society. The present edition represents a complete revision and expansion of the earlier text, or, as Budge himself writes in his preface to this edition from 1925, "the [original] book must be rewritten and, of course, enlarged." In his very direct literary style, Budge begins with an introduction to the land of the two rivers, the Tigris and the Euphrates; its geographical borders;

and the environmental and climatic conditions of the region. As an explorer and adventurer, Budge spent considerable time in Mesopotamia, and his first-hand observations in the late nineteenth century of the life and the environment of the region offer a unique view of traditional societies therein. The book continues as a chronological survey of many of the most important and formative historical events of the ancient Near East, from the beginning of written history in the fourth millennium BC until Mesopotamia became part of the Persian Empire in 539 BC. This survey is rounded off by a detailed description of the city of Babylon—as it was known in 1925—and its many well-known monuments, including the great Ziggurat, the Ishtar Gate, and the so-called Hanging Gardens. In addition to a review of the long history of the city, we learn, in particular, about the extensive and extremely well-conducted German excavations of the site directed by Robert Koldewey from 1899 to 1912. Almost every chapter of *Babylonian Life and History* is full of longer excerpts of ancient texts, in English translations, and the author certainly makes use of his extremely wide field of interests and knowledge in this account of the history, religion, archaeology, and literature of ancient Babylonia. Typically, Budge endeavors to uphold his arguments and views by drawing from a number of diverse sources, including data from archaeological excavations, a multitude of historical or ancient texts, as well as his own personal observations of contemporary practices in the Middle East and the eastern Mediterranean. Budge makes frequent use of the cuneiform records in his book, and the diversity of the primary textual documentation on which Budge relies in *Babylonian Life and History* is quite remarkable. In addition to ample references to preserved cuneiform texts, the book incorporates into its discussions everything from a particular section in the Old Testament or a specific sura in the Koran, to a Syriac manuscript by one of the Patriarchs of the first millennium AD or an ancient Egyptian papyrus kept in some basement of the British Museum.

Ernest Alfred Thompson Wallis Budge was born in London on July 27, 1857. His fascination with the history and languages of Egypt and the Near East led him to Cambridge University, where he studied several ancient languages, including Egyptian hieroglyphics, Coptic Hebrew, Syriac, and Ethiopic. Budge was closely associated with the British Museum from the very beginning of his scholarly career, and he acted as the museum's Keeper of the Department of Egyptian and Assyrian Antiquities for forty years, between 1884 and 1924. Budge directed several archaeological expeditions in Egypt, the Sudan, and the Near East for the British Museum. He also published a truly spectacular number of scholarly and semi-scholarly books and articles of somewhat mixed quality. Nonetheless, in his own time, Budge's campaigns and publications received immense popular attention, and in 1920, he received a knighthood for his significant and long-lasting services to the British Museum. In memory of his wife, who died two years after his retirement in October of 1926, Budge founded two studentships in Egyptology at Christ's College, Cambridge, and University College, Oxford. He died November 23, 1934, in London at the age of seventy-seven and was buried in Nunhead Cemetery in south London, bequeathing his private library to Christ's College, Cambridge.

While Budge was certainly right in his high praise of Koldewey's exemplary excavations and subsequent publications of the city of Babylon, some readers of *Babylonian Life and History* may perhaps find Budge's less flattering picture of the earlier British excavations of the site conducted by Sir Henry Austen Layard in 1850 and, in particular, those of Hormuzd Rassam from 1878 to 1880, rather surprising. Budge's negative account of these earlier attempts to excavate Babylon is easier to understand if one takes into account Rassam's high-profiled and, certainly for the British Museum, scandalous lawsuit against Budge for slander, which took place in London in 1893. Rassam, who claimed £1,000 in damages, obtained a verdict for only fifty pounds. Nevertheless, it is hardly an exaggeration to say that

Budge's relation with his Iraqi colleague and also, at least to some extent, with the famous explorer, archaeologist, and diplomat Henry Layard, who died the year after the lawsuit and on whose recommendation Rassam had been originally appointed, were everything but jovial and cheerful. As we can see in his sometimes rather litigious book *The Rise & Progress of Assyriology* (1925a), the negative outcome of this lawsuit by no means prevented Budge from continuing his quite malicious accusations of Rassam in public.

No one can deny that Budge was and continues to be highly controversial, as a scholar and publicist, as a public figure, and certainly as a private individual. Already as a young boy, he was fascinated with the Orient, and he studied, rather successfully, it seems, both Hebrew and Syriac while he was still in school, partly under the guidance of the Orientalist Charles Seager. During these early years, he was a frequent visitor of the British Museum, where he first met the prominent scholars Samuel Birch and George Smith; and he became actively engaged in the activities of the museum in 1878, at the mere age of twenty-one. The same year his first articles, dealing with the royal inscription of Sennacherib (1878a) and Assyrian incantations to fire and water (1878b), appeared in print in the Society of Biblical Archaeology's annual publication *Records of the Past;* this was also the year when young Budge enrolled as a student at Cambridge, where he would be studying in Christ's College. His first books in Assyriology were soon to follow, with *Assyrian Texts, being extracts from the annals of Shalmaneser II., Sennacherib, and Assur-bani-pal* in 1880 and *The History of Esarhaddon (son of Sennacherib) King of Assyria, BC 681–668* the year after. In addition to Hebrew and Syriac, he also studied Egyptian hieroglyphs, Coptic, and Ethiopic with great success at Cambridge. In 1882, he won the Tyrwhitt Hebrew Scholarship, and shortly afterwards he accepted a position as an Assistant to the Department of Egyptian and Assyrian Antiquities in the British Museum.

In 1884, at the early age of 36, Budge was appointed to the prestigious post of Keeper of Department of Egyptian and Assyrian Antiquities, and served in that position until his retirement in 1924. In this capacity, Budge was involved in numerous archaeological expeditions and he traveled extensively in the Orient in pursuit of all kinds of antiquities. He excavated at numerous well-known sites in Egypt, including Aswan, Gebel Barkal, the Island of Meroe, and Semna, as well as at other sites in Nubia and the Sudan. In Mesopotamia he directed, among others, the excavations in Kouyunjik in 1888–89 and in Dêr in 1890. These archaeological campaigns and explorations were considered, at least in those days, extremely successful, because Budge was able to enrich the British Museum collections with some of its most precious treasures. Budge's acquisitions on behalf of the British Museum included countless large Egyptian statues and many Mesopotamian antiquities. He also brought back several thousands of cuneiform tablets, including the lion's share of the museum's important Tell al-Amarna tablets, which document the prolific international diplomacy and gift exchange among rulers of Egypt and the Near East in the Late Bronze Age (see Bezold and Budge, 1892). In addition, he secured a large number of Coptic, Greek, Arabic, Syriac, Ethiopian, and Egyptian manuscripts which constitute some of the museum's most significant collections to this day.

Despite Budge's success in acquiring antiquities, his confrontational personality did not necessarily always work to his favor back in London. Nonetheless, he certainly knew how to work his way around in the Orient, a fact that should not only be ascribed to his linguistic abilities. The popular and successful publications, campaigns, and adventures of Budge did not go unnoticed: In addition to three doctorates from the universities of Cambridge, Oxford, and Durham, Budge received a medal of honor for his services in the Dongola (Sudan), and he also received the Order of the Star of Ethiopia, which the Ethiopian Emperor Menelik II gave him on account of his *Ethiopic History of Alexander the Great*. Finally, in 1920 Budge was knighted for his considerable services to the country and to the British Museum.

In addition to a large number of scholarly articles published, most importantly in the *Transactions* (*TSBA*) and the *Proceedings* (*PSBA*) of the London-based *Society of Biblical Archaeology*, Budge wrote over one hundred forty books in an extremely wide field of study, including the languages, history, and archaeology of northern Africa and the Near East. This enormous and astonishing level of productivity remains unprecedented in any of the various fields in which Budge was working and publishing. His greatest scholarly contributions were, arguably, in the fields of Ethiopian studies and, in particular, in the field of Egyptology. In Egyptology, Budge wrote the first books oriented toward students of hieroglyphics. These books consisted of the actual hieoroglyphs, the translated texts, and a complete dictionary of the hieroglyphs. According to the most recent *Who Was Who in Egyptology* (Dawson *et al.* 1995: 72), in which Budge has by far the longest list of publications, Budge's largest work was his *An Egyptian Hieroglyphic Dictionary* (1920a). However, Budge is probably best known among the more general readership for his analysis of Egyptian religious practices and rituals in *Osiris and the Egyptian Resurrection* (1911) and in *The Mummy: A Handbook of Egyptian Funerary Archaeology* (1925b), as well as for his translation of *The Egyptian Book of The Dead* (1913), also known as *The Papyrus of Ani*. Budge's longest lasting written legacy to the field of Assyriology, of which *Babylonian Life and History* is part, is represented by the numerous official publications and text editions of the British Museum that were issued under his direction. He realized the extreme importance of making unpublished cuneiform tablets available to the scholarly community, and from 1896 until his retirement in 1924, Budge was actively involved in the publications of no less than thirty-seven volumes of the important British Museum series *Texts from Babylonian Tablets*.

The scholarly communities in the various fields in which Budge published so prolifically have generally not been kind in their assessments of the usefulness and quality of his many publications. Budge's books have often been described as unreliable, and sometimes even misleading, and some passages in *Babylonian Life and History* should therefore be read with caution. The early chronology used by Budge, especially for the third and early second millennium BC, as well as many of his readings of cuneiform signs (and, by extension, therefore also of proper names), are outdated and can be studied better from more recent discourses of the history and literature of the ancient Near East. Nevertheless, while obviously somewhat dated, *Babylonian Life and History*, like many of Budge's other works, has an important place in the development of ancient Near Eastern studies, and readers should keep its historical context in mind. First of all, Budge was living and publishing in an era and atmosphere in which the Near East and Egypt were considered to be little more than exotic (and often primitive) countries full of wondrous objets d'art ready to be shipped to the next major museum in Europe or the United States. All records from these early days of Assyriology and Egyptology reflect this attitude, at least to some degree, and Budge's publications are no exception. While this attitude certainly has changed for the better in more recent decades, this legacy of early western scholarship cannot, and should not, be forgotten or denied; many of the major collections in the West were formed under circumstances that would be considered unethical today. Secondly, the care—or, rather, the lack of it—that Budge took in the details of his books has been a subject of some controversy. Between 1878 and his death in 1934, Budge produced more than one hundred forty books, often in several volumes. With an average production rate of roughly three books per year, Budge was not ready to linger over minor details for too long, and some data in his books are undeniably inaccurate by modern standards. Nonetheless,

Budge's books contain an abundance of accurate and important information that is of much interest, and the real challenge for many non-specialist readers of Budge's works is to separate between the facts and the fiction.

While the criticism of Budge's scholarship certainly is valid in some cases, no one can deny that without the phenomenal energy and devotion of Budge, a large number of primary sources, especially those in Ethiopic, Egyptian, and Akkadian, would not have been made available to the scholarly world. Moreover, it is important to remember that Budge received much of his recognition, not because of his great contributions to the field of Egyptian grammar (which is well-known for having been antiquated already in those days), or for the punctilious accuracy of any of his Babylonian translations, but rather for having invoked the imagination and inspired and amused countless people all over the world through his more popular books. His general works, such as *Babylonian Life and History* and *A History of Egypt from the End of the Neolithic Period to the Death of Cleopatra VII, BC 30* from 1902, in eight volumes, have been, and are, of value to many students and interested laymen and, far more importantly, they have helped to arouse much popular interest to these fields. In addition to this, Budge's numerous guides and introductions to the collections of the British Museum undoubtedly served as considerable enjoyment and gratification to uncountable visitors of the Museum. It is in this light that Budge's contribution to the fields of Egyptology and Assyriology should be considered, not in the unforgiving light of meticulous scholarship. E. A. Wallis Budge was a bold explorer, a cantankerous individual, and a creative author who quite literally devoted his life to writing an absolutely enormous number of scholarly and popular works. For specialist and lay readers alike, *Babylonian Life and History,* like many of his works, remains an inspirational classic that brings the history, archaeology, and languages of ancient Mesopotamia to life.

Magnus Widell studied Assyriology, Classics, and Egyptology at Uppsala University in Sweden from 1991 to 1998. After he received his M.A. degree in Assyriology in 1998, he continued his doctoral studies at the Institute for the History of Ancient Civilizations in Changchun, China, where he received his doctoral degree in Assyriology in 2001. Currently, he is a Postdoctoral Research Associate in the Oriental Institute at the University of Chicago.

PREFACE

In 1883, at the request of the late Rev. Richard Lovett, M.A., General Editor of the publications of the Religious Tract Society, I wrote for their Series of *By-Paths of Bible Knowledge* a little book entitled *Babylonian Life and History*. This youthful production was stereotyped and reprinted several times, but during the Great War the lead stereotype plates were requisitioned by the Government for military purposes and melted down, and the book went rapidly out of print. Early this year the Rev. Dr. C. H. Irwin, the present General Editor, told me that his Society wished to keep the book on their List of Publications, and suggested that it should be revised before they reprinted it. It was quite clear that a book written forty-two years ago would need a considerable amount of revision, especially when the subject treated of in it was Babylonian History. The excavations which have been made by the English, French, Americans and Germans in Babylonia, Assyria and Persia during the last forty years, have yielded up such a mass of new information that Assyriologists have been obliged to rewrite the ancient history of those countries. And philologists in England, Europe and America have been as diligent as the excavator, with the result that a great mass of Sumerian, Anzanite, Babylonian and Assyrian texts have been published, many of them with translations and luminous commentaries. Moreover, Assyrian dictionaries have been compiled, Assyrian and Sumerian Grammars have been written, and the principal features of the great ancient civilizations of Western Asia have been described with a fullness and with a degree of accuracy that the greatest Assyriologists of the "eighties" never imagined to be possible.

In accordance with Dr. Irwin's suggestion for revision I went through my *Babylonian Life and History*, and soon came to the conclusion that no revision would bring the book up to date, or even make a passable job of it. I therefore reported to him that the book must be rewritten and, of course, enlarged. To this he agreed, and the present volume is the result. The facts stated herein are drawn from the works of the best Assyriologists, to whom I beg to express my obligations. The reader who wishes to continue the study of Assyriology will find the general works mentioned in the Bibliography of great assistance. For monographs and papers on special branches of Assyriology he must consult the excellent classified Bibliographies given in the volumes of *The Cambridge Ancient History*, Cambridge, 1923 f.

A popular work of this kind is no place for the discussion of matters which are still the subjects of animated disputes between Assyriologists and theologians. But a reference must here be permitted to the attempts that have been made by the late Prof. F. Delitzsch and his followers to belittle the Religion and Literature of the Hebrews and to prove that they were derived from the Babylonians. It is admitted by all that the Hebrews, together with other Semitic peoples, inherited some of their legends, folk-lore, mythology, customs, laws, etc., from the Babylonians. But he who seeks to find in the Babylonian religious texts any expression of the conception of God Almighty as the great, unchanging, just and eternal God, or as the loving, merciful Father; or any expression of the consciousness of sin, coupled with repentance, or of an intimate personal relationship to God, will seek in vain. The Hebrew's sublime conception of

Yahweh was wholly different from the Babylonian's conception of Bêl-Marduk, or Shamash, or Ashur, and the difference was fundamental. Yahweh was One (Deut. vi, 4); to the Hebrew there was no other; Bêl-Marduk, or Shamash, or Ashur, was only "Lord of the Gods," just as in Egypt Rā or Amen was "King of the gods." The Babylonians may have developed a monotheism comparable to that of the Hebrews, but there is no evidence that they did, and there is no expression of it in their religious texts. And the Accounts of the Creation given in Genesis and the Story of the Flood are not derived from any Babylonian Versions of them known to us. There are many points of resemblance between the cuneiform and the Hebrew Versions, and these often illustrate each other, but the fundamental conceptions are essentially different. The Babylonian God was a development from devils and horrible monsters of foul form, but the God of the Hebrews was a Being who existed in and from the beginning, Almighty and Alone, and the devils of chaos and evil were from the beginning His servants.

A perusal of the Two Lectures by Delitzsch, entitled *Babel und Bibel,* has convinced me that the object of them was to belittle the Hebrew Scriptures, and to exalt the writings of the Babylonians, and to show that, after all, the Prophets of Israel and the Babylonian scribes belonged to the same class of religious teachers, and that the subject matter taught by both was one and the same in kind. Delitzsch's knowledge of comparative Semitic philology was, as was pointed out many years ago, never very profound, and many of the views which he put forward in his *Hebrew Language viewed in the Light of Assyrian Research,* London, 1883, were shown to be incorrect. The Lectures alarmed many both in Germany and in other countries, because it was felt that their general effect would be to undermine the beliefs of those who were unable to verify or control Delitzsch's statements and deductions. The truth is that he could not appreciate or realize the difference between the Religion of Israel and the half-magic, half-religious beliefs of the Babylonians. To him the

Hebrew Scriptures would always remain a monument of a great religious and historical process, whether they were shown to be inspired or not, and nothing more. He himself wrote: "As for myself, I live in the belief that the old Hebrew Scriptures, even though they lose their character as writings 'revealed' or pervaded by a 'spirit of revelation,' will still always maintain their exalted importance, more particularly as an unparalleled monument of a great religious and historical process which extends to our own time."[1] Had Delitzsch known more of Hebrew and Babylonian Literature he would never have written thus.

And we may note here in passing the attempt that has been made in recent years to compare the Myth of Bêl-Marduk with the New Testament account of Christ's death and descent into hell (1 Peter iii, 19). The Babylonian texts connected with the rites that were performed at Babylon and in the city of Ashur during the New Year Festival show that Bêl-Marduk, in spite of his exalted position as "lord of the gods," fell from his high estate and became a prisoner in hell. He was confined in a place where there was neither sun nor light, and twin watchmen were stationed outside it to keep guard over him. His son Nebo was summoned from Borsippa to help him, but was powerless to do so. His wife Beltis went down into hell to try to effect her lord's release, but failed in her attempt. Bêl-Marduk's fall seems to have been brought about by the god Zu, who stole from him the "Tablet of Destinies," by means of which he had ruled heaven and earth. Bêl-Marduk remained in hell until the god Enurta, who had been sent to capture Zu by the god Anshar, returned with the "Tablet of Destinies." Thereupon the gods broke through the door of the prison in which Bêl-Marduk was confined, and brought him out and, presumably, restored to him the Tablet and his former position. We may assume also that the disorder or anarchy which had broken out in Babylon during Bêl-Marduk's absence in hell came to an end as soon as he returned to life and power. According to Zimmern's rendering of the texts,[2]

Bêl-Marduk was made a prisoner, and tried in the judgment hall of the "Mountain" (i.e., Underworld), and beaten, and thrust into prison, whilst of the two evil-doers arrested with him one was killed and the other released. Fighting broke out in Babylon straightway. Bêl-Marduk's apparel was taken from him, his heart's blood poured out through a wound which was inflicted upon him, he was thrust into the darkness of the Underworld, watchers were set over the place where he was, and a goddess went down to seek him, uttering cries of "O my brother! O my brother!" At length Bêl-Marduk is brought back to life, and he issues from the Underworld as the Sun-god of the Spring. The great New Year Festival was celebrated at Babylon in the month of Nisan, and this Spring Festival commemorated the victory of Bêl-Marduk over the powers of darkness, and the death and resurrection of the Sun-god.

Now the value of Zimmern's work on the texts describing the celebration of the New Year Festival at Babylon is very great, but his comparison of the New Testament account of the death and resurrection of the Lord Christ with the Myth of Bêl-Marduk is both unfortunate and unscientific. Apart from the fact that Bêl-Marduk was a mythical being, and Christ a historical Person, it is the narrative of the death and resurrection of Osiris that must be compared with the Myth of Bêl-Marduk, and not the New Testament account of Christ. The great fight between Marduk and Tiâmat finds its Egyptian equivalent in the fight between Râ, the Sun-god and Āpep, the personification of Evil, or that between Osiris and Set, the Archenemy of the gods. Set plotted the overthrow of Osiris, seized him and maltreated him, stripped him naked, caused him to be condemned to death in his Council of Devils, stabbed him and killed him, and thrust his dead body into the dark, airless hell of the damned. Isis, the divine sister and wife of Osiris, in the form of a bird, sought her lord in the Underworld, and tried to lighten his darkness by the sheen of her feathers, and to give him air by the beating of her wings, and the whole time she was "uttering wailings

of distress for her brother."[3] At length the gods, seeing the distur-
bances that had broken out upon earth because of the murder of
Osiris, took action. Working under the instructions of Thoth, the
equivalent of the Babylonian Nabû, who also supplied the necessary *heka*, or "words of power," Isis and Horus, the son of Osiris,
and Anubis restored Osiris to life. The gods in full Council investi-
gated the charges that Set had brought against him, and their
great Advocate Thoth pronounced their verdict, viz., that Osiris
was the Truth-speaker and Set the Liar. They forthwith decreed
that Osiris was to reign as god and Judge of the dead in the kingdom which they had prepared for him, and that his son, begotten
after his death, was to reign on this earth in his stead. During the
celebration of the New Year Festival at Babylon, a sort of miracle
play was performed in which the principal incidents in the death
(or murder) and resurrection of Bêl-Marduk were acted. And
during the great Osiris Festival, which was celebrated annually at
Abydos and other places in Egypt, the suffering, murder and resurrection of Osiris were also acted in a miracle play. The Sun-god of
Spring succeeded his father, Bêl-Marduk, and Horus, the Sun-god
of Spring, also succeeded his father, Osiris, and in due course
fought against Set and was slain by him. Thus the Myth of Bêl-
Marduk and the Myth of Osiris are, *mutatis mutandis,* identical, and
have nothing whatever to do with the New Testament account of
Christ. The substantial identity of the two Myths is proved by their
contents, but there is evidence, of a philological character, which
suggests that Bêl-Marduk and Osiris are one and the same god.
Sidney Smith has shown (*Journal of Egyptian Archaeology,* vol. viii,
pp. 41-44) that Bêl-Marduk of Babylon and Ashur, the great god of
Assyria, who also died and rose from the dead, were one and the
same god, and he thinks the "Asari," an epithet of Bêl-Marduk (as
we know from the tablet giving the Fifty Names of that god), may
be the name from which both the name "Ashur" and the name
"Osiris" are derived. If this be so it is possible, as Smith suggests,

that the Myth of Bêl-Marduk and Ashur and the Myth of Osiris in Egypt had a common origin, both being derived from a Myth which first grew up in Northern Syria, perhaps in the third or fourth millennium BC.

The account of the important excavations in Babylonia given in chapter 11 is based upon the published articles by the excavators in the *Journals* of various learned Societies, and on Mr. Woolley's Report on Ur of the Chaldees for 1924-5, which, by the courtesy of the Trustees of the Joint Expedition of the British Museum and the Museum at Philadelphia, I was permitted to see in manuscript. I am indebted to Professor S. Langdon for the main facts about his excavations at Kish. He allowed me to read the proof sheets of his recently published work on Kish, and from these chapter 12 has been compiled. The importance of the results already obtained justifies the fervent hope that means will be forthcoming to permit the completion of the excavations of the Temenos at Ur of the Chaldees, where the Library still remains undiscovered, and of the other mounds at Kish.

The plates in this book are printed from "electros" which the Trustees of the British Museum kindly allowed to be made from the blocks used for the plates of the official *Guide to the Babylonian and Assyrian Antiquities*, 3rd edition, London, 1922. The "line" illustrations are taken chiefly from that great treasure house, "Cuneiform Texts," published by the British Museum, and Koldewey's invaluable work *Das wieder erstehende Babylon*, Leipzig, 1913, and *The Museum Journal*, published by the University Museum at Philadelphia.

E. A. WALLIS BUDGE
48 Bloomsbury Street,
Bedford Square, W.C.I.

CHAPTER ONE

THE COUNTRY OF BABYLONIA AND THE EUPHRATES AND TIGRIS

THE LAND LYING BETWEEN THE RIVER TIGRIS AND THE RIVER Euphrates is one vast plain, which extends from the mountains of Kurdistan to the Persian Gulf, and has an area of many hundreds of thousands of square miles. The geological formation of the upper, or northern, part of this plain is entirely different from that of the lower, or southern, part. The northern part is higher than the southern, and it in many respects closely resembles the "great and terrible" Syrian Desert which lies to the west of the Euphrates; the southern part consists of alluvium which has been deposited by the Tigris and Euphrates and their branches during countless centuries. Parts of the northern portion of the plain are covered with a layer of desiccated and decayed stones, and after the heavy spring rains a considerable amount of vegetation springs up which affords pasture for sheep and camels. But as there never has existed any means of irrigating it systematically, it has always been impossible to grow crops on any portion of this desert land. On the other hand, the soil of the southern or lower part of the plain being alluvial is extremely fertile, and as it is watered by the Tigris and Euphrates, and by the canals that "take off" from these rivers, its inhabitants from time immemorial have raised crops of grain there, and been able to cultivate the palm with great success, and grow many other kinds of fruit trees. The vast plain between the Tigris and Euphrates runs roughly in a south-easterly direction, and classical writers called its northern part Mesopotamia, and its lower part Babylonia.

Where the northern part ended in the south, or the southern part began in the north, is not known, but it is tolerably certain that, speaking quite generally, the northern boundary of the southern part must have been near the place where the alluvial soil either came to an end or was not deep enough to grow crops upon. The classical geographer Ptolemy seems to have placed the northern border of Babylonia at the Median Wall (mentioned by Xenophon, *Anabasis* ii, 4, 12), which was 100 feet high, 20 feet broad, and 20 parasangs long. Strabo refers to the "massive wall of Semiramis," which reached from the Tigris a little above Sittace to some point near the Euphrates; it is almost certain that he means the Median Wall (*see* Felix Jones, *Memoirs,* pages 226, 263). Arab geographers are not agreed as to where Mesopotamia and Assyria (which they call Al-Jazîrah) ended and Babylonia (which they call Al-'Irâk) began; some say that the boundary line ran from Takrît on the Tigris southwards to Hît on the Euphrates, and others from Takrît to Anbar. The Bible refers to Babylonia, in whole or in part, in the words Land of the Chaldeans (Isai. xxxiii. 13) and Land of Shinar (Gen. x. 10). The plain between the Tigris and Euphrates has much in common with Egypt, the northern part resembling Egypt proper, and the lower part the Delta; the plain was formed by the deposit of the two great rivers, and Egypt and its Delta by the Nile. As the life of Egypt has always depended, and always will depend, on the Nile, so the peoples who have successively inhabited Babylonia have owed their well-being and development entirely to the two rivers, and especially to the Euphrates.

The earliest dwellers in Babylonia known to us, the Sumerians, called the Euphrates BURANUN, 𒀀 𒈗 𒄑 or 𒀀 𒂗 𒆠 𒆠, i.e., "River"; in Gen. xv. 18 we have "the great river, the river Pĕrâth"; the Babylonians and Assyrians knew it as "Pu-rat-tu," 𒌋 𒌋 𒌋. The Euphrates is formed by the junction of two rivers at Diadin, called Frât Su, or Kara Su, and Murâd Su, which rise in the Armenian plateau at a height of over 11,000 feet above the sea; the former is about 275 miles long, and the latter about 415. The length of the Euphrates from its source to the sea is about 1,800 miles, and it falls nearly one foot per mile during the last 1,200 miles. The river begins to rise at the end of March and is in flood towards the end of May; it is navigable for small boats up till the end of September. At Kurnah the Euphrates and Tigris join, and their united streams, which are called Shatt al-'Arab, flow into the Persian Gulf, which is about 80 miles distant. In very early times the head of the Persian Gulf extended about 130 miles further inland; this is proved by the position of the ruins of the city of Eridu, which the cuneiform inscriptions say was on the sea-shore.

The Tigris rises near Lake Geuljik (or Colchis) at a place which is only a few miles from the Murâd Su, and is over 5,000 feet above sea-level. It is formed by the junction of two small rivers at Til, and from this point to Kuṛnah, where it joins the Euphrates, its length is about 1,150 miles. In ancient times it had two tributaries on the west bank, the Tharthar and the Asâs Amîr; its tributaries on the east bank today are the Khâbûr, Great Zâbh, Little Zâbh and the Dîyâlâ. The Sumerians called the Tigris IDIGNA, 𒀀𒇉, adding sometimes ID-DAGAL-LA, "the broad river," and its name among the Babylonians and Assyrians was "I-di-ik-lat," 𒀀 𒁁 𒄿 𒆷; the latter is the base of the Hebrew "Hiddekel" of Gen. ii. 14. The Tigris begins to rise towards the end of September, and its highest floods occur in May; it rises very rapidly when the snows in the hills melt, and in places, especially on the west bank, its waters cover the country for miles. Three ancient Assyrian capitals were built on its banks, Nineveh and Calah (Nimrûd) on the east bank, and Kal'ah Sharkât ("city of Asshur") on the west bank. The Tigris appears to have flowed for several centuries in the bed that it now occupies, but at one time, probably in the seventh or eighth century of our Era, it left its present bed, and flowed down a channel nearly opposite to the present town on the east bank called Kût al-'Amârah. This channel was probably begun by the rush of the waters of the Nahrawân Canal, which took off from the Tigris near Takrît and watered all the country on the east bank for nearly 200 miles. The Tigris entered this channel, which is now known as the Shatt al-Hayy, or "Serpent River," and flowed across the country and past the famous Arab city of Wâsit (site now unknown), and finally poured itself into the Great Swamp, which also received the waters of the Euphrates. The Great Swamp was 200 miles long and about 50 miles broad, and reached nearly as far as Al-Basrah. When for some reason the Shatt al-Hayy became blocked by silt, possibly owing to the neglect of the canals by the Arabs, the Tigris returned to its old bed, probably in the fifteenth century of our Era.

With the Euphrates the case was very different, for there is evidence that it changed its course, in whole or in part, during the historical period, and there is no doubt that its original bed lay more to the east, and that every time the river changed its course it moved westward. It was these movements that affected the prosperity of the towns that were built on the banks of its main stream, or on the arms of it, and there is little doubt that many of them ceased to exist when the river moved away from their walls, or when the canals that took off from it became choked. The lower part of the plain between the Tigris and Euphrates, or, as we may call it, Babylonia, was always, from the point of view of the agriculturist and cattle-breeder, a very desirable country to live in, for crops could be grown easily, and there were abundant water and fodder for cattle and sheep and camels. But there were vast deserts to the east of the Tigris and to the west of the Euphrates, and it is certain that the dwellers in them often cast covetous eyes upon the rich land between the two great rivers, and that, whenever possible, they raided parts of it to obtain food, cattle, and women, and waged systematic warfare upon its well-to-do inhabitants. The dwellers in the country to the north of the alluvial soil which was Babylonia, whether cattle-pasturing nomads or dwellers within walls, were also liable to attack from warlike tribes on the east and west. But while we possess much information about the early inhabitants of Babylonia, we know comparatively little about their contemporaries in the north. As the object of this little book is to give some account of the Babylonians and their life and history, no attempt will be made in it to discuss the peoples of Upper Mesopotamia and Assyria.

The great fertility of the alluvial soil of Babylonia induced men to settle in the country in the earliest times, and we may assume that it has been inhabited, in certain districts at least, from time immemorial. Of the earliest inhabitants nothing is known, but we may assume that they lived in much the same way as men of the Stone Age lived, under similar surroundings and conditions, in other parts of the East. That a Stone Age existed in Babylonia is proved by the objects that have been found in various parts of the country, though they seem to belong rather to the period of the New Stone Age than to that of the Old Stone Age. The oldest settlers in Babylonia known to us were the Sumerians, and when they arrived in the country they were well acquainted with the art of working in metals. The aboriginal inhabitants, whose weapons were made of stone, fared ill in every struggle with men armed with metal weapons, and the new-comers beat down all resistance and occupied the country. The evidence at present available suggests that the invaders came from some part of Central Asia, but author-ities are not agreed about the route followed by them; some think that they entered Lower Babylonia from the highlands of Elam, and others that they came down into the country from some place in the north. Be this as it may, there is no doubt that they settled in Southern Mesopotamia at a very remote period, and that they were masters of the country for many centuries, perhaps even for one or two thousand years, before any record of them that we have was written. The Sumerians divided Babylonia into two parts, which they called "country of Sumer[1] and country of Akkad,"[2] Sumer being the southern part and Akkad the northern. The earliest kings of the whole country called themselves simply "King of the Land," but in the inscriptions of the later kings we find "King of Sumer and Akkad" as the description of their sovereignty and over-lord-ship. The southern boundary of Sumer was the Persian Gulf, but its limit on the north varied from time to time. Speaking generally, the territory of Akkad on the south began a few miles to the north of Babylon, but it is probable that there existed a neutral zone, i.e., a sort of No-man's Land, between Sumer and Akkad, which at one time might come under the rule of the King of Sumer, and at another under that of the King of Akkad.

As soon as the Sumerians had established themselves in the country at the head of the Persian Gulf they began to build dykes and other earthworks, in order to protect their settlements from the floods of the Tigris and Euphrates. At first they lived in huts made of reed-mats fastened to sticks stuck in the ground, and later in little houses of a rectangular (?) shape made of bricks. As they consolidated their position they formed themselves into village communities, each of which had its own god and was practically ruled by the priest of that god. As they extended their territory northwards, their villages grew in size until they became small towns, and these in turn became cities of very considerable extent. And the power of the gods increased as the prosperity of the people increased, and at length they were housed in temples of brick and stone instead of huts made of reed-mats. Among the early Sumerian cities of which we have knowledge may be mentioned: Eridu (the modern Abû Shahrên), the most southerly, which lies to the south of the Euphrates, and was traditionally regarded as the starting-point of Sumerian and Babylonian civilization. It stood at the head of the Persian Gulf, almost on the sea-shore, but its ruins are now about 130 miles from the mouth of the Shatt al-'Arab. A few miles to the east is the mound of Tall al-Lahm, but the name of the ancient city that stood there is unknown. North of Abû Shahrên, and south of the Euphrates, was Ur, the modern Mukayyar, better known as "Ur of the Chaldees," or the "City of Abraham." A little to the west is the mound of Tall al-'Ubêd; but the ancient name of the place is unknown.

On the plain between the Euphrates and Tigris were the following cities: Shirpurla(ki), or Lagash, the modern Tall Lôh, on the east bank of the Shatt al-Hayy, above Shatrah; Tall Zurghul (ancient name unknown); and Umma, the modern Tall Yôkha, to the west of the Shatt al-Hayy. Near the Euphrates were: Tall Abû Sakhâri (ancient name unknown); Larsa, the modern Sankarah; Uruk, the modern Warka; Shuruppak, the modern Fârah; further north were Adab, the modern Bismâya; Nippur, the modern Niffar or Nuffar; and Kisurra, the modern Abû Hatab; the ancient name of the mound called Tall Dalêm (?) is unknown.

Each city was governed by a "Patesi," , who seems to have held a position among its inhabitants comparable to the greatest of the chiefs of the large Nomes in Ancient Egypt, or to the Shêkhs of great Muhammadan tribes in Western Asia and Africa. These Patesis quarrelled among themselves and made war upon each other, and invaded each other's territory, and the Patesi who had succeeded in conquering his fellow Patesis promptly arrogated to himself the title of Lugal, , i.e., "Great Man."

About the cities that existed in Akkad not so much is known, but there is evidence that Kish (Ukhêmar), Agade, the site of which is at present unidentified, Sippar, with its suburb (Abû Habbah and Dêr), and Kuthah (Tall Ibrâhîm) were flourishing centres of commerce and civilization at a very early period. And it is probable that Kish and Agade were older than any of the cities of Sumer mentioned above. It is difficult not to think that the site

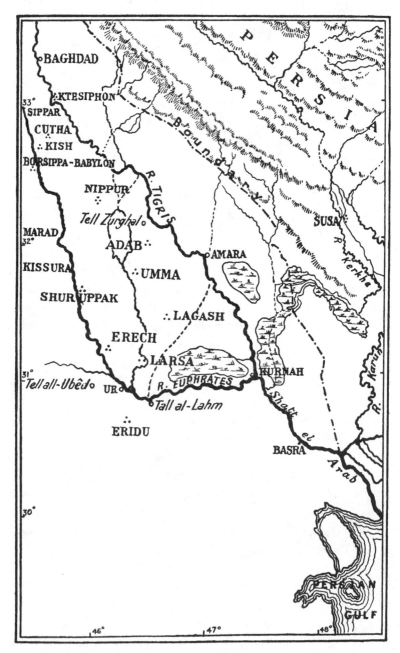

Map showing the positions of the chief City-States in Lower Mesopotamia.

of Babylon was occupied by an Akkadian city before 2000 BC, and the same may be said of the site on the Tigris, close to the mouth of the river 'Adhem, where Upi, or Opis, stood at a later period.

That part of Mesopotamia which we may at the present time assume roughly to represent Babylonia lies between 30° and 35° N. Lat., and is about 230 miles long. Its border on the south is formed by the region of swamps at the head of the Persian Gulf, and on the north the lower rising of the great Assyrian plain which the Arab geographers call "Jazîrah." The distance between the Tigris and Euphrates at Baghdâd is less than 40 miles; at Kût al-'Amârah it is between 80 and 90 miles. If all the land covered during floods or heavy rains by the waters of the Tigris and Euphrates be included, it may be said that the area of the cultivable land of Babylonia was about 14,000 square miles. What the population of Babylonia was cannot be said. Before the Sumerians introduced the canal system, about one-half of Lower Babylonia must have been uninhabitable during the greater part of the year, and the population was, probably, extremely small. But as soon as the rivers were brought under control it increased rapidly. During the reign of Khammurabi, when, under his strong and just rule, trade and commerce flourished, the population increased even more rapidly, and under the Neo-Babylonian Empire the country must have been densely populated. When Babylon ceased to be the central market of the world, the population declined in numbers; and when under the Arabs the canal system broke down, the country became desert and great portions of it became depopulated.

The question of the race to which the Sumerians belonged has been the subject of many discussions by Assyriologists and others; some authorities think that they were Turanians, and others that they were akin to the Chinese. One thing, however, about them is certain: they were not Semites, and their physical forms, features and characteristics, as represented on the monuments, suggest that they were an offshoot of a people who may have lived in some part of Northern India or in the neighbourhood of Elam. Mr. Buxton, Lecturer in Physical Anthropology at Oxford, has examined the skull of a Sumerian which Prof. Langdon dug up at Kish. According to him, the Sumerian was an Armenoid type, and highly civilized, possessing a head of great brain capacity. The Sumerians were the source whence the Semitic peoples of Babylonia and of Western Asia generally derived their civilization, and literally they taught the rest of mankind their letters. The existence of the Sumerian language was discovered by Sir Henry Rawlinson from a tablet which was sent to him by Loftus from Larsa, the modern Sankarah. He first pronounced the language on it to be Semitic, but soon found out his mistake, and then spoke of it as the "Chaldean or Hamitic language of Babylonia." Fox Talbot called it "Proto-Chaldean," and Hincks gave it the name of "Akkadian." Finally, Rawlinson placed it between the African languages and the Proto-Turanian or Finno-Ugrian group. Halévy doubted the existence of the Sumerian language, and thought that it was a species of cryptography, which, like the cuneiform writing in general, had been invented by the Semites. But all Assyriologists now admit that Sumerian is a language; many inscriptions written in it have been published and translated into English, French and German, and elementary grammars in all these languages have been written for the use of students.[3] The Akkadians were Semites, and they spoke, in the earliest times, a language purely Semitic. Some historians hold the view that Semites were in possession of the whole of Babylonia before the immigration of the Sumerians, and that the latter only gained possession of the country by conquest. Whether these hypothetical Semites were acquainted with the art of writing is not known, but it is certain that the Akkadians of Northern Babylonia, where they had ever been, adopted the cuneiform system of writing which was invented by the Sumerians, and used it for at least three thousand years.

CHAPTER TWO

BABYLONIAN CHRONOLOGY
AND HISTORY

THE MONUMENTS FOUND IN THE RUINS OF THE EARLY SUMERIAN cities, and among the remains of the cities built upon them by later kings, supply the names of a large number of Patesis, or kings, but it is extremely difficult to arrange these names in chronological order. The Babylonians themselves knew very little about the lengths of the reigns and the dates of the earliest Sumerian kings, a fact that is clearly proved by the lists of kings and dynasties compiled by them. According to one tradition, ten kings reigned before the Flood for a period of 456,000 years, and according to another, eight kings reigned for a period of 241,200 years. Such impossible figures place these statements in the region of fable. But the names of some of the kings who, according to Berossos, reigned before the Flood, have been identified in the native Babylonian lists, and it is possible that an explanation of such fabulous figures may be found someday. The lengths of the reigns of the kings who followed immediately after the Flood are equally incredible, and though it is very probable that many of them lived in the fourth, or even the fifth, millennium, BC, it is impossible to assign dates to them. The inscriptions, show that the Sumerians were sometimes conquered by the Elamite peoples, whose chief city was at Awan, and sometimes by the Akkadians from Kish, which lay a few miles to the east of Babylon, and sometimes by the warlike tribes (like the modern Kurds and "Hammawind") who lived on the east bank of the Tigris; but they received one of their most serious defeats at the hands of Mesilim, 𒈨 𒆠, King of Kish, before 3000 BC. This king dedicated and deposited in the temple of Ningirsu, the god of the City-State of Shirpurla, or Lagash (Tall Lôh), a mace head, when Lugal-shag-engur, 𒈗 𒊮 𒇶, was Patesi, or king. The authority of Mesilim must have been great, for he settled a serious dispute between the City-States of Lagash and Umma (Yôkha).

At a period which cannot be dated, Lagash once more became a powerful City-State, under the rule of Ur-Ninâ, 𒌨 𒀭 𒊩, about 3000 BC, probably because of the decay of the power of the successors of Mesilim, whose rule passed into the hands of the Patesis of other City-States. Ur-Ninâ, the son of Gunidu, was not of royal birth. His principal work was the rebuilding of the city wall of Lagash; he was a devout worshipper of the old gods of his city, and either reformed or instituted a system of canals which greatly benefited his people. Ur-Ninâ was succeeded by his son Akurgal, 𒀀 𒆳 𒃲, who was in turn succeeded by Eannadu, 𒂍 𒀭 𒈾 𒄭, who was perhaps the greatest king of the Dynasty of Lagash. Soon after he began to reign the Patesi of Umma (the modern Yôkha), disregarding an ancient treaty, plundered certain territory belonging to the god Ningirsu. Eannadu collected his troops and did battle with the aggressors, who had retreated to their city with their loot, and Enlil, the great god of Nippur, gave the men of Lagash the victory, and destroyed their enemies. The king fought in person and, like Rameses II of Egypt, "raged" at his foes, and the number of the slain amounted to at least 3,600 men. The Patesi of Umma, who was called Ush, fled, or was killed, and Eannadu made a treaty of peace with his successor Enakalli, and set up a new frontier state, and dedicated shrines to Enlil, Ninkharsag, Ningirsu and Babbar. To commemorate his victory he caused to be made and set up in a prominent place in his city the large stone stele which is now known as the Stele of Vultures. On the obverse were sculptured figures of the gods and mythological scenes, and on the reverse scenes illustrating the chief events of his wars. A portion of this stele is preserved in the British Museum.

Eannadu was now master of the territory on both sides of the Shatt al-Hayy, and was also overlord of the cities of Uruk (Erech) and Ur, which lay close to the Euphrates, on its south bank. In his inscriptions he describes the defeat of the Elamites, who invaded his territory, and from the prominence which he gives to Elam in his list of conquered countries and cities, we may assume that he was proud of his victory over it. The Elamites, of course, crossed the Tigris and invaded the territory of Lagash in search of grain, cattle and women, but they were driven back by the men of Lagash with great slaughter. Eannadu seems to have pursued the raiders across the Tigris, and to have conquered the people of one or two districts of Elam, and captured two cities, one of which was called "Shakh." Having conquered several other towns or cities in the neighbourhood of the Persian Gulf, and heaped up much wealth, he rebuilt and greatly enlarged the city wall of Lagash, rebuilt the temple of the goddess Gatumdug, and enlarged the precincts of the domain of the goddess Ninâ; and he dug two or more large canals, and made a large tank or reservoir, which was filled with water by the flooding of the river, and the entrance to it was then closed by a dyke. When the river had fallen and water was needed for the crops, the dyke was cut down gradually and the water was allowed to flow out on the fields. The making of this reservoir shows that Eannadu was acquainted with the "basin system" of irrigation. From inscriptions on several of his bricks in the British Museum, we learn that he also obtained water for his city by sinking wells. He defeated the forces of the King of Kish, and marching into his

Inscription in line Babylonian on a stone gate-socket of Enannadu, viceroy of Shirpurla (Lagash), recording the building of a temple to the god Ningirsu. From Cuneiform Texts, Pt. V, pl. 1. B.M. No. 23,287.

city, became King of Sumer and Akkad. He was the greatest king of his Dynasty, and under his rule Shirpurla, or Lagash, attained her greatest power and prosperity.

Eannadu was succeeded by his brother Enannadu (I), ⟨cuneiform⟩, who soon found it necessary to take up arms against Urlumma, the son of Enakalli, Patesi of Umma, who had made a treaty with Eannadu. Urlumma smashed the stele on which the treaty was engraved, and burnt the pieces, and destroyed the shrines of the guardian gods, and then, invading the territory of Lagash, he plundered the people and seized their crops and properties. The resistance made by Enannadu was ineffective, and he did not succeed in breaking the power of the Patesi of Umma, who not only seized but managed to retain possession of certain lands in the territory of Lagash. The power of Lagash began to decline under Enannadu, who was succeeded by his eldest son Entemena, ⊱𝕀 ⚡𝈁 𝈁⊢ ⊢⊣𝈁, who at once found himself involved in a war with Urlumma. Entemena and his army met Urlumma and his soldiers and allies at the frontier of Lagash and utterly routed them; they fled, leaving sixty of their dead on the field. Entemena followed up the fleeing soldiers, invaded the territory of Umma, and then marched on the city, which he captured almost without opposition, and slew Urlumma, the treaty-breaker. He annexed Umma and appointed Ili, a priest, to be the Patesi; he was to administer the newly acquired territory, and to collect and transport to Lagash the tribute in grain which he required from the inhabitants of Umma. Entemena caused a record of his exploits to be engraved on a stele, which was set up in a prominent place in his territory, and to be inscribed on a series of clay cones, which were buried in the foundations of his buildings. He restored the glory and power of Lagash during his reign of twenty-nine (?) years, and the tribute of Umma contributed to the prosperity of his people. Entemena was succeeded by his son Enannadu (II), of whom little is known. After his death a period of inactivity, or perhaps of anarchy, set in, and the next King of Lagash of whom anything is known is Urukagina, ⊱𝈁𝈁 ⊱𝈁⊔ ⊱𝈁𝈁⟨ ⊢⊣𝈁, who was reigning about 2700 BC. But between the reigns of Enannadu (II) and Urukagina, the city of Shirpurla was governed by Enetarzi, Enlitarzi, and Lugal-anda, or Lugal-andanu-shuga, but the rule of all three was of short duration. All were priests, and it is possible that they were usurpers. When Urukagina obtained the supreme power he styled himself Patesi, but after a few years he rejected this title and boldly proclaimed himself King of Shirpurla. He rejected the chief god of his predecessors, and directed his prayers to Ninshakh, instead of to Ningirsu. From his inscriptions it may be gathered that during the rule of the three priest-Patesis a great many serious abuses had crept into the administrative services of the City-State: sacred animals and possessions were used for secular purposes, and bribery, oppression and cruelty were everywhere rampant. Urukagina set to work to abate these abuses, and having restored the properties of the gods to their proper use, he turned his attention to the betterment of the conditions of his people. He abated the privileges of the priests, cut down the numbers of the officials of all grades, and made safe the lives and goods of the peasant classes. In fact, he set out to right what was wrong, and, calling the god Ningirsu to his aid, he drew up a Code of Laws, which has much in common with the laws set out in the famous Code of Khammurabi, which was drawn up some five or six hundred years later. He rebuilt or repaired several temples, founded new shrines, improved the canal system of the city, built a large reservoir, repaired the city wall, and made many improvements in Lagash. In his zeal to benefit the *fallâhîn*, or workers on the land, he curtailed the powers of his higher officials, and he forgot to maintain an army to protect his city against the attack that any neighbouring City-State might make upon it. Moreover, the decay of Lagash had begun before Urukagina made himself king. What was to be expected happened. The Patesi of Umma, Lugal-zaggisi, 𒈗 𒂗 𒍠 𒅆, watched the course of events in Lagash, and when the opportunity offered, invaded its territory, and spoiled the city and destroyed it, and the power of Lagash as a City-State was ended. Lugal-zaggisi attributed his success to Enlil, the great god of Nippur, and on the vases that he dedicated to the temple of this god, he says that he is King of Erech, and "King of the Land," and that the whole country was his from the place of the rising of the sun to that of its setting, and from the Lower Sea and the Euphrates and the Tigris to the Upper Sea. From this last statement some think that his rule extended from the Persian Gulf, in the south, to the Mediterranean Sea, in the north, and that his kingdom included all Akkad and Northern Mesopotamia. Whether this be so or not, it is quite clear that Lugal-zaggisi was a very powerful ruler, and that he was king of the greater part of Lower Babylonia. It is not known how long he reigned, but some think it was as much as twenty-four years.

During the reign of Lugal-zaggisi and the great development of the power of the Sumerians, the power of the Semites of Akkad grew rapidly, and their city, Kish, assumed great importance. The greatest of the Patesis who ruled over it was the mighty warrior Sharru-kin (Sargon), 𒈗 𒁺 𒆠 (𒈗), who reigned for fifty-five years; there is now reason to think that he reigned from 2637–2582 BC. There has been much discussion about the date of his reign because, on a cylinder of Nabonidus in the British Museum, it is stated that Naram-Sin, one of Sargon's successors, reigned 3,200 years before, and if this were so, Sargon must have reigned about 3750 BC. But this statement is not supported by the King Lists, and the date is too high by one thousand years. Assyriologists now think that the scribes of Nabonidus either copied an inaccurate document, or made a mistake and wrote 𒁹𒁹𒁹 𒌋 𒀭 𒁹, 3,200, instead of 𒁹𒁹 𒌋 𒀭 𒁹, i.e., that they added one wedge more than

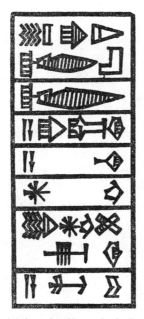

Inscription on a mace-head dedicated to Shamash, the Sun-god, in the city of Sippar, by Sargon of Agade. From Cuneiform Texts, Pt. XXI, pl. 1. B.M. No. 91,146.

was necessary. Sargon defeated Lugal-zaggisi and made himself overlord of all the Sumerian City-States, and established himself at Agade, the site of which has not yet been identified. He marched into Upper Mesopotamia, and conquered all the country west of the Euphrates and east of the Tigris. Tradition says that he crossed the Mediterranean and took possession of Cyprus. According to a legend, which was very popular in Assyria, he was the son of a peasant.

THE LEGEND OF THE BIRTH OF SARGON OF AGADE
From tablets in the British Museum [Nos. KK. 3401, 4470].

Sargon, the mighty king, the King of Agade, am I.

My mother was of humble estate, I knew not my father.

The brother of my father (or paternal uncle) was a dweller in the mountains (a forester?).

My city is Azupirâni, which lies on the bank of the Euphrates.

My humble mother conceived me, she brought me forth in secret.

She laid me in a basket [made] of reeds, she smeared my door with bitumen, she committed me to the river which did not submerge me.

The river carried me to Akki, a man who watered the fields.

Akki, the man who watered the fields . . . lifted me out of the basket.

Akki, the man who watered the fields, brought me up as his own son.

Akki, the man who watered the fields, made me his gardener.

Whilst I was a gardener the goddess Ishtar fell in love with me.

And for . . . four years I ruled the kingdom.

Rawlinson discovered a copy of this legend on a tablet in the British Museum (see *Athenaeum*, Sept. 7, 1867), and George Smith published the cuneiform text in the *Transactions of the Society of Biblical Archaeology* (vol. i, page 46 f.). Both scholars made the legend apply to Sargon of Agade, and not to Sargon II, King of Assyria 721–705 BC. Sargon of Agade is frequently mentioned in the Omen texts, and it is clear that he was regarded as a great and popular national hero for about two thousand years.

Sargon of Agade was succeeded by his son Rimush, ⯮⫶⫶ ⯮⫶ ⯮⫶ (2581 BC), who calls himself "King of Kish," but who apparently added nothing to the territory acquired by his father. He was murdered by his palace servants. In his reign, and in that of his brother Manishtusu (2572 BC) who succeeded him, the Elamites revolted, and were assisted by the people of Barakhsu. The principal monument of his reign is the "Obelisk of Manishtusu," which was found at Shûsh (Susa, or Shushan the

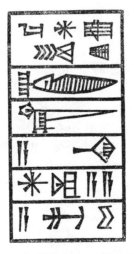

Inscription from a mace-head of Manishtusu, King of Kish. From Cuneiform Texts, Pt. XXI, pl. 1. B.M. No. 91,018.

Palace) by J. de Morgan. The long inscription upon it records the purchase of certain lands by the king. The suppression of the revolt in Elam was a difficult matter, for the king was obliged to fight a league of thirty-two peoples who lived near the Persian Gulf, and he seems to have set up a stele to record his victory over them in his city of Agade. Figures and statues of the king were found at Shûsh, and on one is an inscription stating that it was brought there from Akkad (Agade) by Shutruk-Nakhkhunte, and on another the inscription says that it was brought there by the same king from Ishnunuk. Both were evidently trophies of war.

Manishtusu was succeeded by his son Naram-Sin (⋯𒁹) 𒀭𒌋 𒂍𒌋 𒐐𒀀 𒈾𒁹 ⋯𒐕 𒀭𒌋𒌋, who reigned from 2557–2520 BC, and is mentioned in the Omen texts of a later period. He was a great warrior and a great conqueror, and he describes himself as "King of the Four Quarters" (of the world). He took the city of Apirak and defeated Rîsh-Adad its king; he conquered the land of Magan (west of Babylonia). The inscription on his statue states that he fought nine battles in one year in the country to the north-east of Elam, and defeated a confederation of peoples who had opposed his advance. He set up a stele at Agade to commemorate his victory, and the sculptures upon it illustrate his powers in battle. This stele was found at Shûsh and, in addition to Naram-Sin's own inscription, bears another text which states that it was brought, no doubt as a trophy of war, to Shûsh by Shutruk-Nakhkhunte, a king of the Elamites. Naram-Sin rebuilt the temple of Enlil at Nippur and the temple of the Sun-god at Sippar (Abû-Habbah), and made gifts to the temples of several of the gods of Lagash. A remarkable stele of Naram-Sin was found at Pir Husên, near Diarbakr, and the inscription on it states that the king owed the defeat of his enemies in the four quarters of the world to the god Enki, or Ea. This monument shows that Naram-Sin's rule extended to the region of the upper waters of the Tigris, and is a proof of his great military achievements. The successors of Naram-Sin were: Shar-gali-sharri (⊢▸⌐) 𒂊𒈝 𒅗𒄡 𒌋 𒅗𒄡 ⊣𒐊 (2519–2496 BC), Igigi, 𒌋 𒁹𒐚 𒁹𒐚, Imi, 𒂊 𒌋𒌋, Nanum, ⊢𒐊 ⋏ 𒅗𒐊𒐊, Illulu, 𒂊 𒐼𒐊 𒐼𒐊, Dudu, 𒅆𒐊 𒅆𒐊 (2492 BC), and his son Shudurul (2471 BC), 𒂗 𒆷𒅅𒌋 𒅅. Whilst Naram-Sin was adding country after country to his kingdom, the power of Akkad at home was decaying, and soon after his death the Gutians, who lived on the east bank of the Tigris, began to invade its territory, and Shar-gali-sharri was unable to check them. His successors, one by one, lost their territories, and about 2457 BC the Dynasty of Sargon, which had lasted 181 years, came to an end. The Gutians at length conquered Akkad, and their dynasty ruled the country for 125 years. The names of about twenty of their kings are known. The Gutians were ejected from the country by the Sumerians, who were led by Uru-Khegal, ⊢𒐊 𒀸𒐊 𒂍𒈨 ⊢𒐼𒀸, Patesi of Erech, and the last king of their Dynasty, Tirigan, 𒌋𒀸 ⊢𒅗𒐊 𒅗𒄡 𒐊𒐊 ⊢𒐊, fled. From 2456–2427 BC a Dynasty of five kings reigned. For a period, the exact length of which is unknown, there was no central power in Babylonia, and each Patesi and chief did what seemed good in his own eyes. The Patesis of Lagash gradually attained to something of their former power, and for a short time the city became rich and prosperous. The names of about fourteen of the Patesis of Lagash at this period are known, and a few of them were men of remarkable ability, and the monuments that they have left prove them to have been a highly cultured folk. The early Patesi of this new Dynasty of Lagash were Lugal-ushumgal, Ur-e, Puzur-mama, Ugme and Ur-mama, but little is known of them. The next Patesi was Ur-bau, 𒐼𒐊 ⊢𒌋 ⊢𒅗 𒅗𒄡𒂊, who enlarged the temple of E-ninnû, the great temple of Ningirsu at Lagash, and set up a small statue of himself in it. He rebuilt or enlarged many other temples. He gave his energies to consolidating the power of his city, and did not attempt to make conquests abroad.

The next important Patesi was Gudea, ⬦⬦⬦ ⬦⬦⬦ ⬦ under his rule the city attained its highest point of renewed prosperity. He was a man of large and sumptuous ideas, as his buildings and statues testify, and spared no pains in making his city beautiful; as his architectural ability was great he no doubt succeeded. The materials used in his buildings were brought from many remote countries, and among them are cedar wood, gold, silver, copper, marble and variegated stones, and costly woods of various kinds. His caravans traded with Syrians, Arabians and Elamites, and he provided barges and made roads to his quarries; in fact, he was a merchant Patesi in a very large way of business, and the tradesmen with whom he dealt in far countries evidently had no doubt about his solvency. The statues of him found at Tall Lôh are very remarkable specimens of Sumerian sculpture, and their makers were highly skilled handicraftsmen. The baked clay cylinders, now in the Louvre, on which he recorded his works, are his best memorial, for though they afford us little or no historical information, they are connected compositions, complete in themselves, and of indescribable value for the student of the Sumerian language. The

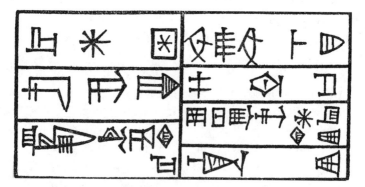

Inscription from a cylinder seal containing an address to Ur-Nammu by Khashkhamex, viceroy of the city of Ishkun-Sin. From Cuneiform Texts, Pt. XXI, pl. 6. B.M. No. 89,126.

objects found at Tall Lôh show that Gudea loved fine buildings, and that his chief object in life was to make his city beautiful. He was a patron of the arts and crafts known in his day, and in developing them he spent the great wealth that he derived from his trafficking caravans. In many respects he was to Lagash what Amenhetep III was to Egypt. Gudea was succeeded by his son Ur-Ningirsu, 𒉈 𒀭 𒃲 𒀭 𒀭; his reign was short, and with his deposition or death the glory and power of Lagash departed.

The next rulers of Babylonia were the five Patesis of Ur (Mukayyar), whose reigns lasted for about 108 years (2294–2187 BC). The first of these was Ur-Engur, 𒉈 𒀭 𒂍, or Ur-Nammu,[1] who reigned eighteen years. He fortified his city, and then, one by one, attacked the cities of Erech, Larsa and Nippur, and he seems to have made himself master of the southern states of Akkad. He rebuilt the temples of the gods of the cities which he had taken, and so secured the support of their priests. He was succeeded by his son Dungi, (𒀭) 𒀭𒀭 𒀭𒀭, or Shulgi, who reigned for about forty-five years. He extended the borders of his country in Elam and along the east bank of the Tigris, and established his rule over Akkad. For some unknown reason he revived the glory and importance of Enki, the old god of Eridu, a city which stood on the sea-shore near the head of the Persian Gulf, and was one of the oldest Sumerian cities. Not content with seizing Akkad, he marched to Babylon, and plundered the temple of E-Zida, and sacked the city; he laid waste the shrine of its god, and of course degraded its priests. He seems to have attempted to rule permanently the countries which he conquered, and to establish law and order in them; to raid a country, strip it bare, and then leave it and march home laden with spoil was no part of his policy. He standardized the weights and measures of Babylonia, and established a system for dating documents. Dungi deified himself, and his descendants followed his example. He was succeeded by his son Bur-Sin, or Amar-Sin, 𒀭 𒆠 𒀭 𒀭 𒀭, his grandson

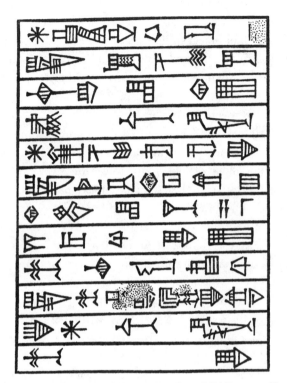

Inscription on a cylinder seal dedicated to the god Shidlam-ta-uddua by Kilull-guzalal, containing a prayer for the life of Dungi. From Cuneiform Texts, Pt. XXI, Pl. 9. B.M. No. 99,131.

Gimil-Sin, or Shu-Sin, and his great-grandson Ibi-Sin, . Bur-Sin, during his short reign of about eight years, did little for his country, and seems to have been of a peaceful, or indolent, disposition. His son Gimil-Sin, whose reign also was very short, found that the Semites from the north were encroaching on his dominions, and was obliged to build a great wall on the west of Ur to keep them from invading the city lands. However, the third Dynasty of Ur was brought to an end

List of eleven temple-estates, with measurements and statistics compiled in the reign of Bur-Sin, King of Ur about 2230 or 2220 BC. B.M. No. 18,039.

not by such encroachments, but by the Elamites, who raided Ur and carried off Ibi-Sin as a prisoner. There was no one in Ur to succeed him, and so the sovereignty of Babylonia passed from Ur to Isin, 𒀭𒈗𒊺𒀭𒆠, I-SI-IN (KI), which became "a city of royalty." The exact site of this city is unknown, but it probably lay a little to the north of Nippur. The Dynasty of Isin was founded by Ishbi-irra, 𒀭𒈗𒆠𒀭𒀸𒊏, who reigned thirty-two years (2186–2154 BC) and expelled the Elamites, who appear to have formed settlements in Babylonia. The kings of Isin were fifteen in number, and they reigned for 226 years, i.e., from 2186–1961 BC; the most important of them were Ishme-Dagan, ⟨➤⟩ ⟦⟧ ⟦⟧ ⟦⟧ ⟦⟧ ⟦⟧, Libit Ishtar, ⟨➤⟩ ⟦⟧ ⟦⟧ ⟦⟧ ⟦⟧, Ur-Enurta ⟨➤⟩ ⟦⟧ ➤ ⟦⟧ ⟦⟧, and Bur-Sin, ⟨➤⟩ ⟦⟧ ➤ ⟦⟧ ⟦⟧.

Contemporary with the Dynasty of Semites at Isin was the Dynasty of Larsa, which consisted of sixteen kings who reigned for 287 years (2187–1901 BC). The founder of this Dynasty was Naplanum, ➤⟧ ⟦⟧ ➤⟧ ⟋ ⟦⟧. About 1997 BC, when the power of the kings of Isin was decreasing rapidly, the Elamite king

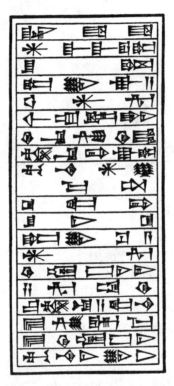

Reverse of an inscription of Khammurabi recording the building of a temple to Ishtar in the city of Khallab. From Cuneiform Texts, Pt. XXI, pl. 44. B.M. No. 90,939.

Kudur Mabug, who had made himself master of the eastern lands of Babylonia, established his sons Warad-Sin and Rim-Sin as kings in Larsa, and they reigned there for twelve years and sixty years respectively. Rim-Sin broke the power of the King of Isin and captured his city, and his dominion over Sippar and Babylon came to an end.

About 2057 BC the First Semitic Dynasty of Babylon began to rule in the city of Babylon under its founder, Sumuabum, who reigned for about thirteen years. The Dynasty consisted of eleven kings, and they reigned for three hundred years. Under the kings Sumulailu, Sâbum, Apil-Sin, or Awêl-Sin, and Sin-muballit, the power of the Babylonians increased greatly, but it was under the rule of Khammurabi, 𒄷 𒂅 𒈨 𒂖 𒌋, who was the sixth king of the Dynasty, and reigned for about forty-two years, that Babylon attained its greatest influence and splendour, and became the first city in Babylonia. He marched against Rim-Sin, who had captured Isin, and took Larsa, and made its king a prisoner, and thus the power of Larsa came to an end. He conducted campaigns in Sumer, Upper Babylonia and Assyria, and was victorious everywhere; among the cities taken by him were Nineveh and Ashur. He was not only a great warrior, but a great organizing ruler, who thought that nothing concerning the welfare of his kingdom or people was too small or unimportant to deserve his personal supervision. His desire to make his subjects a law-abiding people is shown by the Code of Laws that he compiled, and it is clear from it that he realized no kingdom could stand that was not ruled by justice coupled with wisdom and humanity. He was undoubtedly the greatest king of Babylonia and perhaps the greatest man the country ever produced. That his Code was based upon existing Sumerian Codes of Laws does not detract from its merit as containing the most comprehensive series of wise and humane laws that has come down to us from an Oriental King. Some writers think that Khammurabi is to be identified with "Amraphel, King of Shinar," who, with Arioch of Ellasar, Chedorlaomer, King of Elam, and

Tidal, King of Goiim, invaded Palestine (Gen. xiv.). "Amraphel" may well be a garbled form of the name Khammurabi, and Tidal seems to be a good Hittite name, and the mention of a King of Babylon with a Hittite king need not surprise us. There is an Elamite ring in the sound of "Chedorlaomer," yet though Ellasar may represent Larsa, its king Arioch is difficult to identify. But it is very probable that the statement in Genesis has a historical foundation.

Khammurabi's Letters and Dispatches prove that he devoted much care and attention to the affairs of his kingdom, and the decisions which he made show that he ruled the people with justice and with due regard to what he believed to be their best interests. He insisted that all difficult questions should be referred to him for his personal consideration, and he considered no detail of administration too small or unimportant for his attention. This is made clear by the series of his Letters which was admirably published by the late L. W. King in his *Letters and Inscriptions of Khammurabi*, 3 vols., London, 1898–1900, and from this work the following example is taken. From the tablet in the British Museum (No. 12,812) we learn that the Patesi Sin-idinnam had removed from his post Gimillum, a baker of Emutbalum, and transferred his services to another department. Khammurabi had written to Sin-idinnam and informed him that he had received a report from Ibni-Martu, the scribe of the bakers of Emutbalum, concerning four bakers. In answer to Khammurabi's letter, Sin-idinnam replied that the four bakers had been assigned to him under the authority of the seal (i.e., a document bearing a seal), and that he was sending one of the four bakers, Gimillum, to appear before the king (i.e., Khammurabi). In due course Gimillum arrived, and, going into the presence of the king, he stated his case. Khammurabi heard what Gimillum had to say, and enquired into his statements, and then decided that he must be restored to the position that he had formerly held among the bakers of Emutbalum. Thereupon he ordered a Dispatch to be written to Sin-idinnam, and having

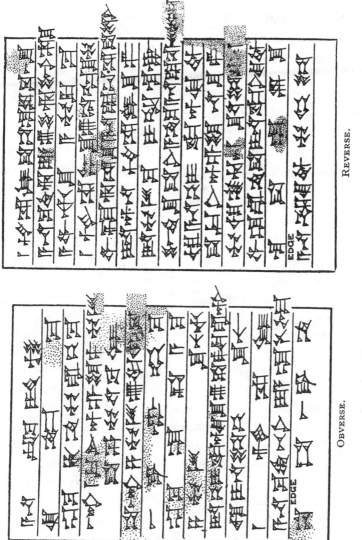

REVERSE.

OBVERSE.

Letter from Khammurabi to Sin-idinnam. B.M. No. 12,812.

quoted the actual words which Sin-idinnam had used in his letter to him, told him that Gimillum must be restored to his former position, and that he must send some other man to take his place in the Department to which he had transferred him. A reproduction of the text is given on page 28.

Khammurabi was succeeded by Samsuiluna, Abiêshu', Ammiditana, Ammisaduga and Samsuditana, but none of them possessed his power and ability. Under his firm and just rule the commerce of Babylon had increased greatly, and the numerous contract tablets which are in our museums testify to the magnitude and variety of the transactions of the great merchants of Babylon at this period. On Khammurabi's death he left few countries that his successors could conquer, but several of the Sumerian states seized the opportunity which that event gave them, and began to throw off their allegiance to Babylon. Nearly one hundred years before the end of the First Dynasty of Babylon, i.e., about 1900 BC, a Dynasty of Kings of the Sea-Country began to reign, and according to the King Lists it lasted until 1517 BC; the names of twelve of its kings are known, and they are said to have reigned for a period of 368 years. These kings formed the so-called Second Dynasty of Babylon. The power of the First Dynasty of Babylon was broken by the Hittites, who in the reign of Samsuditana, its last king, invaded Akkad and captured Babylon and sacked it. As the Kassite king Agum-kakrime brought back to Babylon from Khana on the Euphrates the shrine images of Marduk and Sarpanitum, it is probable that the Hittites also plundered the temples. It is not probable that the Hittites occupied Babylon for a very long time. Before they could settle there they would have had to break the power of the Kings of the Sea-Country in the south, and it may be assumed that realizing this fact, they loaded themselves with spoil and retraced their steps by the Euphrates to their own country. Babylon suffered sorely from the Hittite Invasion, together probably with many of the cities in the south whose interests were bound up with hers.

For a few years after the departure of the Hittites there was no strong central power in Babylonia, for the Kings of the Sea-Country, who were of Sumerian origin, were unable to make their power effective in Akkad, and many of the old Sumerian cities, e.g., Lagash, Umma, Shurruppak, Kisurra, Adab, etc., had either collapsed entirely, or were in a moribund condition.

About 1750 BC the chieftains who lived on the east bank of the Tigris began to cross that river and settle themselves on the rich lands in Lower Mesopotamia, and they succeeded in making the natives do their will. Increasing their power gradually, these chieftains made their way to Babylon, and in a comparatively short time, Gandash, 𒀭 𒂍 𒀭, one of these Kashshu people (commonly called Kassites), made himself king of Babylon and founded the Third or Kassite Dynasty of Babylon. There seems to have been no series of invasions of Babylonia by large armies of Kassites, or any great and widespread destruction of the lives and property of the natives by the new-comers. The only Kassite raid we know of took place in the reign of Samsu-iluna between 1912 BC and 1875 BC. And the evidence available shows that their immigration into Babylonia had been going on quietly for many years. They belonged to some Asiatic race that was civilized, and their rule was wise and on the whole beneficent. They abolished the system of dating by events, and dated all documents by the years of the king's reign. They owed their success in Babylonia chiefly to the horse, which they introduced into Babylonia, for the natives had never ridden any animal that moved faster than a camel or ass. As with the Hyksos in Egypt, the mobility which the horse gave them made them masters of the country in a comparatively short period. Though they honoured their native gods, and kept their own names, and always retained their chief native customs, they adopted, to their great advantage, much of the civilization of the Babylonians. The King Lists state that the Kassite kings were thirty-six in number, and that they reigned 576 years, i.e., from about 1746–1171 BC.

Very little is known of their history. Three of them were called Agum, ⟨cuneiform⟩, four Kashtiliash, ⟨cuneiform⟩, three Kurigalzu, ⟨cuneiform⟩, two Meli-Shipak, ⟨cuneiform⟩, two Nazi-Maruttash, ⟨cuneiform⟩, two Kadashman-Kharbe, ⟨cuneiform⟩, two Burnaburiash, ⟨cuneiform⟩, and two Kadashman-Enlil, ⟨cuneiform⟩. From the Tall al-'Amârnah Tablets we learn that two Kassite kings, Kadashman Kharbe I (1388 BC?) and Burnaburiash II (1369 BC?), corresponded with Amenhetep III, King of Egypt, and his son Amenhetep IV. Both Kassite kings describe themselves as "King of Kar-Duniash," which shows that the Kassite kings called Babylonia Kar-Duniash, ⟨cuneiform⟩. The Kassites ruled Babylonia, it is true, but they did nothing to help her to regain her former position of power and splendour. They modified the system of land-tenure which had been in existence from time immemorial, but they seem to have allowed commerce to follow its natural course and Babylonian merchants and owners of caravans to enjoy considerable freedom of action.

For the first two or three centuries of their rule the Kassite kings succeeded each other as a matter of course, but in the fifteenth century BC they realized that a mighty power had grown up in Northern Mesopotamia, and that their hold on Babylonia was threatened by it. This power was Assyria. About 2200 BC the Assyrians regarded the Kings of Ur in Lower Babylonia as their lords paramount, and 250 years later Khammurabi enumerated the cities of Nineveh and Ashur among his possessions, and included Assyria in his kingdom. But Assyria asserted her independence soon after the death of Khammurabi, and about 1525 BC the Kassites found it advantageous to make treaties with the kings of Assyria. They knew, too, that the Hittites also were becoming a powerful people, and naturally they were alarmed when the Mitanian Dynasty established itself on the Euphrates (about 1450 BC). And the conquests of Thothmes III giving them further cause for alarm, they, in the fourteenth century BC, began to seek an alliance with the Egyptians. The Assyrian kings, like the Kassites, were afraid of the Mitanians and Hittites, and although they coveted the fertile lands and the wealth of Babylonia, they made no attempt to invade that country. The Mitanian Dynasty came to an end in the fourteenth century BC, and the still growing power of the Hittites received a check from the Egyptians in the thirteenth century BC. Then came the opportunity of the Assyrians, who invaded Kassite territory, and the Kassites were obliged to fight the Assyrians. About 1250 BC, Tukulti-Enurta I 𒁹 𒂍 𒀭 𒈨 𒌋𒌋 𒌦, King of Assyria, defeated the army of Kashtiliash II, King of Babylonia, captured the city of Babylon, and Babylonia became a province of Assyria. The Kassites never forgot that Ashur-uballit, King of Assyria (1380–1340 BC), had invaded their country and slain their nominee to the throne, Kurigalzu III, and that Adad-Nirari I, King of Assyria (1310–1280 BC), had seized a portion of Babylonian territory after his defeat of Nazi-Maruttash, and on the death of Tukulti-Enurta I they rebelled. Their leader, Rammân-shum-nâsir, 𒁹 𒈬 𒀭 𒀀 𒈨𒌍, collected troops and marched against the Assyrians, who were led by Bêl-kudur-usur, 𒁹 𒌦 𒉽 𒂍 𒂍 𒌋. The armies met near Ashur, the Assyrian king was slain, and the Kassites regained their independence for some years. Between 1175 and 1141 BC, Ashur-dân I, 𒁹 𒈬 𒈪 𒀝 𒈪 𒌦, attacked the Kassite king, Zababa-shum-iddin, and defeated him and recovered the territory which the Assyrians had lost. The Kassite Dynasty was brought to an end by Shutruk-Nakhkhunte, King of Elam, who invaded Babylonia, slew Zababa-shum-iddin, and sacked the city of Sippar.

The Fourth Dynasty of Babylon was established by Marduk-shâpik-zêri, 𒁹 𒌦 𒊬 𒌋 𒂅 𒈨, about 1170 BC; it consisted of eleven kings, who reigned 132 years. The greatest king of the dynasty was Nebuchadnezzar I, 𒁹 𒈬 𒀭 𒂍 𒂍 𒉿 𒈨𒌍, whose troops marched into Elam, burning and destroying as they went. The campaign was led by Ritti-Marduk, a captain of the chariots, and the Babylonians were victorious. The Elamite king was slain, and Ritti-Marduk and the army returned laden with spoil. Nebuchadnezzar rewarded his brave officer, and the *kudurru*, or landmark, inscribed with a list of the gifts and privileges which he bestowed upon him, is in the British Museum (No. 90,858). The Assyrians invaded Babylonia again under Ashur-resh-ishi I about 1120 BC, but were driven back by Nebuchadnezzar, who pursued them to Zanki. The Babylonians, however, were obliged to retreat, and their subsequent attempts to conquer Assyria were unsuccessful. The successors of Nebuchadnezzar I ruled very little outside the walls of Babylon. One of them, Marduk-nadin-akhê, had some success in an encounter with the troops of Tiglath-Pileser I, but the Assyrian invaded Babylonia with his army, and captured Opis on the Tigris, Dûr-Kurigalzu, Sippar of Shamash, Sippar of Anunitum, and Babylon itself. Tiglath-Pileser made no attempt to occupy Babylonia, and his successors even maintained friendly relations with the kings of Babylon.

The Fourth Dynasty of Babylon was followed by two or three short-lived Dynasties, but none of their kings was able to arrest the decay which was destroying the power of the Babylonians. About 1000 BC, perhaps even earlier, raids were frequently made into Babylonian territory by the half-nomad Semitic tribes who are grouped under the name Sutû. These, like the Shasu of the Egyptians, lived by pasturing flocks and herds and by highway robbery; they flocked into Babylonia from Northern Mesopotamia, and plundered villages and even towns, without let or hindrance. The Chaldeans on the Lower Euphrates caused serious trouble, for having seized much territory they divided it among their tribes, and in their districts the owning of land by towns and individuals came to an end. The chiefs of the tribes became masters of the country, and no king of Babylon was strong enough to overthrow the new system of land ownership. The Eighth Dynasty of Babylon began about 990 BC; it consisted of twenty-two kings, who reigned about 258 years, i.e., until 732 BC. The founder of the Dynasty was Nabu-mukinapli, 𒁹 ⸺𒁹 ⸺𒆪 𒍪 𒉌, who probably reigned about thirty-five years. The Sutû tribes in his reign held all the rich lands around Babylon, and their power was sufficiently great to stop the celebration by the king of the great New Year Festival by preventing the priests from carrying the statue of the god Nabû (Nebo) from his temple at Birs-i-Nimrûd across the Euphrates into Babylon.

Nabu-shum-ukin I was succeeded by Nabu-apal-iddina, 𒁹 ⸺𒀭 ⸺𒆪 𒉌 𒂗 ⸺𒁹, about 885 BC, and he has earned fame as the rebuilder of the great temple of the Sun-god Shamash at Sippar, which the Sutû, or Arameans, had plundered and laid waste. The old temple was wrecked probably in the reign of Rammân-apaliddina (1083–1062 BC), and was repaired by Simmash-Shipak (1038–1031 BC), but the service of the god was discontinued until the reign of E-ulmash-shakin-shumi (1016–1000 BC) of Bît-Bazi, who partly re-endowed the temple. Nabu-apal-iddina rebuilt the temple, restored the sculptures, endowed the priesthood, and established regular services and offerings. He re-decorated the figure of the Sun-god with gold and lapis lazuli, and then found the ancient stone with a figure of the Sun-god upon it and had a careful copy made of it. He covered the sculptured portion of this Tablet with a layer of clay to preserve it, and then buried it in a safe place in the foundations of the temple. In the inscription on the Sun-god Tablet (*see* Plate IV) the king described the ruin that the Sutû had brought upon the country, and gives a list of the offerings that he dedicated to the god, and enumerates at length the various vestments that the priests are to wear on festival and holy days. The temple was again restored by Nabopolassar (625–604 BC), who during the course of his work found the Tablet. He provided the sculptured portion of the Tablet with a new clay covering (B.M. No. 91,002), and in the inscription on the back of it he says that he dedicated offerings to the god and provided new vestments for the priests. The Tablet, which is now in the British Museum (No. 91,000), was found in a large baked clay box (B.M. No. 91,004), together with the old and the newer clay covering, and two inscribed barrel cylinders of Nabonidus (555–538 BC). Whether the box was the work of Nabopolassar or Nabonidus is not known.

Now the Sutû, who continued to descend both the Tigris and Euphrates and settle in the fertile plains of Lower Mesopotamia, troubled the Assyrians as much as they did the Babylonians, and their inter-tribal fights disorganized all attempts to rule of both Governments. As Babylon could not bring these fights to an end, the Assyrians undertook the task, and Ashur-nasir-pal, 𒈨𒈨𒈨𒈨 (883–859 BC), and his son Shalmaneser III, 𒈨𒈨𒈨𒈨𒈨 (859–824 BC), sent their soldiers to Babylon and the country to the south to restore order. The Assyrian method of quelling rebellion was short and effective; the towns and villages of the rebels were burnt, their fields were laid waste, the rebels themselves were slain, or burnt alive or impaled, and their women and cattle and sheep were carried off into captivity. The Assyrians were a brutally cruel people, and when the Babylonians saw their acts on the battlefields, they could do nothing except make themselves tributaries of Assyria. Between 851 and 828 BC. Marduk-zakir-shumi I, 𒈨𒈨𒈨𒈨𒈨, became the vassal of Shalmaneser III. His son Marduk-balatsu-ikbi, 𒈨𒈨𒈨𒈨𒈨 (827–825 BC), refused to submit to this state of affairs, and he collected Elamites and Chaldeans and others and set out to drive back Shamshi-Adad VI (824–810 BC), King of Assyria, who had been plundering the Babylonian cities in all directions. The Babylonian and Assyrian armies met at Dûr-Pap-sukal, and, as was to be expected, the former was defeated utterly. But the Babylonians were a stiff-necked people, and they rebelled against the Assyrians and attacked their soldiers whenever opportunity offered. At length the Assyrians determined to conquer

The Sun-god Tablet sculptured with a scene representing Nabû-apal-iddina, King of Babylon, about 870 BC, worshipping in the shrine of the Sun-god of Sippar. The inscription records the restoration of the temple by this king. B.M. No. 91,000.

Babylonia, and Tiglath-Pileser III, 𒁹 𒂍 𒍦 𒌋 𒈨𒌍 𒀀 𒈗 (745–727 BC), marched on Babylon, took the city, and made its king, Nabu-nadin-zeri, 𒁹 𒀭 𒉺 𒊭 𒈨, prisoner, and proclaimed himself King of Babylon about 729 BC. He ruled in Babylon under the name of Pulu, 𒁹 𒇽 𒂍 (*see* 2 Kings xv. 19; Chron. v. 26). His successor, Shalmaneser V (727–722 BC), ruled in Babylon under the name of Ululai, 𒁹 𒊩𒆷 𒂍 𒉌 𒀀 𒀀. A little later Merodach-Baladan, King of Bît-Yakin, a district at the head of the Persian Gulf, made a league with Khumbanigash, King of Elam, and besieged the Assyrians in Dêr on the Tigris, and defeated an army of Sargon II (722–705 BC) there. Merodach-Baladan then went on to Babylon and became King of Babylonia. His attacks on the Assyrians roused the wrath of Sargon, who marched on Babylon and expelled Merodach-Baladan, and took the city and reigned over it until his death. Then the Babylonians again revolted and placed at their head Merodach-Baladan, who once more began to trouble Assyria. Sennacherib, 𒁹 𒌍 𒀾 𒋀 𒌷𒌋 (705–681 BC), appeared with his army at Babylon and defeated the rebellious Babylonians and their allies the Elamites. The new King of Babylon, Bêl-ibni, 𒁹 𒀭 𒌋 𒊒, made an alliance with a prince of Kaldu called Mushezib-Marduk, and rebelled against Assyria. Sennacherib again appeared at Babylon, slew the rebels and transported Bêl-ibni and his supporters to Assyria, and made his own son Ashur-nadin-shumi King of Babylon. When Esarhaddon, 𒁹 𒊹 𒈨𒌍 𒋩 𒀭 (681–669 BC), became King of Assyria, he adopted a new policy in dealing with the Babylonians, and he made friends with the priesthood and began to rebuild parts of the city; he restored the services in the temples, and re-established the priestly orders. He made one of his sons, Shamash-shum-ukin, 𒁹 𒌓 𒌋 𒄴 𒊭 𒌋𒌋 𒀭 (668–648 BC), King of Babylon, and another, Ashur-bani-pal, 𒁹 𒀭 𒀀 𒊒 𒌋 (668–626 BC), King of Assyria. Shamash-shum-ukin obtained allies among the Elamites and rebelled against his

Brick inscribed with the names and titles of Nebuchadnezzar II,
King of Babylon, 604–561 BC. B.M. No. 90,112.

brother's authority with some success. Ashur-bani-pal had already
defeated the Elamites and slain their king, Teumman, and when
he marched against Babylon he determined to make an end of the
rebels who were there and in Elam. He captured Babylon without difficulty, and Shamash-shum-ukin was burnt to death in his
palace. Ashur-bani-pal then invaded Elam, laid waste the country,

marched on its capital, Susa, and captured it and slew its inhabitants. He plundered the temples and palaces and then destroyed them; he wrecked the tombs of the Elamite kings, and what could be burnt he burnt. Thus he became King of Babylonia, and his rule over that country and Assyria remained practically unchallenged for the rest of his life. His campaigns in Egypt and Elam had materially weakened his military power and had seriously drained his resources, and during the last years of his life the Scythians and Medes and other peoples invaded parts of his kingdom unchecked.

The Babylonians watched the decay of the Assyrian power, and when Ashur-bani-pal died they set on the throne Nabopolassar, 𒀭 ⸱⸱⸱ ⸱⸱⸱ ⸱⸱⸱ (625–604 BC), who seems to have been a shrewd and capable ruler. He married his son Nebuchadnezzar II, 𒀭 ⸱⸱⸱ ⸱⸱⸱ ⸱⸱⸱ (604–561 BC), to the daughter of Cyaxares, King of the Medes, and when they invested Nineveh for the third time he sent no troops to help the Assyrians to defend their capital. Nineveh fell 612 BC, as Mr. C. J. Gadd, of the British Museum, has proved, and its king, Sin-shar-ishkun, 𒀭 ⸱⸱⸱ ⸱⸱⸱ ⸱⸱⸱ ⸱⸱⸱ (620?-612 BC), was burnt to death in his palace. On the downfall of the Assyrian power, the Babylonians became independent, and Nabopolassar established an army and strengthened his capital. When he heard that the Egyptians had marched into Palestine with the view of recovering their territory in that country which the Assyrians had seized some years before, he sent his son Nebuchadnezzar with an army up the Euphrates to occupy Syria and Palestine. Nebuchadnezzar defeated Necho, King of Egypt, at Carchemish and routed his army, and all Palestine submitted to his yoke. Josiah, King of Judah, had marched to Megiddo, presumably to help the Assyrians, but was slain there (2 Kings xxiii. 29). The people of Judah then paid tribute to the Babylonians; but after a time they revolted, and Nebuchadnezzar II came to Jerusalem, which he captured and plundered, and he carried off to Babylon

INSCRIPTION ON A BRONZE STEP OF NEBUCHADNEZZAR II
IN THE BRITISH MUSEUM

Found in the ruins of the Temple of Nabû at Birs-i-Nimrûd.

1.

Na - bi - um - ku - du -   ur - ri - u - su - ur
Nebuchadnezzar

shar   Ka - dingir - ra   (KI)[2]
the king of Babylon (the gate of god)

2.

za- ni - in   E   SAG - ILA   u   E   ZI - DA
the restorer of the temple Sagila and the temple Zida

3.

ablu   asharidu   sha   Nabû - apla
the   eldest   son   of   Nabu -pal-

u - su - ur   shar Tin - tir (KI) a - na - ku
usur   the king of Babylon (the seat of life) am I.

4.

a - na   Na - bi - um   bil - ni   si - i - ri
For   the   god   Nabû   the   supreme   lord

5.

mu - sha - ri - ku   u - um   ma - la - ki - ya
the lengthener of the day of my rule (or kingdom)

6.

E - ZI - DA   bît - su   i - na   Bar- si - pa (KI)
E-Zida   his temple   in   Borsippa

esh - shi - ish   e - pu - ush
afresh   I made.

the king and his mother and family and all the craftsmen in the city, 596 BC (2 Kings xxiv. 1–17). About ten years later the people of Jerusalem again rebelled, and Nebuchadnezzar marched against Jerusalem once more, threw down the walls, burnt the

Temple and houses, and carried off Zedekiah and the remainder of the people to Babylon, 587 BC (*see* 2 Kings xxv.). Apries, Necho's successor, attempted to relieve Jerusalem, but failed. Nebuchadnezzar took all Palestine and Syria and the cities on the seacoast, including Tyre, which fell after a siege of thirteen years (573 BC). Whether he invaded Egypt is doubtful, but on the authority of a mutilated inscription in the British Museum, some think that in the forty-first year of his reign he fought against Amasis II, King of Egypt. The inscriptions of Nebuchadnezzar are numerous, but none of them contains any account of his wars and conquests, and in this respect they are different from those of the earlier kings of Babylonia and Assyria. But they supply a great deal of information about his building operations, which were on a very large scale. He rebuilt the great temples and palaces of Babylon, and strengthened its walls and fortified them strongly. A brief account of these will be found in the following chapter on the city of Babylon. Nebuchadnezzar seems to have thought as lightly of his great conquests as Khammurabi, his great predecessor on the throne of Babylon, thought of his. The principal object of these kings was to record their devotion to Bêl-Marduk and the other gods, and their restorations of the temples throughout the land.

Nebuchadnezzar II was succeeded by his son Awel-Marduk, 𒀭𒈬 𒈗 𒊩 𒌑 𒊩𒌆 (Evil-Merodach), 561–559 BC, a man of evil reputation, and by his son-in-law Neriglissar, 𒀭 𒋻 𒆗 𒉌𒊓 𒊹, *Nergal-shar-usur* (559–556 BC), who has been identified with Nergal-sharezer, the Rab-mag who, according to Jer. xxxix. 3–13, was with Nebuchadnezzar's army at Jerusalem. Labâshi-Marduk, son of Neriglissar, was deposed and slain, and the priests set upon the throne Nabonidus, 𒀭 𒀝 𒈾𒀉 𒄿 𒈾𒀉 (555–538 BC), who was a great builder and repairer of temples. But he was neither a soldier nor a practical man of affairs, and he studied the past history of the religious institutions of his country more than the means by which the power of Babylon was to be maintained or the right government of his subjects. Much interesting light has been thrown on the character of Nabonidus and his reign by a tablet in the British Museum (No. 38,299), the text of which has been published, with transliteration, translation and critical notes, by Sidney Smith, of the British Museum, in his *Babylonian Historical Texts*, London, 1924. When complete it contained an account of the reign of Nabonidus, and described the events that led up to the conquest of Babylon, 538 BC. According to the text, the rule of Nabonidus was unjust and the people became discontented; devils took possession of him, and he built a sanctuary which the Babylonians refused to recognize as such. He set up a statue of Sin the Moon-god, who was represented in a state of eclipse, and stated his reasons for so doing, saying that the legends of the gods described their acts incorrectly. He decided to build a temple, E.Hul.Hul, to the Moon-god of Harran, and forbade the celebration of the New Year Festival until the period of mourning which he had proclaimed and the work of building were ended. He built the temple, set up the statue, made his son Bel-shar-usur viceroy, and set out on a campaign against Tema', in the land of Amurru. He took the city, slew the king, and built a palace for himself like that at Babylon. He is charged with claiming in his inscriptions victories over lands which he had never conquered, and though he proclaims the might of Cyrus, boasts that he will conquer the Persian. During the celebration of the New Year Festival, 538 BC, he committed several impious acts that showed his utter contempt for the sacred symbols of the Babylonian god Sin and the god Bêl. In the last column of the tablet we read of the restoration of the old rites in Babylon, the completion of the great wall Imgur-Enlil, and the return of the gods to their cities. The work of Nabonidus was destroyed everywhere, and all records of him that could be found were broken. The text ends with a curse on Nabonidus, who is consigned to the prison in the Underworld, and with a prayer for Cyrus.

From the paragraph above it is clear that Nabonidus tried to introduce into the worship of the Moon-god at Babylon certain changes which would make it resemble entirely the manner of the worship of that god at Harran (for explanations of the mythological allusions the reader should consult Sidney Smith's work, pages 68 ff.). He set up a statue of the god which the Babylonians refused to worship, and thereby drew down upon himself the revilings of his people, who seem to have declared openly that he was not a fit and proper person to officiate at the New Year's Festival. It is possible, too, that the Babylonians did not look with favour on the king's act in dedicating his daughter Bêl-shalti-Nannar to the service of Sin and Nergal at Ur, and rebuilding rooms and shrines for her at E.Gɪ.Pᴀʀ, or Bît Gipari. This building lay inside a gate in the *temenos* wall, opening on to the enclosure at the foot of the *zikkurat,* or temple tower, and the public women of the temple lived in it. Nabonidus incurred the anger of his people by his restoration of the building, which seems to have been altered, probably as a result of a change in ritual, by Nebuchadnezzar II. Mr. C. L. Woolley, during his excavations at Ur in 1922–23, noticed a complete change in the design of the building in the time of Nebuchadnezzar II. On the whole, it seems that Nabonidus was somewhat of a religious fanatic, and that he would have fulfilled his purpose in life better as a priest than a king. It is possible that the king of Babylon who is said to have gone mad in the Book of Daniel was not Nebuchadnezzar II but Nabonidus.

When Cyrus, 𒀭 𒆤 𒅖 𒌨 (538–529 BC), had defeated Croesus, King of Lydia, he turned his attention to Babylon, and sent his general Gobryas to take the city. Gobryas, who has been identified with Gubaru, an officer of Nebuchadnezzar II, found himself opposed at Opis by Prince Belshazzar, the son of Nabonidus, who had been appointed by his father to defend Babylon, but the Babylonian army was routed and Nabonidus fled. At this time Sippar revolted, and welcomed the Persians, and

Gubaru marched into Babylon and, with the connivance of the priests, occupied it without fighting. In due course Cyrus entered the city and was welcomed and greeted as the saviour of the people. He made Gubaru governor of Babylon, and it seems that Belshazzar was put to death.

AN ACCOUNT OF THE CAPTURE OF BABYLON BY CYRUS (538 BC).
From a cylinder in the British Museum [No. 12,049].

Marduk sought me out [me] a righteous prince and a man after his own heart, whom he could take by the hand. He proclaimed my name "Cyrus, King of Anshan," and declared my name for sovereignty over the whole world. He (i.e., Cyrus) compelled the land of Kutî, and all the tribes thereof, to bow down at his feet; all the Black Heads (i.e., Babylonians) whom Marduk had delivered into his hands he governed with justice and righteousness. Marduk, the great lord, the protector of his people, looked on his beneficent deeds and his righteous heart with joy. Marduk commanded him to go to his city of Babylon; he made him to set out on the road to Babylon, and he marched by his side as a friend and helper. His countless soldiers, with their armour girded on them, advanced by his side like a wide-spreading flood. Without fighting, and unopposed, Marduk made him to enter into his city of Babylon, and he refrained from sacking it. He delivered into his hand Nabonidus, who did not worship him [Marduk]. All the men of Babylon, all the people of Sumer and Akkad, and their princes and governors bowed down before him and kissed his feet; they rejoiced in his sovereignty,

Baked clay cylinder of Nabonidus, King of Babylon, 555–538 BC, mentioning Naram-Sin. B.M. No. 91,109.

their faces were bright. They bowed down in reverence to him, and adored the name of Marduk, the lord, who by his power had raised to life the dead, and had saved all from destruction and want.

I am Cyrus, King of the world, the great king, the mighty king, the king of Babylon, king of Sumer and Akkad, king of the four quarters of the world, the son of Cambyses, the great king king of Anshan, grandson of Cyrus, the great king, king of Anshan, descendant of Teispes, the great king, king of Anshan, the everlasting seed of royalty, whose reign Bêl [of Babylon] and Nabû [of Borsippa] love, and whose sovereignty they desired with joyful hearts. When I had entered Babylon, I entered under favourable auspices; I made my abode in the Royal Palace, a splendid building, amid shouts of gladness and cries of joy. Marduk, the great lord, the darling god of the Babylonians, inclined graciously to me, and daily did I duly worship him. In vast numbers my soldiers marched peacefully into Babylon. I took care that all the people of Sumer and Akkad, a great race, should suffer no molestation; I had respect for the tribulation of Babylon and all her cities. And the gods of Sumer and Akkad which Nabonidus had brought into Babylon, whereat the wrath of the lord of the gods was roused, by the command of Marduk, the great lord, one and all I restored to their shrines, and made them to inhabit once again the places in which their hearts rejoiced. May all the gods whom I have brought into their own cities pray daily before Bêl and Nabû for the lengthening of my days! May they speak the word which shall bring me prosperity, and may they say unto Marduk, my lord, "Let King Cyrus, who worshippeth thee, and his son Cambyses [be prosperous]!"

Thus the Babylonian Empire came to an end, and Babylonia became a satrapy of Persia. The Babylonians rebelled during the reign of Cambyses (529–521 BC), but were easily reduced to subjection by Darius I (521–485 BC); at his death they rebelled again. This brought on them the wrath of Xerxes I (485–465 BC), who marched to Babylon, broke down its walls, and destroyed many buildings and temples, including E-zida, the great sanctuary of Bêl-Marduk, which he plundered and left in ruins. On the defeat of Darius III (336–331 BC), Babylon became the capital of the Asiatic Empire of Alexander the Great; and at his death Mesopotamia became a province of the kingdom of Seleucus I Nicator (312–281 BC). So much of Babylon had been destroyed by Xerxes that Seleucus founded the city of Seleucia, on the west bank of the Tigris, near Baghdâd, and the doom of Babylon was sealed. The Parthians set up Arsaces as their king, 249–248 BC, and the Era of the Arsacidae began. They built their capital Ctesiphon on the east bank of the Tigris, a few miles south of Baghdâd. The Sassanians (Persians) overthrew the Parthian Dynasty about AD 226, and they founded their capital Al-Madain (i.e., "the Cities") between Ctesiphon and Baghdâd. The Arabs defeated the Sassanians at the Battle of Kâdîsîyah, on the Euphrates, AD 635, and made Baghdâd their capital. Babylonia then became a Muhammadan Province, and remained so until about AD 1517, when it became a Turkish Pashalik and was ruled from Constantinople.

CHAPTER THREE

THE CITY OF BABYLON

THE NAME OF THE FOUNDER OF BABYLON AND THE DATE WHEN IT was founded are alike unknown. Its position caused it at a very early period to be a kind of central market for caravans from the west, north and east, and the caravans from the south found it at all periods a useful terminus. Some of the objects discovered in the lowermost strata of the ruins which now occupy the site suggest that a settlement existed there in the Neolithic Period. Babylon owed everything to its geographical position, and it was this that enabled the city to survive the series of destructive attacks which were made upon it during the four or five thousand years of its existence. Its true value was recognized by that great and wise law-giver, Khammurabi, who enlarged it, strengthened it, and made it his capital. In the opening lines of his Code he tells us of the great things that he did for the temple of Enlil at Nippur, and how he restored the city of Eridu, perhaps the oldest city in Babylonia, and he goes on to say that he "magnified the renown of Babylon, and rejoiced the heart of Marduk his lord," and what he did for Esagila, the greatest of all the temples of Babylon.

The Sumerians called the city KA DINGIRRA(ki), 𒆍𒀭𒊏𒆠, i.e., the "Gate of God," and TINTIRA, 𒁷𒋾𒆠𒀀, the "Grove of Life." The Akkadians, i.e., the

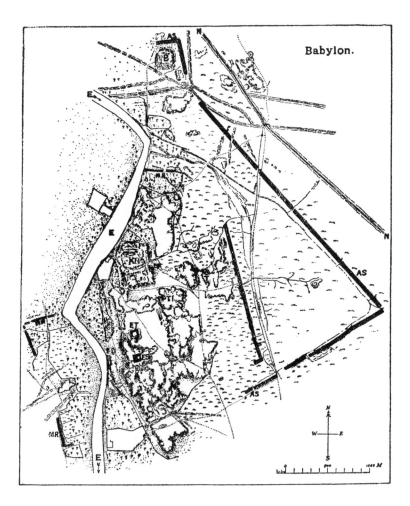

Plan of the ruins at Babylon. After Koldewey, Excavations at Babylon, London, 1914.
 A—The mound of 'Amrân.
 AS—Outer wall of Babylon.
 E—River Euphrates.
 EM—The Temple of Ninmakh.
 ES—E-Sagila, the Temple of Bêl Marduk.
 ET—The Zikkurat, i.e., the Tower of Babylon.
 K—The Kasr (Fortress of Babylon or "Babylon Castle").

The Sirrush, or "Dragon of Babylon," with the head and tail of a serpent, erect horns, spiral combs, scaly body, forelegs of a lion (?), claws of a bird, and hair. From Koldewey, The Excavations at Babylon, London, 1914, pages 46–49.

Semitic Babylonians, translated the old Sumerian name KA DINGIRRA(ki) by Babilu, ⌐⌐ ⌐⌐⌐, a name also meaning "The Gate of God" (*Bâb ili*), and from this the Greek name for the whole country, Βαβυχωνία, is derived. The Jewish Rabbis, remembering the confounding or confusion of tongues that took place when the building of the Tower of Babel was stopped, made a pun on the name "Bâb ili," and rendered the two words by one and called the city "Bâbhel," which means a "mixing up," or "confusion."

The Arab geographers knew well where Babylon had stood, but among European travellers one of the first to identify its site was Benjamin of Tudela, a Jewish Rabbi, who visited it in 1173. Then came Beatus Odoricus, a friar (fourteenth century), Cesare Federigo, Bolbi, John Newberrie, John Eldred, Ralph Fitch, W. Leedes, John Story and Rauwolf (sixteenth century), Pietro della Valle, Emanuel de Saint Albert and F. Vincenzo Maria (seventeenth century), Niebuhr, J. Beauchamps and Olivier (eighteenth century). The natives took Beauchamps under the ruins of the ancient buildings whence they were digging out bricks, and showed him the famous basalt lion which still lies there. Like Pietro della Valle, he took some of the bricks, packed them up and sent them to Europe. In 1811, C. J. Rich, the first British Consul at Baghdâd, examined and partly excavated some of the ruins, and made a map of them. Layard (1850), Rawlinson (1854), Rassam (1878–80) carried out excavations at Babylon, but it was not systematically excavated until Dr. Koldewey had dug there from 1899 to 1912, when he reported that about one-half of the site had been excavated. The largest mound at Babylon is Bâbil, which is 22 metres high and has an area at the base of 250 metres; it contains the remains of a palace of Nebuchadnezzar II. The next building on the south is the Kasr, or "Castle," or "Citadel of Babylon," which was built by Nebuchadnezzar II. Here is what Koldewey calls "Bâbil Street," which the same king paved with slabs of limestone 3 feet 6 inches square, and here were the enamelled or glazed brick walls which were decorated with figures of lions and fabulous animals. Close by is the Ishtar Gate, the walls of which (12 metres high) still stand; on them are figures of bulls and fabulous animals. The "dragon" has scales, a serpent's head, horns and spiral combs; the tail is a serpent's, the forelegs are those of an animal, and the hind legs those of a bird. To the east of the Ishtar Gate is the Temple of Ninmakh, with a well in the forecourt. From the ruins a plan of the temple has been made. The Vaulted Building in the Southern Citadel contains, according to Koldewey, the well with three shafts that enclosed the machinery for watering the famous Hanging Garden, about which so much has been written; and the building itself represents the substructure of the Hanging Garden. Classical writers (Diodorus and Strabo) would have us believe that the Hanging Garden ascended in terraces 6 feet high, 32 feet wide, and 400 feet long, looking like a great flight of stairs, or the tiers of seats in a theatre. It was planted with trees and flowers, and was watered by a hydraulic screw, which went down from the highest terrace to the level of the Euphrates. Every one who has seen the ruins (i.e., of the Vaulted Building) will admit that a garden of this size and kind never existed at Babylon.[1] There may have been there a terrace, with trees and plants, of the same kind as the Bît Gipari which Nabonidus made for his daughter at Ur, and it was probably used by the temple women like the terrace at Ur (see S. Smith, Bab. Hist. Texts, page 57, note 1).

In the Kasr is a large hall, 52 metres long by 17 metres broad, with one of its walls 6 metres thick. Rassam and other excavators have suggested that this was the "banquet house" in which Belshazzar "drank wine before the thousand" of his lords, and saw the writing on the wall (Dan. v. 1–25). In the south-west corner of the Kasr, Koldewey found a large pottery coffin, and he wonders if the person who was buried in it was the king's father Nabopolassar. Between the palace and the moat wall of Imgur-Bêl stood the Apadânâ, or Persian Palace. Further to the south stood the great *zikkurat,* or "temple tower," or "stepped tower," which was called by the Babylonians E-Temen-An-ki, i.e., the "House of the Foundation Stone of Heaven and Earth," 𒀭𒌍 𒍝𒋫 ✳ ⊕, but is more commonly known as the Tower of Babel. The area in which it stood had two doors and ten gateways, and adjoining it were a series of houses which were used by the priests and pilgrims and several store-rooms. Herodotus says (i. 181) that "in the middle of the precinct there was a tower of solid masonry . . . upon which was raised a second tower, and on that a third, and so on up to eight." A tablet translated by George Smith (see *Athenaeum,* Feb. 12, 1876), formerly in the possession of Madame Fennerly, supplies the dimensions of all the stages of this tower, with the exception of the sixth, which is probably due to inadvertence on the part of the scribe. The text has been published by Scheil in the *Mémoires de l'Institut,* vol. xxxix, pages 293 ff. According to it:

Stage 1 was 15 x 15 x 5½ *gar*, i.e., 300 feet square and 110 feet high.
Stage 2 was 13 x 13 x 3 *gar*, i.e., 260 feet square and 60 feet high.
Stage 3 was 10 x 10 x 1 *gar*, i.e., 200 feet square and 20 feet high.
Stage 4 was 8½ x 8½ x 1 *gar*, i.e., 170 feet square and 20 feet high.
Stage 5 was 7 x 7 x 1 *gar*, i.e., 140 feet square and 20 feet high.
Stage 6 [omitted on tablet].

Stage 7 was 4 x 3½ x 2½ *gar*, i.e., 80 feet long, 70 feet broad, and 50 feet high. This was the Temple of Bêl, and in it was the statue of the god.

Assuming that the height of Stage 6 was the same as that of Stages 3, 4 and 5, i.e., I *gar*, or 20 feet, the total height of the Tower of Babel was 300 feet, i.e., its height was equal to the length of one side of the lowest stage. A distinguished mathematician, Mr. Marcel Dieulafoy, held the view that the *gar* was equal to 11 feet and not to 20 as Smith had supposed, and if this be correct, all Smith's figures must be reduced by 45 per cent. (see *Mémoires de l'Institut*, vol. xxxix, pages 310 ff.). This "stepped tower" was undoubtedly the Tower of Babel, not the "stepped tower" of the Temple of Nabû (called in the Middle Ages and at the present day Birs-i-Nimrûd) as many have supposed.

The city of Babylon was joined to a large suburb on the west bank of the Euphrates (the site of which is now partly occupied by the town of Hillah) by a bridge about 123 metres in length. Its piers were 9 metres apart and were 21 metres long and 9 metres wide, and it was approached by the "Procession Street," which was paved by Nebuchadnezzar II. In a direct line with the Tower of Babel stood Esagila, the great temple of Bêl-Marduk; the northern front, where stood the shrine of the god Ea, was about 70 metres long, and the western front, where stood the shrine of Marduk, was about 85 metres long. On the walls, in groups of three, were towers, and in each side wall was a gateway with protecting towers. To the south is the mosque-tomb of 'Amrân ibn 'Ali, and east of it are the remains of the Temple of Enurta, a part of which dates from the time of Nabopolassar, and a little to the north were situated the offices and houses of the Government servants. The mounds of Humrah mark the site of the Temple of Ishtar of Agade, and of the Greek theatre, which may date from the time of Alexander the Great. The northern mound of Humrah was formed by a colossal mass of *débris* from the ruined Temple of Babel, which, Strabo says (xvii. 1. 5), had been destroyed by Xerxes. Alexander the Great intended to have it rebuilt and gave orders to that effect, and he expended 600,000 days' wages in removing the *débris;* but the work came to an end when he died, and the building remained a ruin. Strabo actually speaks of the "tomb of Bêl," but the measurements of the building which he gives certainly refer to some very high building such as the Tower of Babel.

Many classical writers have described the "broad walls" of Babylon, as Jeremiah calls them (li. 58), and given measurements of them, but none of them agree with the evidence derived from their ruins. Herodotus says (i. 178, 179) that the city was square, measuring 120 stadia each way, i.e., that its circuit was 480 stadia, or about 54 miles, which is impossible. Other writers make its circuit to be 360, or 365, or 385 stadia, and none of their measurements agree with those of Koldewey. Again, Herodotus gives the width of the walls of Babylon as being 50 royal cubits, and says that a covered shelter ran along each side, leaving space enough for a four-horsed chariot to drive along between them. As the royal cubit was equal to half a metre, the walls were 25 metres wide, i.e., about 83 feet. Now, Koldewey has shown that Babylon's great wall consisted of *two* walls, 7 and 7.8 metres wide, respectively, that these walls were 12 metres apart, and that the space between them was filled up with earth, the total width being 26.8 metres. The space between the walls, being 12 metres, or about 40 feet, would be quite wide enough for a four-horsed chariot to drive along. Thus the statement of Herodotus about the width of the walls is approximately correct. Outside this double wall was the moat, each side of which was lined with a layer of burnt bricks, 10 feet thick, set in bitumen, and the outer wall was built of the same material. The inner wall was built of unbaked bricks, and before the reign of Nebuchadnezzar II was the only defensive wall of the city. The outer wall was built by Nebuchadnezzar II. Astride of the wall of unburnt bricks, at intervals of 52.5 metres, were towers 8.57 metres wide, which projected beyond each side of the wall. The circuit of the walls was about 18 kilometres, or 10 miles, and not 25 as the measurements of Herodotus would make it. For a full account of the excavations at Babylon *see* Koldewey, *Das Wieder-Erstehende Babylon,* Berlin, 1913, or the English translation by A. S. Johns, London, 1914.

Babylon must have been in existence in the fifth or fourth millennium before Christ, and it must have been an important commercial centre even in the time when Kish, which lay eight miles to the east of it, flourished under the rule of its great Sumerian kings. The oldest ruins at Babylon accessible to Koldewey were of the time of Khammurabi. The Assyrian kings built the wall of the Southern Citadel, and laid down pavements and restored some of the temples. Nebuchadnezzar II intended to rebuild the whole city, and he actually restored the temples of E-Makh, Enurta and Ishtar, and the Tower of Babylon, and built the bridge over the Euphrates at 'Amrân. The final decay of Babylon seems to have been due to the Euphrates in the time of the Persian kings (538–331 BC). Up to that period the river had only flowed by the west side of the Kasr, but then it changed its course and flowed round the eastern side of it. Probably it was the alterations made in the city by this change of bed by the river that induced Seleucus I to found Seleucia near the Tigris; at all events, as the new city grew, Babylon declined. During the early centuries of the Christian Era the district about 'Amrân was inhabited by a miserable remnant of its people, and by a number of Jews who cultivated divination and witchcraft. And popular tradition asserted that the mounds were peopled by hosts of evil spirits led by the two great devils, Harût and Marût, who were sent on earth by God to tempt men and to teach them magic. The town of Hillah, on the west bank of the Euphrates, was founded AD 1101–2, and in a few years Babylon was left without an inhabitant. The natives did not even spare her ruins, for they began to tear down the walls of her temples and palaces and fortifications, and carry away the bricks to build the towns and mosques of Kifl, Kûfah and Karbala. In following the courses of the walls they reached the foundations of the Kasr and other buildings, and it is grievous to think of the many valuable historical documents and evidences which they destroyed in the process. The Abbé Beauchamps reported in the *Journal des Sçavans* for 1791 that a native admitted to him that he had often found inscribed baked clay cylinders among the ruins, but that he had always thrown them away because they were useless for building purposes!

The chief sanctuary of Babylon was Esagila, the seat of the god Bêl, or Bêl-Marduk, which had been built by the hands of angels or gods, and stood within the city walls. But there was an extra-mural sanctuary of great importance, namely, Ezida, 𒂍𒍣𒁕, which was the seat of the god Nabû (Nebo) of BARZIPA(KI), 𒀭𒁀𒌅, or Borsippa, which was called the Second Babylon, 𒆍𒀭𒊏𒆠. The ruin is now called Birs-i-Nimrûd. It stood on the west bank of the Euphrates a few miles from Babylon, and during the New Year Festival the god Nabû was carried in solemn procession across the Euphrates into the sanctuary Esagila, and his priests performed important functions in connection with the annual ceremonies. That Bêl and Nabû were regarded as of equal importance is shown by the words "Bel boweth down, Nebo stoopeth, . . . they stoop, they bow down together; they could not deliver the burden, but themselves [or, their soul] are gone into captivity" (Isai. xlvi. 1, 2). Close to the temple was the great *zikkurat*, or "stepped tower," called E-UR-IMIN-AN-KI, 𒂍𒌉𒅎𒀭𒆠. This building was in seven stages, like the Tower of Babel, and Rawlinson stated that each stage was dedicated to a planet, and had a different colour, thus:

Stage.	Height.	Square.	Colour.	Planet.
1	26	272	Black	Saturn
2	26	230	Red-brown	Jupiter
3	26	188	Red	Mars
4	26	146	Gold	Sun
5	15	104	Yellow	Venus
6	15	62	Blue	Mercury
7	15	20	[Silver?]	[Moon]

Specimens of coloured inlay from this building were presented to the British Museum a few years ago. All that now remains of the *zikkurat* is a mass of semi-vitrified brickwork about 35 feet high, which stands on a mound nearly 120 feet high; Felix Jones made the total height of mound and brickwork 153½ feet. Legend says that the vitrification was caused by fire which fell from Heaven and destroyed the *zikkurat*. Benjamin of Tudela saw the sloping pathways up the sides of the stages by which the top was reached, but all these, and much else disappeared, probably centuries ago. When Rassam stopped work at the Birs-i-Nimrûd in 1854, the natives flocked to the ruins, which they ransacked with great thoroughness, and carried off many thousands of the bricks of Nebuchadnezzar II, which were promptly used by the authorities to repair the barrage of the Hindîyah Canal. A greatly exaggerated importance has been given to this ruin through the mistake made by Benjamin of Tudela (*see* the Hebrew text, ed. Asher, page 65), who thought it was the Tower of Babel, which was destroyed when the speech of mankind was confounded. But the statements of Arrian (*Anabasis* vii. 17) and Strabo (xvii. 1. 5) seem to me sufficient to justify the belief that the *zikkurat* of Babylon was in ruins when Alexander the Great entered Babylon. If this be so, neither Benjamin of Tudela nor any more modern traveller can ever have seen the true Tower of Babel. It is true that Muslim tradition states that the Birs-i-Nimrûd is the remains of the tower that was built by Nimrod, a contemporary of

Abraham, so that he might ascend to Heaven to see God. Nimrod persecuted Abraham, but God protected the patriarch, and destroyed Nimrod's tower by fire. Nimrod died miserably, for a gnat entered his head through his ear or nose, and caused him agony which lasted for four hundred years. The importance which Nebuchadnezzar II attached to the sanctuaries of Bêl and Nabû is illustrated by the following paraphrases of extracts from his great inscription in the India Office.

> Marduk, the glorious chief, the captain of the gods, heard my petition and received my prayer. His Lordship showed compassion, he set the fear of his godhead in my heart, he made my heart to incline to the love of his laws. By his august help I marched into remote countries, and made long journeys over the difficult lands that lie between the Upper Sea (i.e., the Mediterranean) and the Lower Sea (i.e., the Persian Gulf), where there are no roads and the going is painful and laborious, and I subdued those who would not obey my will, and bound the rebels in fetters. I administered the country, and made its inhabitants prosperous, and I divided the loyal folk from the disloyal. I gathered together silver, gold, precious stones, copper, precious woods, and costly things of every kind, and whatsoever was in the mountains, and the products of the seas, and carried them to Babylon, and laid them as a rich gift before his Lordship in Esagila. I decorated the shrine of Marduk with them, and inlaid its walls with gold and precious stones. A former king had inlaid it with silver, but I plated it with gold. The vessels of Esagila I covered with gold, and I decorated the Boat of Marduk with precious stones and inlayings. I made the summit of

E-temen-an-ki (the Tower of Babel) to rear itself up in
burnt brick and fine stone, and I toiled hard to establish Esagila. I used the finest cedars which I had
brought from Lebanon to roof the shrine of his
Lordship, and I plated the beams with gold. I beauti-
fied Barzipa (Borsippa), and I restored Ezida, and
decorated it with gold and silver and precious stones.
I roofed the house of Nabû with cedar wood and
plated the beams with gold. The roof of the Gate of
Nanâ I plated with silver, and I made to shine with
silver the bulls, the doors, the gate, the lintels, the bars
and bolt, the ends of the roof-beams, etc. The paths
to the shrine and the building I paved with glazed (?)
bricks. The interior of the shrine was of carved silver
work. I made the building so beautiful and fitted it
with so many things of beauty that those who looked
upon it would marvel. I built and restored the temple
of Borsippa, and I made the zikkurat to rear its
summit in burnt brick and limestone. The sides and
cabin of the Boat of the god, the Boat which was
carried in the New Year Festival to Babylon, I inlaid
with precious stones." [Then follows an account of
the buildings that he made for the Great Goddess who
made him, Sin, Shamash, Rimmon, Gula and other
gods and goddesses in Babylon and Borsippa.] "My
father Nabopolassar had begun to build the two great
walls of Babylon, Imgur Bêl and Nimitti Bêl, and to
make the brick walls of the moat and the dykes on the
Euphrates, and to pave the sacred way from the Gate
of Beltis, but he did not finish the work of any of
these. But I, Nebuchadnezzar, his son, his heart's
darling, finished the building of the walls Imgur Bêl
and Nimitti Bêl, and also the building of the walls of

the moat. And I embanked Aiburshabu, the sacred way of Marduk, and paved it with tiles (?) and stone, and I repaired this road from the Upper Gate to the palace of Ishtar, who crushes her foes. I completed all that my father had begun. I reset the gates of Imgur Bêl and Nimitti Bêl with bricks and bitumen. I made for them roofs of cedar, and doors of cedar plated with copper, and provided them with hinges and copper frames. I set up by them huge bronze bulls and serpents to the admiration (?) of the people. I built a rampart 4,000 cubits long, and dug a wide moat for it, which I lined with bricks set in bitumen and then filled with water, so that no enemy might approach Babylon. I rebuilt Tâbisubûrshu, the wall of Borsippa, and dug a moat for it, and lined it with brick set in bitumen. Ever since Marduk created me to be a king, and Nabû committed his people to my rule, I have loved like my own life the work of building their cities. The brickwork of the canal which Nabopolassar had made from the bank of the Euphrates to Aiburshabu became weak and cracked, and I dug down to the bottom of it and repaired the lining with bricks set in bitumen. And I built a rampart for the wall Nimitti Bêl. Between the walls I built a palace, roofed it with cedar, provided doors made of precious woods, framed in silver and gold and plated with copper. I built a huge wall round it, and faced it with stone. I made the walls of Babylon to frighten the enemy, and made Babylon as strong as the forest-clad hills." [Then comes a prayer of Nebuchadnezzar.] "O Lord Marduk, prince of the gods, thou didst create me and commit to me the sovereignty of the host of thy people. Like my life, I love the supremacy of thy cities. I have no other city in the country like unto thine. As I love thy godhead, so do I seek (?) thy lordship. May the house that I have made endure, like thine, to all eternity, O Marduk, thou compassionate one. May I be satisfied with the fullness thereof, and may I reach old age therein. May I be satisfied with offspring. May the kings who rule over all mankind [bring] heavy tribute, and may I receive it therein. From the foundation of heaven to the heights thereof and from the rising [to the setting sun] may I have no foes, may I have no enemies. And in it may my posterity rule over men for ever and ever.

The rectangular, thick slab of hard black stone on which Nebuchadnezzar II caused his "Standard Inscription" to be cut in archaic Babylonian characters in ten columns is in the India Office; there is a cast of it in the British Museum, and another in the Library of the Royal Asiatic Society. It was found at Babylon, and was acquired by Sir Harford Jones in 1808, and sent home by him to the India Office. The Hon. the East India Company published a facsimile of the text, which was reproduced in Rawlinson's *Selection*, vol. i.

CHAPTER FOUR

THE BABYLONIAN STORY
OF THE CREATION

THE SUMERIANS AND BABYLONIANS, IN COMMON WITH THE Egyptians and other peoples of antiquity, frequently speculated on the origin of the heavens and earth and things in general, including themselves, and we know that different thinkers in different parts of Babylonia arrived at different conclusions as the result of their cogitations. In the cuneiform texts, as in the Book of Genesis, we have two versions of the Story of Creation, and various passages in the Legends that have come down to us show that other versions existed. The shorter, simpler version, which is known as the "Bilingual Version" of the Creation Legend, is found on a tablet in the British Museum (No. 93,014). It begins by describing a time when the house of the gods did not exist, when neither trees nor plants were in existence, when neither a house nor a city had been built, and when no being had been fashioned. That time was so far remote that the temple of Enlil at Nippur and the temple of Erech had not been built. Even Eridu, the oldest city in the land, had not been founded. No land was visible, the sea was everywhere. Then Eridu was formed, and Esagila, the sanctuary of Bêl-Marduk at Babylon, was founded, and in due course both these sanctuaries were completed. Then Lugal-dul-Azuga, a form of Marduk, created the Anunnaki gods, who proclaimed the sovereignty of the city of Babylon in which they delighted to dwell. The world was created by Marduk, who formed it by kneading earth and spreading it over a mat made of rushes, which he laid on the face of the waters. This formed an abiding place for the gods of which they approved. Marduk then fashioned man, and the goddess Aruru with him created the seed of mankind. He created the beasts of the field and all the small creatures of the field. He created the rivers Tigris and Euphrates, and assigned to them their places in the land, and announced their names. He created vegetation, the plants that grow in the marshes, the seed-bearing plants and bushes, and the herbage of the field; lands, marshes and swamps; he created the cow and her calf, the ewe and her lamb, and the sheep of the field; gardens (?) and shrub-land. He created the he-goat and the wild goat. The lord Marduk built a dyke in the sea, he enclosed a swamp . . . he created plants and trees . . . he laid bricks and built up brickwork, he constructed houses and founded cities, he built cities and peopled them. He made the city of Nippur and built her temple E-Kur, he made Erech and built her temple E-Anna. It is interesting to note that this text, like that of the Egyptian story of the Creation as found in the Papyrus of Nesi-Amsu (*see* Budge, *Legends of the Gods,* London, 1912, pages 2 ff.), was sometimes used for recital as an incantation. And its recital was supposed to produce some important result.

The other version of the Story of the Creation is found in the Seven Tablets of Creation, large portions of which are preserved in the British Museum.[1] According to this, in the beginning nothing existed, except an inert mass of watery matter, of boundless extent, called Apsu. Ancient writers make no attempt to show how this came into being, or when; like the Egyptian Nenu, it was supposed to have existed always. Out of Apsu came hideous devils of composite forms, and gods in the forms of men; the former lived in Apsu and the latter above it. The place where the gods lived we may call heaven, and the space immediately below it, together with Apsu, we may call earth. The two oldest gods to spring from Apsu were Lakhmu and Lakhamu, but about them we know nothing. After a long and indefinite period the gods Anshar and Kishar appeared, and heaven and earth were established as separate entities. Next there came into being Anu, ⸻ ⸻ ⸻, the god of heaven and the sky, and the god Ea, ⸻ ⸻ ⸻, god of the "House of Water," and several other gods. The disposition of things, which the text calls the "Way of the gods," was displeasing to Apsu, who is here made to be the predominant being in Apsu, and he took counsel with the monster she-devil, Tiâmat, ⸻ ⸻ ⸻, with the view of finding a way of overthrowing the order which had taken the place of chaos. Tiâmat was imagined to be a composite creature, part animal, part serpent, part bird, revolting in appearance, and evil in every way. But at the same time she was the Universe-Mother, and she had in her possession the Tablet of Fate. Nowhere in the texts is any description of this Tablet given, but we probably find a parallel to it in the Book of the Dead and in the Kur'ân. In the former there is a mention of a "brick," or tablet "of iron," ⸻ ⸻ ⸻, on which the decrees of Ptah-Tanen concerning the destiny of Osiris were inscribed (Chap. clxxxiii. l. 15), and in the latter we have the "Preserved Tablet" (Surah x. 62), on which the destiny of every man was written at or before the creation of the world. Tiâmat was the personification of chaos, night, darkness and inertness, and of every kind of evil. Apsu and Tiâmat having taken counsel together determined that, with the help of Mummu, they would fight the gods and abolish their arrangement of heaven and earth. When Ea knew of their decision he went forth to do battle with the powers of darkness and chaos, and gained a victory over them, but we have no details of the encounter. One text says that he used a "holy incantation," which, of course, possessed great power; the recital of it cast a spell on the allies of Tiâmat, and they were rendered impotent. The Egyptian texts relate the same thing of the god Her-Tuati, who recited words of power against Āpep, the equivalent of Tiâmat, and the monster was rendered helpless. But Ea's spell, unlike that of Her-Tuati's, produced a permanent effect on Apsu and Mummu, and seems actually to have killed Apsu.

For a time Tiâmat was dismayed at the death of Apsu, but she recovered, and her anger against the gods increased. She called to her help the female devil Ummu-Khubur, who at once spawned a brood of monster devils and put them at her disposal. Tiâmat next summoned her male counterpart Kingu, and placed under his command the evil powers of the air, to which the texts give the names of the Viper, the Snake, Lakhamu, the Whirlwind, the Ravening Dog, the Scorpion-man, the Storm Wind, the Fishman, the Horned Beast, and all these were armed with an invincible weapon. These, together with Kingu and Tiâmat, probably represent the primitive Twelve Signs of the Zodiac, which were powers of evil. Kingu was the king and leader of all the powers of the kingdom of darkness, and Tiâmat, when she appointed him to be the captain of her hosts, recited over him a spell which would make him invincible, and preserve him from wounds and death. She gave him also the Tablet of Fate which she carried in her bosom, so that his words would possess almighty power. Thus Kingu and his hosts of devils were ready to renew the fight with Ea and, if necessary, with the other gods.

When Ea heard what Tiâmat had done, and how she had collected a mighty army of devils with Kingu at their head, he felt that he was not strong enough to do battle with them, and he went to Anshar and told him about Tiâmat. Anshar, like Ea, was troubled, and called Anu, the Sky-god, to help him. When Anu came, Anshar sent him to Tiâmat, perhaps with the belief that he would be able to persuade her to abate her anger and her hostility to the gods. But when Anu came to her, Tiâmat raged at him, and on seeing her hideous form and features he turned and fled. On his return to report his failure to conciliate Tiâmat, a council of the gods was called by Ea, and his son Marduk came with the rest, and offered to go as the champion of the gods to fight Tiâmat. Anshar ordered a banquet to be prepared in Upshukkinaku, the chief abode of the gods, to which he invited all the gods; when they had come, and saluted each other, they sat down, and ate bread and drank hot wine, and discussed what was to be done. They appointed Marduk to be their champion, and conferred upon him magical powers of all kinds, and saluted him as their king and gave him the sceptre and the throne, and put on him all the outward symbols of sovereignty. This done, they commanded him to go and slay Tiâmat.

Then Marduk armed himself with a bow, a spear, and a club, and filled himself with fire, and set the lightning before him. He took in one hand a net wherewith to catch Tiâmat, and he grouped the four winds of heaven about him, to prevent her flight; in the other hand he grasped the thunderbolt, and created by means of it violent tempests and storms to help him. Then he mounted the [Chariot of] the Storm, which was drawn by four horses, and set out to capture Tiâmat. Meanwhile Kingu had taken up his place in the middle of Tiâmat, and when he saw Marduk clothed with thunder and girt about with lightnings entering in there, he was terrified and staggered about helplessly, and all his followers sank down in a stupefied state. As Marduk came on Tiâmat cursed him, and when he attacked her she raged, and began to recite a spell which she believed would paralyse him. Marduk threw his net over her, and when a gale of wind entering through her mouth distended her body, he drove his spear into her hide, which at once burst asunder. Her fiends and devils tried to escape, but were prevented by the four winds; and having caught them all in his net Marduk trampled upon them. He took the Tablet of Fate from off Kingu's breast and, setting his seal upon it, placed it on his own. He then crushed the skull of Tiâmat with his club, and scattered her blood to the north wind. He split her body into two parts; of the hide of the one he made the vault of heaven and of the hide of the other he made the abode of Ea. The plenishing of heaven and earth next occupied his attention, and he began by establishing abodes for Anu, god of the heavens, Bêl, god of the earth, and Ea, god of the deep and the underworld.

The regulations that Marduk made for the heavenly bodies were set forth in the Fifth Tablet of Creation, of which only a very fragmentary copy has come down to us. From the text available it is evident that Marduk fixed stations for the great gods, the Lumashi,

*Portion of a tablet inscribed with a version of the legend of the fight
between Marduk and Tiâmat. B.M. No. 93,016.*

or Signs of the Zodiac, the Year, the three stars of each month (i.e.,
the Dekans), Nibiru (see Langdon, *Epic of Creation,* page 155), the
Moon, etc. The gods, however, appear not to have been wholly satisfied with what Marduk had done for them, chiefly because there was

no one to present offerings to them and to worship at their shrines. When Marduk heard their complaint he decided to create man out of "blood and bone," and announced his decision to Ea, who suggested that one of the gods should be sacrificed to provide "blood and bone" for the man who was to be made. Thereupon Marduk asked the gods in council who was the cause of the rebellion of Tiâmat and had made war, and they named Kingu, the husband of Tiâmat. And they bound Kingu with fetters, and brought him to Ea, and having chastised him they let out his blood, from which mankind was made. The Anunnaki gods then proposed to build a shrine for Marduk, and when Marduk heard this he was pleased, and said that he wished the shrine to be in Babylon. The gods spent a year in making bricks, and built Esagila and its *zikkurat* with their own hands. When the temple was finished Marduk took up his abode therein, and assigned places to the gods, and the Anunnaki sang a Hymn of Praise to him. A little later the gods met there in council and bestowed upon him the Fifty Names, which indicated that the power and wisdom of every god were collected in him. On the origin of the Creation Legend as told in the Seven Tablets, and the various forms of it current in Babylonia and Assyria, the reader should consult the little work, *Babylonian Legends of the Creation and the Fight between Bêl and the Dragon*, London, 1921, published by the Trustees of the British Museum. It must be pointed out that there is no evidence at all that the Two Accounts of the Creation which are given in the early chapters of Genesis are derived from the Seven Tablets, the contents of which have been summarized above. "There are many points of resemblance between the narratives in cuneiform and Hebrew, and these often illustrate each other, but the fundamental conceptions of the Babylonian and Hebrew accounts are essentially different" (*Babylonian Legends,* page 30).

CHAPTER FIVE

THE BABYLONIAN STORY OF THE FLOOD AS TOLD IN THE GILGAMISH EPIC

THE ACCOUNT OF THE FLOOD GIVEN IN THE BOOK OF GENESIS IS NOT borrowed from the Babylonian Version, as has so often been stated. It is quite true that the Accounts in cuneiform and Hebrew agree in many places very closely, but the variations in them show that their writers, or editors, were dealing with a very ancient legend which had found its way among all the Sumerians, Semites and other peoples in Western Asia. Exactly how old the legend is cannot be said, but there is reason for thinking that it was in existence before the Sumerians overcame the aboriginal inhabitants of Lower Mesopotamia. The Sumerian scribes treated the old indigenous legend in one way, the Babylonians in another, and the Hebrews in yet another, and it is pretty clear that variant versions of it existed among the Sumerians and Babylonians in the third millennium BC. Scheil has published (*Recueil de Travaux*, vol. xx., pages 35 ff.) the text of a part of a Babylonian Version from a tablet dating from the reign of Khammurabi, and Poebel has edited and translated (*Hist. Texts* and *Hist. and Gram. Texts*, Philadelphia, 1914) a portion of a Sumerian Version which was written in the reign of Ammisaduga, about 2000 BC. The scribes who wrote these texts did not invent the Legend of the Flood, and they must have had archetypes to copy, and how old these were no man can say. In its simplest form the legend described what was probably only a local flood in Lower Babylonia, due to a wide-spread inundation of the Tigris or Euphrates, or both, which coincided with torrential rains in the district. Such floods have occurred in Lower Mesopotamia from time immemorial, and they have not been unknown during the last fifty years. In primitive times the reed-huts and mud-houses were swept away, whole villages were destroyed, and men and cattle were drowned. The flood which is referred to in the legend must have been peculiarly destructive, for to both Sumerians and Babylonians it served as a sort of never-to-be-forgotten chronological landmark in their King Lists. Berossos (ed. Schnabel, page 261) states that ten kings reigned before the Flood for 120 *sars*, i.e., for 432,000 years; and of some of the kings whom he mentions the cuneiform equivalents are forthcoming. Thus, Enedôrachos is Enmeduranki, ⟨cuneiform⟩, Opartes is Ubara-Tutu, ⟨cuneiform⟩, and Xisûthros is Atrakhasis, The ⟨cuneiform⟩. Legend of the Flood has nothing to do with the exploits of the mythical hero Gilgamish, and it is difficult to see why it is included in the history of them. It is possible that its incorporation in the Epic of Gilgamish is due to the scribes of Ashur-bani-pal. One fact is worthy of note: every editor of the Legend tries to inculcate a moral lesson in his version. The city of Shuruppak was destroyed because of the wickedness of its people, which brought down upon them the wrath of Bêl, the god of middle heaven; and Uta-Napishtim being, like Noah, a righteous man, was warned by a divine power of the destruction that was to fall upon mankind; the sinner and all his possessions were to perish, but the righteous man should be saved alive; the gods see and know everything. The great moral lesson of the Epic of Gilgamish is that the greatest and mightiest king must die, for all men are born to die; no man can enjoy immortality on earth. But this lesson is not what the Legend of the Flood as told by Berossos teaches. For, according to him, when Xisûthros found that the ark had come to a standstill he looked out and saw that it was resting on a mountain side. Therefore he and his wife and daughter and the pilot left the ark, made adoration to the earth, and built an altar and offered up sacrifices to the gods and then disappeared. When those who remained in the ark found that he and his wife and daughter and the pilot did not return to them they left the ark with many lamentations, calling continually on the name of Xisûthros. They saw him no more, but they could hear his voice in the air and his admonitions to be religious. The voice told them that it was on account of his piety that he had been translated to live with the gods, and that his wife and daughter and the pilot had received the same honour. The voice also told them to return to Babylonia, to search the writings at Sippara, which they were to make known to mankind. They offered sacrifices to the gods and journeyed towards Babylonia (see Cory, *Ancient Fragments*, London, 1832, pages 26 ff.).

The History of Gilgamish was written upon a Series of Twelve Tablets which were preserved in the Library of Nabû at Nineveh; the Eleventh of the Series contained the Legend of the Flood. According to a King List, Gilgamish, ⊱⊣⊨ 𒈥 ⊁, was the fifth king of a Sumerian Dynasty that ruled at Erech, and he reigned 126 years (*see* Gadd, *Early Dynasties of Sumer and Akkad*, London, 1921, page 36). The contents of the tablets describing his exploits may be thus summarized: Gilgamish was a great, wise and learned king, and was well acquainted with antediluvian history. He was a great traveller and a mighty hero, and he had a record of his deeds inscribed on a stone stele. He built the great wall of Erech and the temple E-Anna. He was part-god and part-man, two-thirds of him being god and one-third man. His people suffered so greatly from the *corvée* which he imposed upon them that they cried out to the gods to send them a deliverer, and the gods ordered the goddess Aruru to create one. She washed her hands, took some clay, spat upon it, and made a man, who was covered with hair; he lived in the forests with the beasts, which he ruled by reason of his mighty stature and strength. He was called Enkidu, ⸢𒂗⸣ 𒆠𒆕. This name was formerly read Eabani. When Gilgamish heard of him, he sent out a woman to the forest, and she lured him into Erech, where he and Gilgamish became great friends. One day the two friends quarrelled because Gilgamish wished to go to visit the goddess Ishkhara, and in the fight that took place between them Enkidu was the victor.

It was reported to Gilgamish that a mighty being called Khumbaba lived in the Forest of Cedars; his voice was like the roar of a storm, his breath was a whirlwind, and his mouth was like that of the gods. Gilgamish and Enkidu set out to attack Khumbaba, and having reached the Forest of Cedars, they overthrew him there. When Gilgamish returned to Erech he arrayed himself in royal apparel, and the goddess Ishtar saw him and fell in love with him and promised him a gold chariot and horses, the service of kings and nobles, abundant flocks and herds, and the tribute of foreign nations, if he would become her lover. Gilgamish rejected her advances, reviled her for her inconstancy, and hurled abusive words at her. Ishtar went to Anu, the Sky-god, and Antu, her mother, and having complained bitterly of the insults of Gilgamish, she entreated Anu to make a bull that would destroy him. Anu created a fire-breathing bull which went to Erech and killed many people in the city. Then Gilgamish and Enkidu went out and killed the bull and presented his horns to the god Lugalbanda. Soon after this Gilgamish had a dream in which it seemed that disaster was about to fall upon Enkidu, and shortly afterwards that mighty hero fell sick, and died on the twelfth day of his illness. When Gilgamish saw his dead body he thought at first that Enkidu was asleep, but when he found that he was dead his grief made him roar like a lioness robbed of her cubs, and he bitterly lamented his brave friend, the "panther of the desert." When his burst of grief was over and he was wandering about the country, the thought struck him that he himself would die one day, and would then be even as was Enkidu. He dreaded the very idea of death, and determined to consult his ancestor, Uta-Napishtim, who had become immortal, as to the means he must take to escape from it. Where this ancestor lived he did not know, but it was somewhere in the West, and he set out without delay. He marched to Mount Mashu, fought with animals and men, talked with the Scorpion men, and then went on through a region of darkness, until he arrived in a beautiful garden, in which he saw the tree of the gods. Here he met the goddess Siduri-Sabitu, and he asked her how he was to find the way to Uta-Napishtim. The goddess told him that the immortal lived in a place beyond the Waters of Death, which no one except the Sun-god had ever crossed, but that Ur-Shanabi, the boatman of Uta-Napishtim, was in her dwelling, and that he should see him. Gilgamish sought and found the boatman and, having followed his instructions, set out with him in his boat, and reached the abode of Uta-Napishtim in one month and fifteen days. Uta-Napishtim saw the boat coming and went down to meet Gilgamish. When they had talked together and Gilgamish had told him that he did not wish to become dust like his friend Enkidu, and asked him how he could escape death, Uta-Napishtim told him that the gods had decreed the fate of every man, and that death was the lot of all men. Then Gilgamish asked him how it came about that he had obtained immortality, and in answer Uta-Napishtim told him the

BABYLONIAN STORY OF THE FLOOD

The gods who dwelt in Shuruppak, a city on the Euphrates, persuaded the great gods Anu, Enlil (Bêl), Enurta, Ennugi and Ea to make a mighty storm. The god Ea spoke in a dream to Uta-Napishtim, who was sleeping in a reed hut, and told him to tear down his house, to build a ship, to abandon his goods and possessions and to save his life by means of the ship. It was to be as broad as it

Portion of a baked clay tablet inscribed with a version of the Babylonian account of the Deluge. B.M. No. K. 3375.

was long, and to have a roof, and he was to load the ship with all kinds of grain. Uta-Napishtim replied that he heard and understood his lord's commands and would fulfil them, but he asked Ea how he was to explain his action to his fellow-townsmen. Ea told him to say that he had incurred the wrath of Enlil, that he must leave Shuruppak and never see it again, and that he was going to sail on the ocean to his lord Ea. The next morning Uta-Napishtim made men bring him bitumen and other materials for building the ship; it was 120 cubits high, and the roof had the same dimensions. He plastered it with bitumen, made a steering-pole and its fittings, and provided water-bolts. He slaughtered oxen and sheep for the workmen and supplied them with beer, oil and wine, and celebrated the completion of the ship by making a great feast like that held on New Year's Day, and anointed himself with unguent. He then loaded the ship with all his goods and possessions, gold, silver, grain, and sent into it his family and kinsfolk and servants and cattle. The god Shamash warned him that the great storm would break at eventide and, when the night fell and the storm drew nigh, Uta-Napishtim went up into his ship and shut the door, as Shamash had commanded him; and his pilot Puzur-Bêl took charge of the ship. At dawn the storm was raging, black clouds covered the sky, lightnings rent the heavens, thunders pealed, and the whirlwind carried away the post of the ship. Darkness was everywhere, and torrents of rain poured down, and the waters reached to the mountains. The flood swept away the people, who struggled against it as if they were fighting a battle. The gods themselves were terrified at the storm and fled to the highest heaven and cowered by the wall like dogs. Ishtar lamented bitterly when she saw the bodies of the drowned folk filling the sea "like little fishes," and the gods joined their wailings to hers and sat down and wept. The rains descended and the cyclone raged for six days and six nights, but they ceased on the seventh day. When Uta-Napishtim looked out through the air-hole of the ship he saw water everywhere, for the land was laid flat and men had become mud; and he sat down and wept.

Twelve days later they saw an island, and the pilot steered the ship to the land of Nisir, and when it reached the slope of Mount Nisir it grounded and remained fast for six days. On the seventh day Uta-Napishtim sent out a dove from the ship, and though it flew away it came back, for it could not find land on which to alight. He then sent out a swallow, which flew away, but, like the dove, finding no land on which to alight, came back to the ship. Next he sent out a raven, which flew away, and, finding ground from which it could peck food, it did not return. Then Uta-Napishtim came out of his ship and offered up a sacrifice, and poured out a libation on the top of the mountain. The gods smelt the sweet savour of the sacrifice, and gathered together about it like flies. At this moment Ishtar came, and, lifting up her necklace of lapis-lazuli (i.e., the rainbow), which her father Anu had made for her, she swore that she would never forget the days that had just passed, and invited all the gods to partake of the sacrifice, except Enlil, who had made the flood and destroyed her people. But Enlil came, and when he saw the ship and the man who had escaped alive from the flood, he was filled with wrath, and declared that the man should die. Then Ea asked Enlil how it came about that he refused to be advised and made the flood. Let the man, he said, who is a sinner suffer for his sin, and the transgressor pay for his transgression; Enlil should be merciful and compassionate, otherwise man and everything else would be destroyed. "I would" (he said) "that a lion, or a wolf, or famine, or plague had come upon man rather than thy storm." And in order to save the life of Uta-Napishtim, Ea told Enlil that he had not revealed to Uta-Napishtim the decision of the gods to make a storm, but had only sent him a vision through which the man had found it out. Enlil apparently agreed to spare the life of Uta-Napishtim, for Ea went up into the ship and, taking him by the hand, led him out with his wife. Then Ea made them to kneel on the ground facing each other, and he stood up between them and blessed them, and pronounced the decree that Uta-Napishtim and his wife, who were mortals, should henceforward be immortal, like the gods, and he assigned to them a place at the mouth of the rivers in which they were to dwell. In accordance with Ea's decree, Uta-Napishtim and his wife were taken to a remote place at the mouth of the rivers, and there they dwelt.

Thus Uta-Napishtim obtained immortality, not for any special merit of his own, but because Enlil, having promised the gods of Shuruppak that he would send a storm to destroy the city and its people, would not permit the man who had escaped from the storm which he sent to continue his life as a man. Enlil's word and decree were absolute and must be held to be so by gods and men.

THE SUBSEQUENT ADVENTURES OF GILGAMISH

We are not told what Gilgamish thought of Uta-Napishtim's Story of the Flood, but it is clear that he was not content with the statement that all men must die at one time or another. And when Uta-Napishtim asked what god would unite him to himself and make him immortal, Gilgamish had nothing to say. Knowing the weakness of man's physical nature, Uta-Napishtim told him to do without sleep for six days and seven nights, but as soon as Gilgamish sat down he became drowsy and fell asleep, and slept for six days. When Uta-Napishtim pointed this out to his wife, she had pity on Gilgamish and asked her husband to help him to get back to his home; she baked bread and carried it to the ship, and Uta-Napishtim told Ur-Shanabi to take him back to the place whence he came. During a conversation about death, Gilgamish asked his host for advice as to his future proceedings in his quest of immortality. Uta-Napishtim told him that a certain plant, which grew at the bottom of the sea, would, if he ate of it, renew his youth. Gilgamish tied stones to his feet and sank himself down to the bottom of the sea and found the plant, and pulled it up and returned to the boat. On his way back to Erech he and Ur-Shanabi passed a pool of cold water, and Gilgamish decided to take a bath. He placed the plant that renewed youth in a safe place before he entered the pool, but whilst he was in the water a serpent discovered its whereabouts by its smell and ate it. Gilgamish cursed and wept over his wasted labour and, tired and depressed, he continued his journey. In due course he and Ur-Shanabi reached Erech. But the haunting fear of death continued to harass Gilgamish, and he still hoped to find a way to attain to immortality, and thought that he might discover it among the dead. He consulted the priests, who were ready to help him on certain conditions; what these were we know not, but it is clear that they were unacceptable to him, and that he could not enter the abode of the dead to find immortality. Then he remembered that his friend Enkidu was among the dead, and he believed that, if only he could see him and talk to him, he might obtain some useful information. As the priests could not help him, he petitioned Enlil (Bêl) to permit the spirit of Enkidu to come to him, but the god did not answer; Gilgamish petitioned Sin, with the same result. He then petitioned Ea, who, pitying him, ordered Enurta to bring the spirit of Enkidu up to earth. Enurta opened the ground, and the spirit of Enkidu came up; but such answers as it gave to the questions of Gilgamish afforded him very little satisfaction, and helped him in no way. Of the history of Gilgamish after this event nothing is known.

CHAPTER SIX

BABYLONIAN RELIGIOUS BELIEFS

THE STORY OF THE CREATION HAS BEEN TOLD IN A PREVIOUS chapter, but its author, being more concerned to glorify Marduk, whom he makes to be the Creator of the heavens and the earth and all therein, than to instruct his readers, has left many important details of the work of Creation unexplained. Heaven, we are told, was made out of one-half of the skin of Tiâmat, and earth out of the other. The Babylonians believed, even as Diodorus said (ii. 31.7), that the form of the earth was that of a hollow round bowl turned upside down which resembled in shape the *kuffah*,[1] or round boat which is in use today on the Tigris and Euphrates, and that heaven had the form of a fixed hard hemisphere inverted over it. Heaven was usually divided into three parts, viz., the heaven of Anu, the heaven of Bêl, and the heaven of Ea, though some theologians held the view that there were seven heavens. Heaven rested upon a foundation which was firmly moored to posts in the surrounding ocean, and was provided with a girdle-wall like a temple or fort. On the outside of the vault of heaven was the region where the sun passed the night and the moon stayed during the days when she is invisible to man. On the east was the mountain of sunrise, and on the west the mountain of sunset, and each had a door. The sun opened the eastern door in the morning and disappeared through the western door in the evening. Representations of these doors are to be seen on cylinder-seals. The stars had their places in the vault of heaven, and likewise the celestial originals of the great cities and rivers of Mesopotamia. Below heaven was the earth, also divided into three parts (or seven parts), which were inhabited by Ea, men, and the gods of the Underworld. The highest part of the earth formed the seat of the god Enlil, and was called "E-kur," or "House of the Mountain," and the mountain itself was divided into four parts, i.e., the four quarters of the earth. East of this was the Mountain of the Sunrise, and near it was Upshukkinaku, where, in the chamber Duku, the gods arranged the affairs of the world at the beginning of each year. Below the earth was the subterranean sea called "Apsu," which could be reached by an opening made in the ground; it was surrounded by a sea that enclosed all earth and heaven. In the latter sea were eight islands. Near the Mountain of the Sunset was the entrance to the Underworld, which was called Kurnugia, or Arali, and occupied the uttermost depths of the earth. This region was divided into seven parts by seven girdle-walls, each of which was provided with two doors. It was ruled over by a goddess called Allatu, or Ereshkigal, who, with the help of the Six Hundred Anunnaki, took charge of the spirits of the dead. Another view is that as there were Seven Heavens there were also Seven Hells, and that the lowermost Hell was reserved for the spirits of those who had been the greatest sinners on earth.

The gods and goddesses of the Babylonians were many, and their names fill one of the largest tablets of the Kuyûnjik Collection in the British Museum. The earliest people in Babylonia believed that everything possessed a spirit, and such religion as they had can perhaps be best described by the word Animism. Some spirits were benevolent and some malevolent, and the latter must be propitiated by gifts or supplications, or by both. The oldest of such spirits

was the "house spirit," or household-god. When men formed themselves into village communities the idea of the "spirit of the village"
was evolved, and later came the "god of the town or city," and the
"god of the country." Each of the elements, earth, air, fire, and
water had its spirit or "god," the earthquake, lightning, thunder,
rain, storm, desert whirlwind, each had likewise its spirit or "god,"
and, of course, each plant, tree, and animal. As time went on men
began to think that certain spirits were more powerful than others,
and these they selected for special reverence or worship. Accident,
or design on the part of interested persons, enhanced the popular-
ity of these, and Local-gods and Nature-gods came into being.
Primitive man was too careful of his own welfare to abandon his
belief in the spirits who were not selected for special reverence,
because there was always the possibility that at some time or other
they might have the opportunity of hurting him or of doing him
good, and he therefore assigned to them a position in the world of
unseen beings, although one of inferiority. The length of the
animistic period of religion in Babylonia is not known, but there is
abundant evidence that, in the fourth millennium before Christ,
the Sumerians had formulated a system of gods in which each held
a well-defined place. The gods were usually represented in human
forms, but some had the forms of animals, birds, etc.; each had his
own attributes, and each performed certain duties and work. At a
comparatively late period the powers and attributes of all the gods
were assigned to Marduk, the son of Ea, and some have thought in
consequence that the Babylonians were Monotheists, but such was
not the case. The monotheism of the Babylonians and Assyrians
(for the national god Ashur was in Assyria what Marduk was in
Babylonia) entirely lacked the sublime, spiritual conception of
God that the Israelites possessed, and was wholly different from the
monotheism of Christian nations. Among the Sumerian and
Babylonian gods may be mentioned the following:

Anu, the Father and King of the Gods, the God *par excellence* in fact. He was not a popular god in Babylonia, for he was too great and too remote to be called upon by worshippers to help them in the affairs of daily life. His position astronomically was the Equator of Heaven and his number was the perfect number Sixty. His oldest sanctuary was in Uruk (Warka), and his temple there was called E-Anna. His wife was called Ninzalli, and his concubine Ninursalla; in later times the name of his wife is given as Antu. Her position was usurped by Ishtar, to whom Anu gave a name corresponding to his own. A somewhat similar story is found in Egyptian, in which Isis succeeds in making Rā tell, or give, her his secret name. The goddess Nanai, or Nanâ, was the daughter of Anu, and the seat of her cult was Uruk.

Enlil, or Ellil, whom the Semites call Bêl, was the god of the wind which brought with it rain and floods. He lived on the "Great Mountain" in the heaven of Bêl, which united heaven with earth. The centre of his cult was Nippur, and his temple was called E-Kur, i.e., House of the Mountains. He also was the Father and King of the Gods, and he was the Keeper of the Tablet of Fate, which was, however, stolen from him by the Bird-god Zû. Though he protected kings, he was not especially benevolent towards mankind, for be created the dragon Labbu and caused the Flood. His principal wife was Ninlil, who possessed many of the attributes of the World-Mother. In Assyria the god Dagan, who was of foreign origin, was regarded as a sort of counterpart of Enlil; his wife also bore a foreign name, Shalash.

Ninurta was the son of Enlil and a god of war and the chase. He seems to have represented the sun at midday; as a planet he was Saturn, and as a fixed star Sirius. He dwelt in E-Shumedu in Nippur, but had sanctuaries in other great towns in Babylonia, and at Calah in Assyria. He was equipped with a sword, shield, bow, net and girdle. One of his wives was called Gula.

Nusku, a Fire-god and Light-god, was sometimes identified with Sin, the Moon-god. His wife was called Sadaranunna. The Cosseans identified him with their god Shuqamuna.

Makh, a Mother-goddess, was known as Ninmakh, Mama, Nintu, Aruru, and Ninkhursagga; she presided over the conception and birth of children and was their constant protector. She created the gods and suckled kings, and terracotta figures of her represent her suckling a child at her left breast. The consort of this goddess was Shulpa'e, of whom Jupiter was the symbol, and her son was called Lil.

Ea, also called Nudimmud, was the son of Anu by Nammu of E-Kur. As the lord of water in all forms, rivers, lakes, seas, the water in the earth and the celestial ocean, he was called Enki. The chief seat of his cult was Eridu, which in early Sumerian times was at the head of the swamps leading to the Persian Gulf, or on the sea itself. He was the god of wisdom and all knowledge, and instructed men in handicrafts, and invented the characters used in writing. He also taught man to overcome their enemies by the use of spells and incantations, and was the arch-magician and master of the art of divination. By the use of a spell he paralysed Mummu, as we have already seen, and so defeated the champion of Apsu. His chief temple was E-Apsu in Eridu; the animal sacred to him was the ibex. His wife was Damgalnunna, or Damkina, and Adapa was their son. A god closely associated with him was Gibil, the Fire-god.

Marduk was also a son of Ea. The original seat of his cult was in Eridu, and he represented, like one of the forms of Horus in Egypt, the early morning sun. At an early period he was chosen as the chief god of Babylon, and after Khammurabi enlarged that city, the renown of the god increased, until at length he became the lord of all the land. Like his father, he engaged in battle against the powers of evil who were the enemies of all mankind, and as his father conquered Mummu, so he conquered Tiâmat, and he was made king of the gods as the result. The animal sacred to him was the serpent-gryphon, and his sacred number was Ten; his star was

Jupiter. His chief shrine was Eagila in Babylon, and his statue was made of pure gold ornamented with precious stones. His wife was called Sarpânîtu, which the Semites turned into Zêr-bânîtu.

Nabû (Nebo), i.e., the "Announcer," was the son of Marduk, and was also called Tutu. He was endowed with great wisdom, like his father, and he acted as scribe to the gods; he had charge of the Tablet of Fate of the gods, and had the power of prolonging the days of men. Like the Egyptian Thoth, his eyes travelled over the circuit of the heavens and over all the earth. He was the personification of knowledge, and as a god of vegetation he caused the earth to produce abundant crops. His chief shrines were in Borsippa (Birs-i-Nimrûd) and in Calah (Nimrûd) in Assyria. His star was Mercury, and his symbol was a scribe's stilus. His wife was called Tashmitu.

Sin, the Moon-god, the first-born son of Enlil, was also called Enzu and Nannar. When invisible on earth he was supposed to be in the Underworld, and during an eclipse he was thought to be fighting against evil spirits. He marked the lengths of the day, the month and the year, and as lord of the month his number was Thirty. His chief shrines were E-gishshirgal in Ur and E-khulkhul in Harran. Like Nabû, he was a god of vegetation. His wife was called Ningal, or Nikkal, and she is said to be the mother of the Sun-god; Nin-Mar, the goddess of the town of Mar, was associated with Sin, and by him she is said to have had twelve children.

Shamash, the Sun-god, who is also called Utu and Babbar, was the son of Sin. In primitive times he was supposed to stride over the heavens on foot, but in later times to do so in a fiery chariot which was drawn by animals driven by one Bunene. He was regarded as a gracious god, for he helped all who were in trouble, gave life to the dead, and set free him that was in bonds. Possessing the power to see everywhere, he knew all things, and judged men rightly. He is represented as an old, long-bearded man, from whose shoulders rays of light come forth, and as a disk with a star, or a disk with wings, like the winged disk of Horus of Edfû, which is seen sculptured over the door of his temple at Edfû. Shamash's chief sanctuaries in Babylonia were at Larsa (Sankarah) and Sippar (Abû Habbah), and the seat of his cult in Assyria was the "city of Asshur." His wife was called Aia and Shenirda.

Mer, or Ishkur, the god of storms, was called by the Semites Rammân (Rimmon) and Adad, and some think that he was the equivalent of the Hittite god Teshub, and Amurru of the Syrian peoples. His chief shrines were in Babylon, Borsippa, the "city of Asshur," and Bît-Karkar (site unknown). His wife Shala was the goddess of the snow-clad mountains.

Dumuzi, i.e., Tammuz, united in his person the attributes of two gods, viz. Shamash and a son of Ea. He was in part a Water-god and in part a Vegetation-god; his cult was already old in Sumerian times, and he was honoured among the people until a very late period. The texts do not help us to decide whether he was killed by the fiery love of Ishtar, or, like Adonis, by a boar's tusk. One portion of the year he spent in the Underworld and, according to a legend, Ishtar went down there and brought him back to earth. During his absence all sorts of calamities had taken place in the world, but they came to an end on his return. During his annual visit to the Underworld women wept for him, and to this custom we have an allusion in Ezek. viii. 14. The mother of Tammuz was Sirdu, and his sister was Geshtin.

Ishkhara was an ancient, and perhaps foreign, goddess; the dragon and scorpion were sacred to her. She was a Mother-goddess, and the seat of her cult was Kisurra (Abû Hatab).

Ishtar, or Ninni, or Innina, was the daughter of Sin, the Moon-god; she usurped the position of Antu as the wife or concubine of Anu. She was the goddess of love, but in one of her forms her lovers suffered pain and death. She was also a goddess of battle, and one form of her was the goddess Anunitu, who dwelt in E-Ulmash and was the tutelary deity of Akkad. Her star was the planet Venus, and her sacred animal was the lion.

Lugalbanda was a son of Enlil, and his wife was called Ninsun.

Urash was the first-born son of Enlil, and was identified sometimes with Ninurta; his city was Dilbat and his star was Centaurus. His wife was called Nin-uru and Nin-egal, and his son Lagamal.

Zamana, or Zababa, was a son of Enlil, and was a god of battle; the seat of his cult was his temple E-Meteursag, in Kish; his wife was Ba'u.

Abu appears to have been a form of Ninurta. His wife was Gula, a goddess of medicine and healing. In Isin she was known as Ninkarrak.

Ningirsu, a son of Enlil, was a form of Ninurta and was a god of battle.

Nin-tinugga was a goddess of healing; her consort was En-dagga.

En-anum also was a goddess of healing; her consort was Pabilsag.

The gods of the passage to the Underworld, or the "Land of no return," were Birtu and Manungal. To reach the Underworld the spirits bound thither had to cross the river Khubur and pass through the Seven Gates, which divided it into seven parts, like the Seven Ārits of the Book of the Dead. Its goddess was Ereshkigal, whom the Babylonians called Allatu; a temple called E-Urugal at Kuthah was dedicated to her. Her husband is sometimes called Gugulanna and sometimes Ninazu. Her minister was Namtar, and it was his duty to introduce the dead to his dread mistress. He had it in his power to strike men with sixty different kinds of sicknesses, and he and his wife Khushbisag produced a family of devils who caused diseases in man. Namtar is said to be the son of Enlil by Ereshkigal. The scribe of the Underworld was Bêlit-sêri. Ninazu is also said to be the husband of Ningirda and the father of Ningishzida, the tutelary god of Gudea, whose symbol was two serpents twined about a staff. His star was Hydra.

Tishpak was a foreign god who was introduced into Babylonia at a very early period.

Nergal, who in early times represented the destructive power of the sun, and was a Plague-god, became at a later period the god of the Underworld. His father was Anu, or Enlil, or Ea, and his mother was Kutusar. His temple was in Kuthah, and his star was Mars. His wife was either Ereshkigal or Mammitu.

Irra was a god of pestilence, fire, battle and the desert; his wife was called Ninmug, or Shubula.

The Sumerian gods enumerated above are mentioned in a List of Gods from Nippur which has been published by Deimel in his *Schultexte aus Fâra*. These gods have been ably described and discussed by Meissner in his *Babylonien und Assyrien*, Bd. ii. pages 1 ff. Another useful summary of the gods is given by Jastrow (*The Religion of Babylonia and Assyria*, New York, 1898), who distinguishes between the early Sumerian gods and those who were worshipped in the time of Khammurabi, about 1950 BC. The Babylonians and Assyrians adopted the greater number of the Sumerian gods mentioned above, but the latter adopted as their chief national god Ashur (Ashshur) the War-god, who was probably unknown to the Sumerians. He was originally the Local-god of the "city of Asshur" (Kal'ah Sharkât) and was of little importance outside its walls. As the power of Marduk became predominant when Babylon grew into a great city, so the power of Ashur waxed great when the Assyrians became a strong and warlike nation. He is called in the texts the self-begotten king of the gods, and he became to Assyria what Enlil had been and Marduk was to Babylon. His wife was called Ninlil and Ishtar. He dwelt at first in E-Sharra, and later in E-Kharsag-kurkurru. He is represented usually as a Warrior-god, wearing a pair of horns and carrying a bow and a quiver and standing within a winged disk. His short skirt is of feathers and has the form of a tail of a bird. Another Assyrian Local-god was Shulmanu, whose wife was called Shulmânitu.

The gods were divided into two main groups; the one group had dominion in heaven, and the other on earth and in the Underworld. The gods of heaven were called the Igigi, and those of earth Anunnaki; the former were in number three hundred, and the latter six hundred. A text published by Ebeling (*Keilschrifttexte aus Assur*, No. 164) makes the number of the gods to be 3,600. From first to last the attributes and characters of the gods remained practically unchanged for at least three thousand years. Besides these there were many spirits of various kinds, some good-natured and some ill-natured, some in human form and some in the forms of birds, animals, etc. Among the former class were the Shedu and Lamassu; and the colossal lions and man-headed bulls which protected palaces were representations of benevolent beings. Evil spirits were Labartu, Lilû, Lilîtu (the Lîlîth of Isai. xxxiv. 14), Asakku, Alû, Etimmu, Gallû, etc.

The Babylonians ascribed to their gods human attributes as well as human forms, and as they conceived of a time when the gods came into being or were born, like men and women, so they also thought it possible that a time would come when they would cease to be, or die, like men and animals. The Creation Legend described in a preceding chapter shows that the gods of evil could be killed and cease to exist. And a ritual text published by Meissner makes it clear that the priests of Bêl-Marduk at Babylon held the dogma that their god died, went down to hell, and then raised himself to life again. This god was believed to be able to raise dead gods to life by reciting a certain spell or incantation. One interpretation of the text suggests that the god sacrificed himself and cut off his own head, so that from his blood man might be fashioned. The priests also held the view that Marduk had to cross the river in the Underworld, and to go to the kingdom of the dead therein, where he remained for some time in close captivity. He was delivered by the gods, and then became the King of the gods and Lord of heaven. For a full description of the text on which these views are based, see Zimmern, *Zweiter Beitrag zum Babylonischen Neujahrsfest,* Leipzig, 1918, and an article by Sidney Smith in *the Journal of Egyptian Archaeology,* vol. viii, parts 1 and 2, 1922.

The gods considered man to be, in some respects, akin to themselves, for though man's body was made of clay it was animated by a divine soul, and was made in their likeness and image. The gods were man's overlords, and men were their vassals; but the gods were also men's fathers, and men were their sons, and it was believed possible for a god to dwell in his son. But the gods who were thus closely related to men were gods of the lower orders of the celestial hierarchy, and there is no text which suggests that Anu, or Enlil, or Ea, ever became incarnate in man. Since men were vassals as well as sons of the gods, it was their bounden duty to render service to them, and it is clearly indicated that man was created in order to worship the gods and make offerings to them. To neglect the service of the gods, or to perform it carelessly or imperfectly, or to act in any way contrary to the well-known wishes of a god or goddess, was sin of the first order. Any breach of the Religious Law entailed serious penalties on the delinquent and even death.

The Moral Law demanded truth-speaking, straight-dealing, and the honouring of parents; lying, deceit, murder, adultery, robbery of the orphan, were abominable acts. A man should avoid his neighbour's house and the polluting of the water supply. It was his duty to maintain and honour and keep together the members of the family, and to avoid all words or deeds that would break up a family or cause strife in the house or town, etc. The Civic Law forbade the use of false weights and measures and the use of metals with alloy in them as currency, trespass on the property of the god or the neighbours, the removal of landmarks and boundary stones, the stealing of a neighbour's plough, the destruction of growing crops, the cutting down of reeds and thickets, the stopping of a watercourse, and, in short, any act or deed that would tend to disgrace the Local-god or cause unhappiness, injury, misery or loss in any shape or form to a neighbour.

Offences against any law could only be atoned for by offerings of various kinds and prayers to the gods made under the direction of a priest. The sinner suffering under the punishment of disease or sickness or loss of property, which he believed to have come upon him for his sin, no doubt prayed with groans and tears; but there is no text containing any suggestion that the Babylonian prayed for the change of mind that would prevent him from repeating his sin. He prayed that his god would change his wrath to compassion or mercy, but he never asked him to create in him a "clean heart" and a "steadfast spirit" (Psalm li. 10). The Babylonians in general, like the Egyptians, did not understand the importance of repentance in our sense of the word. The inscrutability of the will of the gods was recognized by the thinking and philosophical class, and some of them no doubt believed, like the Christian ascetics of the Scete Desert, in the immortality of the soul and the possibility of its union with the Divine Being. But ordinary folk in Babylonia cared little for theorizing on such matters, and knowing that the gods created man to die they endeavoured to enjoy life to the fullest extent. To eat one's fill, to make every day a day of pleasure, to dance and sing by day and by night, to wash the head and body and to wear clean apparel were the aim of most people. Though man must die, the day of his death is unknown to him, therefore pray to the gods to lengthen thy life, and forget that death must come one day. The life of a man is cut off like a reed, and the man who is alive and well in the evening may be dead in the morning.

And the doctrines of the priests encouraged men to enjoy life to the full, for their descriptions of the Underworld were terrifying indeed. Once arrived there man's body turned into mud, and his spirit took the form of a bird and flitted about in darkness. The Underworld, which was usually called Kigallu, or Arallû, or Irkalla, was situated under the earth, and the spirit of the dead entered it through an opening in the earth in the West. The first obstacle was the river Khubur, which was crossed in a ferry worked by the ferryman Khumuttabal, who had a bird's head and four hands and feet. The Book of the Dead shows that the Egyptian soul was ferried over a river by a ferryman whose name was "Face-behind-him." When the spirit left the ferry it entered Dead Land, where it was judged by a company of gods. Then it had to pass through Seven, or Fourteen, Doors (like the Egyptian Arits and Pylons), each of which was guarded by one of the sons of the goddess Enmesharra. The porter announced the name of the soul to the goddess, who gave it permission to enter. The spirit was then, like Ishtar when she descended into the Underworld in quest of Tammuz, stripped of all clothing and it entered into the presence of the goddess naked. The doors passed, the spirit entered the dark house of Irkalla. He who once enters this house never comes out again, and never can return by the road by which he came. Those who are in it are without light, they feed upon dust and they eat mud; they never see the light, but sit in darkness; they wear feathers like the birds and the dust lies thick on the door and its bolts. In the House of Dust dwell Etana, Samugan and the Queen of the Underworld, Ereshkigal. She lives with the three hundred, or six hundred, Anunnaki, and like the spirits of the dead, eats mud and drinks dirty water, but, in her own way, she compassionates those who have left the world and come to dwell with her. Her husband Ninazu, or Nergal, wears a crown, carries weapons of war, and has a following of fourteen devils, who cause disease and sickness in men. The names of the dead are written down by the goddess Bêlit-sêri. Her chief minister is Namtar, the Plague-god; his wife Namtartu (?) has the head of a bull and the feet and hands of a man. Besides these, many devils and demons who cause sicknesses in men, and bring upon them calamities, dwell in the Underworld. After the spirit had appeared before Ereshkigal, it seems that the Anunnaki sat in judgment upon it, and with Mammitu, the goddess of the destinies of men, proceeded to discuss the good and evil deeds that it had done in the body. The details of this judgment are not known, but it seems to resemble the Egyptian judgment of the dead which took place in the hall of Osiris. One section of the Underworld must have been set apart for the spirits who were not condemned by the Anunnaki, for we read of some who reclined on couches and drank water, and of others who had their fathers and mothers to support their heads, and their wives to sit by their sides.

Presumably such spirits lived upon the spirits of the offerings made to the dead by the living, and the libations poured out in this world found their way to those in the Underworld. It seems that the spirits of the dead whose bodies were unburied wandered about the villages and lived on such fragments of food as were thrown out into the streets. There must also have been a place set apart in the Underworld for those who were condemned in the judgment by the Anunnaki, where punishment was inflicted on them. The spirits of the dead were sometimes permitted to return to earth (we know that Enkidu was allowed by Nergal to appear before Gilgamish), and sometimes the spirits of the wicked escaped to earth, where, in the form of demons of sickness, they troubled mankind. But the only divine beings who went into the Underworld and came out of it and remained out of it were Ishtar and Bêl-Marduk. Among the Babylonians the belief in the immortality of the soul (or spirit) was fundamental, and the doctrine of annihilation appears to have been wholly unknown to them.

The Babylonians believed that man had lived on the earth for some hundreds of thousands of years, and the length of the reigns of the ten kings who flourished before the Flood they estimated at 241,200 years according to one list, and at 456,000 years according to another. According to Berossos, the period from the time of the first king to that of Alexander the Great was 468,000 years. Classical writers state that the Babylonians believed the world would last for one World-Year, i.e., 144 sars, or 518,400 years. Of this period, the kings before the Flood reigned 120 sars, or 432,000 years, and the period between the Flood and Alexander the Great was 36,000 years. Therefore when Alexander died there were about fifty thousand years to run before the world could come to an end. The view of Berossos that the period between the Creation and the death of Alexander was 468,000 years finds an echo in *De Divinatione* of Cicero (I. 19), who speaks of records which the Babylonians had kept for 470,000 years, and Diodorus (II. 31) speaks of the astronomical observations which the Babylonians had made for 473,000 years. A belief existed that, when the World-Year was ended, the world would be destroyed by a universal fire which would be followed by a flood. It is probable that these views were derived from Babylonian sources, but the cuneiform texts now known contain no mention of them.

LIST OF THE PRINCIPAL GODS AND GODDESSES

⊢, older ✳, is the ideogram for god and is always placed before a god's name.

Anu or **Anum** ⊢ 𒀭 𒌋, the god of the highest heaven.

Bêl ⊢ ⊣ or **Enlil**, ⊢ 𒆷 𒇸, the god of earth, god of Nippur.

Ea ⊢ 𒂗 𒀭, the god of the abyss, lord of wisdom; also called **Nudimmud**, ⊢ 𒌑 𒌋 𒀭.

Sin ⊢ 𒌍,
Enzu ⊢ 𒍪 𒀭, } the Moon-god.
Nannaru ⊢ 𒂍 𒌋,

Shamash ⊢ 𒌓, the Sun-god.

Adad
Rammânu } ⊢ 𒅎, the Wind-god.

Marduk or
Bêl-Marduk } ⊢ 𒀫, the great god of Babylon.

Nabû (Nebo) ⊢ 𒀝 or ⊢ 𒀭.

Enurta ⊢ 𒎗 𒊩, or ⊢ ⊢, god of battle.

Nergal ⊢ 𒄊, god of the Underworld.

Gibil { ⊢ 𒉈 𒀭, a Fire-god.
{ ⊢ 𒉈 ⊢.

Nusku ⊢ 𒉀, a Fire-god.

Irra ⊢ 𒀀 𒊏, a Plague-god.

Ashshur ⟊ ⟊, the national god of Assyria.

Tiâmat ⟊ ⟊, a primeval Dragon-goddess.

Apsu ⟊ ⟊, a god of sweet water.

Lakhmu ⟊ ⟊, a Serpent-god.

Lakhamu ⟊ ⟊, consort of Lakhmu, a goddess of moisture.

Anshar ⟊ ⟊, father of heaven.

Kishar ⟊ ⟊, father of earth.

Mummu ⟊ ⟊ (attributes unknown).

Kingu ⟊ ⟊, husband of Tiâmat.

Ishtar ⟊ ⟊, ⟊ ⟊, goddess of love and battle.

Ninlil ⟊ ⟊, wife of Bêl.

Damkina ⟊ ⟊, wife of Ea.

CHAPTER SEVEN

THE CODE OF LAWS OF KHAMMURABI

IN PRIMITIVE TIMES IN BABYLONIA EACH COMMUNITY OR EACH tribe formulated its own laws and administered them according to custom, which was probably already age-old. The laws at that time were few and simple, and were drawn up chiefly to protect the property of the god and the community. Of these we know nothing. When the Sumerians conquered Babylonia and settled down in it, they observed their own laws, and it is possible that they adopted some of those of their predecessors in the country. When the City-States like Eridu, Ur, Shuruppak, etc., came into being, the local conditions in each place made it necessary to formulate a number of new laws, which were duly observed, together with the older, well-established laws. The Sumerians had a Code of family laws, some of which are preserved on a tablet in the British Museum (K. 251); of these the following are examples: "If a son saith unto his father, 'Thou art not my father,' they shall brand him, bind him in fetters, and sell him for money as a slave." "If a man saith unto his mother, 'Thou art not my mother,' they shall brand him on the face, and forbid him the city, and drive him out of the house." "If a wife hateth her husband and saith unto him, 'Thou art not my husband,' they shall throw her into the river." "If a husband saith unto his wife, 'Thou art not my wife,' he shall pay [to her] half a *maneh* of silver." Among the Sumerian laws there were many of a tribal origin. Neither king nor governor could override the laws of a city. Though on all essential matters relating to property the Law must have been the same in all the City-States, many different codes existed, and in the outlying districts their customs were their laws, and aliens in the City-States observed the laws of their native countries, provided they did not affect their neighbours harmfully.

When Khammurabi had conquered the whole of Babylonia and reduced the countries to the east of the Tigris to subjection, he formulated a Code of Laws, by which he intended all his subjects to regulate their lives and affairs. The Laws were not invented by him, but were drawn up from earlier codes which had been in existence for many centuries, and had been observed in all well-governed City-States. He had this Code cut upon a large stone stele, which was set up in the Temple of Marduk in E-sagila, so that any and every man could consult it there when in doubt or difficulty about any point of law. The condition of peace which existed through the country under the firm, just and vigorous rule of Khammurabi made the application of the Laws of the Code comparatively easy. The property of the rich and the rights and privileges of the poor were alike safeguarded, and during the time that the Code was observed a woman could travel unmolested from Babylon to the Mediterranean Sea. The text of the Code was edited for use in schools, and was studied as a text-book for many centuries after Khammurabi's death.

The Stele on which the Code is engraved is a large block of black diorite which tapers towards its rounded top, and is about eight feet high. It was carried off to Shûsh (Susa) by a king whose name is unknown, and a part of the text was erased by him to provide space for an inscription of his own, which was, however, never engraved upon it. It was discovered in a broken condition

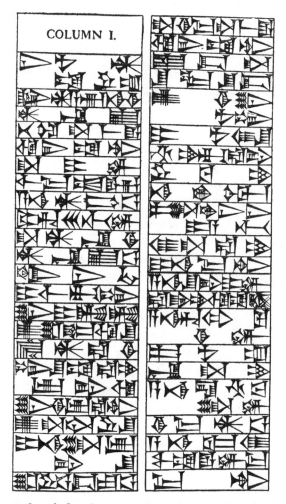

Extract from the Introduction: to the Code of Laws of Khammurabi.
From Harper, Code of Khammurabi, Chicago, 1904, Plate II.

by J. de Morgan in 1902 among the ruins of Susa, and the text was
published in the same year by Father Scheil, with a transcription
and French translation in Vol. IV of *Textes Élamites-Sémitiques* in

the *Mémoires de la Délégation en Perse,* Paris, 1902. On the upper part of the obverse is sculptured a scene in which the king is represented standing before a seated figure of Shamash, the Sun-god, god and judge of heaven. The king stands with his right hand raised and his arm resting on his left breast. The god is seated on a throne set on the mountains. He has on his head a conical head-dress with horns, and he holds in his hand a rod and circle, which may symbolize eternity. Flames rise from his shoulders, and he wears the usual garment with many flounces. The stele is covered with an inscription in forty-four columns containing 3,614 short lines. It may be divided into three parts: in Part I the king describes the benefits that he has conferred upon the temples and cities of Babylonia, and the following extract from it illustrates its general character:

> [Col. I] When the exalted Anu, the King of the Anunnaki, and Enlil (Bêl), the lord of heaven and earth, the determiner of the destiny of the land entrusted to Marduk, the eldest son of Enki (Ea), the lordship, of the multitudes of men—when they magnified him among the Igigi, and proclaimed the exalted name of Ka-Dingirra-ki and made it renowned among the Four Quarters of the World and established in the midst thereof an everlasting king-dom whereof the foundations were as solid as [those of] heaven and earth—at that time they (i.e., Anu and Enlil) called me Khammurabi, the exalted prince, the reverer of the gods, to make justice to prevail in the land, to overthrow wickedness and evil, to relieve the weak from the oppression of the strong, to rule the Black Heads like Shamash, to illumine the land, and to promote the well-being of men. I am Khammurabi, the Shepherd (i.e., Governor) proclaimed by Enlil, who

perfected prosperity and abundance, who provided in full measure whatsoever was [required] for the city En-lil-ki (Nippur) and the city of Dûr-ilu, the glorious restorer (?) of the temple E-kur [in Nippur], the wise king who restored Nun-ki to its place, who cleared out [Col. II] the shrine of the temple E-ZU-AB, who conquered the Four Quarters of the World, who made great the fame of Babylon. . . . etc.

[Here follow the names of the towns and sanctuaries which he repaired or rebuilt.]

Part II gives the text of 282 Laws; and Part III contains a blessing on the man who observes these Laws, and a curse on him who disregards them. The following renderings of some of the Laws will illustrate their general character:

1. The man who casts a spell on a man, and cannot justify his action, shall be put to death.
2. If a man casts a spell on a man and does not justify his action, the man who is under the spell shall go to the sacred river and cast himself in, and if the river drowns him the caster of the spell shall take his house as his property. If the river does not drown him the caster of the spell shall be put to death, and the innocent man shall take his house.
3. If a man threatens the witnesses in a capital case, and fails to justify his statements, he shall be put to death.
5. If a judge has passed a verdict, and reverses it subsequently, he shall be tried, and shall pay twelve-fold the sum which he had ordered to be paid, and shall be removed from his office and never again sit on the bench.
6. He who steals from the temple or palace shall be killed, and the receiver of the stolen goods shall be put to death.

7. If a man buys silver, gold, a servant, an ox, a sheep, an ass, etc., from a man's son or his slave, or receives them on deposit without a witness and bonds, he has acted as a thief and shall be killed.

8. If a man steals an ox, or a sheep, or an ass, or a pig, or a boat from the temple or palace, he shall pay thirty-fold. The poor man shall pay ten-fold. If the thief has no money, he shall be killed.

14. If a man has stolen the son of a free man, he shall be killed.

15. If a man has enticed a maid of the temple or palace, or the slave or maid of a poor man outside the gate, he shall be killed.

16. The man who has given a refuge to a runaway servant, and refused to produce him on demand, shall be killed.

17. The house-breaker shall be killed and buried in the hole he dug.

18. The highway-robber when caught shall be killed.

19. The man who is caught stealing during a fire shall be thrown into the fire.

29. The woman who acts in business for her son who is a minor shall receive one-third of the produce of the field and shall maintain her son.

30. The governor or judge who sends a hired man on the king's business in place of the royal envoy shall be killed.

40. A native or alien may sell his business and the buyer carry it on.

109. If a wine-merchant allows riotous men to assemble in his house and does not expel them, he shall be killed.

110. If a temple-woman opens a wine shop or enters one, she shall be burnt.

117. If a debtor has handed over his wife, son and daughter to his creditor, or to work for him, they shall do so for three years and then be free.

127. The man who makes an accusation against a temple-woman or a man's wife, and fails to justify it, shall be branded.

129. A man and a woman caught in adultery shall be cast into the water, but the husband of the woman may save her, and the king may save the man.

130. If a man forces a betrothed maiden living in her father's house, the man shall be killed and the woman shall go free.

133. If there be provisions in the house of a man who is taken captive, and his wife goes to another man, she shall be cast into the waters.

134. If there be no provisions in the house and she goes to another man and bears him children, if the husband returns she shall go back to him, and the father of the children shall keep them.

136. If a man forsakes his city and his wife, and then returns, his wife shall not return to him.

137. If a man puts away his concubine or his wife who has given him children, he shall return her dowry and add thereto, and she shall rear the children.

138–140. If a man puts away his childless wife, he shall give her back her dowry two-fold. If there was no dowry, he shall give one *maneh* of silver; if he is a poor man, he shall give her one-third of a *maneh*.

141. If a wife spends her time out of the house, behaves foolishly, wastes her husband's goods, and holds him in contempt, he can say "I divorce her," and send her away without paying back to her her dowry; if he does not say "I divorce her," he shall marry another woman, and the wasteful wife shall live in his house as a servant.

142. If a blameless wife has been reviled by her husband, she shall take her dowry and return to her father's house.

143. If a wife is not blameless, and has wasted her husband's goods and reviled him, she shall be thrown into the waters.

194. If a man's child has died under the care of the nurse, and the nurse substitutes another without the consent of his father and mother, the breasts of that nurse shall be cut off.

195. If a man strikes his father, his hands shall be cut off.

196. If a man destroys the eye of another, his own eye shall be destroyed.

197. If a man has broken another man's limb, his own shall be broken.

198. If a man has destroyed an eye or a limb of a poor man, he shall pay one *maneh* of silver.

199. If a man has destroyed an eye or a limb of the servant of another man, he shall pay one-half of a mina.

200. If a man has made the tooth of another to fall out, one of his own teeth shall be knocked out.

201. If the tooth be that of a poor man, he shall pay one-third of a *maneh* of silver.

202. If a man strikes a gentleman, he shall receive sixty stripes with a cow-hide whip.

203. If a gentleman strikes a gentleman, he shall pay one *maneh* of silver.

204. If a poor man strikes a poor man, he shall pay ten shekels of silver.

205. If a servant strikes a free man, his ear shall be cut off.

206. If a man wounds a man in a quarrel accidentally, he shall pay the doctor.

207. If the wounded man be a gentleman, and the striker be a gentleman, he shall pay half a *maneh* of silver.

208. If he be a poor man, he shall pay one-third of a *maneh* of silver.

209. If a man strikes a gentlewoman and she miscarries, he shall pay ten shekels of silver for her loss of offspring.

210. If the gentlewoman dies, the striker's daughter shall be killed.

211. If the woman be the daughter of a poor man, the striker shall pay five shekels for her miscarriage.

212. If the poor man's daughter dies, the striker shall pay half a *maneh* of silver.

215. The doctor who treats and cures a gentleman's wound, or has operated on the eye with a copper lancet, shall charge ten shekels of silver.

216. If the patient be a poor man, the doctor shall charge five shekels of silver.

217. If the patient be a servant, his master shall pay the doctor two shekels of silver.

218. If a doctor operates on a wound with a copper lancet, and the patient dies, or on the eye of a gentleman, who loses his eye in consequence, his hands shall be cut off.

226. If a man brands a slave indelibly, without his master's consent, the hands of the brander shall be cut off.

227. The man who wrongfully causes the brander to brand a slave indelibly shall be killed and buried in his house, and the brander shall swear, "I did it unwittingly."

229. The mason who builds a house which falls down and kills the inmate shall be put to death.

230. If it be the son of the master of the house who is killed, the son of the mason who built it shall be killed.

231. If it be a slave who has been killed, a slave of the mason shall be killed.

234. The fee of the boatman who has sailed a ship for sixty *gur* shall be two shekels of silver.

235. If a boatman hires a ship and sails it carelessly and runs it aground, or loses it, he shall replace it for the owner.

241. If a man takes an ox for debt, he shall pay one-third of a *maneh* of silver.

244. If a lion kills a hired ox or sheep, the loss shall fall on its owner.

245. If a man maims or kills a hired ox, he shall restore ox for ox to its owner.

246. If a man crushes the hoof of a hired ox or cuts its neck, ox for ox the hirer shall restore to the owner of the ox.

247. If a man hires an ox and blinds it, he shall pay one-half of its value to its owner.

249. If a man hires an ox, and God strikes it and it dies, he shall take an oath and not be liable for the ox.

CHAPTER EIGHT

BABYLONIAN RELIGIOUS AND MAGICAL LITERATURE, LEGENDS, ETC.

FROM FIRST TO LAST ALMOST EVERY BRANCH OF BABYLONIAN, AND even Assyrian, literature which is made known to us by the cuneiform inscriptions bears upon it a strong impress of religious influence and teaching; in fact, it may almost be said that all Babylonian literature is religious. Royal inscriptions are filled with phrases in which the king's devotion to the gods and their temples is insisted upon, historical texts contain frequent mentions of the gods individually or collectively, and allusions to events in the lives of the gods and goddesses, and even the contracts which men made with each other in the ordinary way of business, when written down were given a religious complexion. The longest texts we have deal with legends and myths of the gods, and it is clear that the priests contrived to make the attempts of all seekers after the knowledge of natural things subservient to existing religious ideas and beliefs. It is possible, though it is difficult to believe it, that some kind of profane or secular literature existed in Babylonia, but no examples of it have come down to us. The Sumerian agriculturists and workmen must have sung popular songs and told amusing tales to each other, but after these were edited by the priests little of their original plainness of speech and sparkle remained in them. The earliest and most persistent form of Sumerian and Babylonian literature is a rhythmic prose. Rhyming was unknown. The earliest song consisted of what we may call verses, each of which contained two halves with the same form and expressing the same sense; two such verses formed a distich. Nearly all poetic compositions were written in this form, which was also used in exorcisms, incantations, and even in historical inscriptions. The greater part of Babylonian poetical literature consists of Hymns and Prayers in which the gods are praised extravagantly, and their help demanded by the suppliant. In the earliest times these hymns were sung on high days and holy days by priests and worshippers, but at a later period they were used as exorcisms and recited by the priests alone to drive out from a suppliant a devil or a spirit of a disease. After singing a hymn of this kind a worshipper often recited a prayer on his own behalf, in which he entreated the favour of the god addressed by him, and petitioned him to remove some sickness, caused by "black magic," from which he was suffering, or to deliver him from tribulation of some sort. To petitions of this kind the name of Penitential Psalms has been given. The phraseology of such compositions is always the same, and it seems that they might be addressed to any god. The following is a specimen of an early hymn to Anu:

> O Prince of the gods, whose utterance ruleth over the obedient company of the gods; Lord of the horned crown, which is marvellously splendid; thou travellest hither and thither on the raging storm; thou standest in the royal chamber, to be admired as a king.
>
> The ears of the Igigi are directed to hear thy pure utterance; the Anunnaki in a body come to thee, being full of reverence for thee.
>
> At thy word the gods cast themselves on the ground in a body like a reed on the stream; thy command blows like the wind and causes food and drink to thrive; at thy word the angry gods turn back to their habitations.

May all the gods of heaven and earth appear before thee with gifts and offerings; may the kings of the countries bring to thee heavy tribute; may men stand before thee daily with sacrifices, prayers and adorations.

May the great gods pray to thee to cause thy heart to be at rest; may men in their habitations recite prayers to thee to make thy liver to be at peace.

May the great gods make thy heart to be at rest through concord and prayer; may they make thy liver to be at peace by prayers and bowings.

To Uruk (Erech), thy city, do thou show [abundant] favour; O great god Anu, avenge thy city in hostile lands.

(Thureau-Dangin, *Rituels Accadiens,* page 70)

The following is a specimen of the prayers that were said by a suppliant after singing a hymn of praise to the god Marduk:

Among all the multitudes of men who exist and have names, who is there that can of himself have knowledge? Who has not erred? Who has not transgressed? Who is there that knows the Way of the God? I will worship; I will not handle wickedness; I will seek out the regions of Life. Before thee I have worked iniquity; I have transgressed the mark set by the god. Forgive me the sins which I have committed, wittingly or unwittingly, from my youth up. Let not thy heart despair, destroy my sin, do away my faults, lighten my turmoil, illumine my gloom. Let the sins of my father, my grandfather, my mother, my grandmother, my family and the members of my house, both male and female, not come nigh to me, may they pass on one side.

Speak to me, O my god! May he make me white like the Arantu flower. Let the merciful hands of my god order my well-being, so that I may always stand before thee with prayer and tears and a fervent [heart]. May the wanton folk who live in various parts of the country worship thee; destroy my sin, do away my sin.

O brave Marduk, destroy my sin, do away my sin.

O great goddess Erua, destroy my sin.

O Nabû, of fair name, destroy my sin.

O great goddess Tashmit, destroy my sin.

O brave Nergal, destroy my sin.

O ye gods who dwell in the heaven of Anu, destroy my sin.

Dissipate thou the great sins which I have committed from my youth up, and destroy thou them seven times.

May thy heart, as the father who begot me, and the mother who bore me, be at peace; then, O brave Marduk, will I worship thee with lowly submission.

(King, *Babylonian Magic,* No. 11)

The following extract from a Hymn to Shamash is of special interest:

[O Shamash,] thou stridest over the wide and deep sea, the uttermost depths of which the Igigi have never known. Thy beams of light go down into the Ocean, and the vast mass thereof seeth thy light.

[O Shamash,] thou fetterest as with a cord, and thou dost envelop [everything] like the breath of the storm; thy broad shadow casteth down the lands.

Never by day dost thou cast gloom, thy face never becometh dark; thou fillest thyself all the night long, and lettest light stream forth from thee.

Thou dost hasten over an unknown and remote course, leagues uncountably long, O Shamash; thou journeyest by day and turnest not back by night.

Among the Igigi there is none who exerteth himself more than thyself; and among all the gods of the universe there is none who surpasseth thee.

When thou goest forth in the morning the gods of the countries gather themselves together; thy fierce splendour casteth down the lands.

Thou knowest the designs of all the lands concerning which tongues tell; thou watchest their steps.

O Shamash, all men rejoice in thee, and they all long for thy light.

Thou makest the diviner to apprehend the meaning of a dream in the cup of divination, in the preparation of the cedar wood.

Thou sustainest the envoy whose way is difficult; thou givest courage to the seafarer when he feareth the storm.

Thou leadest the hunter through impassable paths; he proceedeth, marching onwards like the Sun-god.

If the evil man seizeth thy weapon, he hath no deliverer; in his contest his father will not appear.

In the case before the judge his brethren will not answer [for him]; and as with a brazen snare he will be thrown down without knowing it.

Thou bringest to nought the horn of the man who soweth iniquity; the territory of him that pondereth to make deceit to flourish shall become the property of another.

Thou makest the unjust judge to see the fetters [of prison]; he who taketh bribes doeth wrong, thou wilt have him punished.

He who taketh not bribes and who supporteth the case of the weak is well-pleasing to Shamash; he shall live long.

The chief judge, who judgeth with righteous judgment, maketh the Palace complete; the dwelling of the Prince is his habitation.

With bowing, kneeling, whispered prayer and prostrations, the weak cry to thee with a full throat [i.e., voice].

The wretched, the weak, the afflicted, the poor, approach thee with prayer and offerings, bearing themselves humbly.

He whose kinsfolk are afar off, and whose city is remote [and] the shepherd approach thee with the produce of the plain.

The shepherd in the tumult of fighting, the herdsman among enemies, and the caravan [men] when overwhelmed by fear, apply to thee, O Shamash.

The travelling merchant, the man of business who carrieth money, apply to thee, O Shamash; [and] the fisherman with the net.

The hunter, the butcher who seizeth the cattle, the fowler in [his] hiding place, approach thee.

The house-breaker, the thief, although he be an enemy of Shamash, [and] the highwayman of the desert, approach [or, entreat] thee.

The wandering [i.e., unburied] dead man, the spirit of the dead who hath escaped, approach thee, O Shamash, and lament before thee.

A comparatively small but very important section of Babylonian literature is the Creation Epic and the Gilgamish Epic, both of which have been described in preceding chapters; a brief summary of the Legends and Myths may now be given. Some of the earliest legends deal with fabulous monsters. When Enlil began to rule, the earth was in the possession of a monster called Labbu, which came up from the sea. Many gods had tried to kill it and failed, but at length there arose one who armed himself with the Seal of Life and slew it; it took three years, three months, one day and two hours for it to bleed to death. Both Babylonian and Egyptian texts tell of a monster serpent which finds its equivalent in modern times in the "Sea-serpent." The Zu bird, the symbol of storm and tempest, was a god of evil who waged war against Enlil, the holder of the "Tablet of Fate," whereby he ruled heaven and earth. Zu coveted this Tablet, and determined to take it and rule in his stead. Zu watched his opportunity, and one morning when Enlil had taken off his crown and set it down on a stand, and was washing his face with clean water, Zu snatched the Tablet from him and flew away with it into the mountains. Anu called on the gods to go out against Zu and take the Tablet from him, but one and all refused, and the affairs of heaven and earth fell into disorder. At length Lugal-banda announced his readiness to go and attack Zu and the gods sent him to do so and, with the help of Zu's wife, he obtained possession of the Tablet of Destiny.

The Legend of the Descent of Ishtar into the Underworld, presumably to bring back Tammuz, was well known in the third millennium before Christ, and it is possible that it was acted as a sort of miracle play. When Ishtar arrived at the first gate of the Underworld she demanded admission. The porter announced her arrival to Ereshkigal, who ordered her to be admitted. As she passed through each of the Seven Gates, the porter removed from her some part of her apparel or some ornament, and when finally she passed into the presence of Ereshkigal she was naked. The two goddesses gazed upon each other with furious anger, and as Ereshkigal was mistress of the region, she ordered her minister Namtar to take Ishtar and shut her up in prison and to smite her with sixty kinds of sicknesses. As soon as Ishtar left the world, beast and man became unable to perform their natural functions, and the messenger of the gods went to Ea and described, with streaming eyes, what had happened in the world, and demanded his help. Ea listened and then fashioned a man addicted to love-making called Abûshu-namir, and told him to go down into the Underworld, and to speak kindly to Ereshkigal, and to induce her to let him drink from the leather bottle of the water of life. Abûshu-namir went down to the Underworld, and, when he had uttered this insolent request, was cursed, and was himself detained in the kingdom of the dead. But Ereshkigal understood that Ishtar was to be released, and, when Namtar had sprinkled her with the "water of life," and received a gift from her, set her and Tammuz free. As Ishtar retraced her steps and passed through the Seven Gates, the porter of each gave back to her the article of apparel, or the ornament, which he had taken from her previously. After their return to earth Tammuz was ordered to bathe in clean water, to anoint himself with scented unguents, and to array himself in festal attire, presumably as a preparation for his marriage with Ishtar.

According to the copy of a text found at Tall al-'Amârnah in Egypt, the god Nergal also went down into the Underworld, under the following circumstances. One day, when the gods in heaven were banqueting, they sent an invitation to Ereshkigal, goddess of the Underworld, to join them. In reply she sent her minister Namtaru, the Plague-god, and all the gods stood up before him except Nergal. When Ereshkigal heard this she was furiously angry, and sent her minister back to heaven with the command, That god who would not rise up before my minister, bring to me that I may kill him. The gods agreed that Nergal should depart from them, and Ea gave him an escort of fourteen demons who caused sicknesses. When Nergal arrived, the porter announced his presence to Namtaru, who recognized Nergal as the god who would not stand up before him, and told Ereshkigal that Nergal had arrived. She gave orders that he was to be admitted that she might slay him. Nergal posted one of his escort of devils at each of the fourteen doors, and then, having overpowered Namtaru, he marched into hell, seized Ereshkigal by her hair, and dragged her down from her throne on to the ground to cut off her head. Then Ereshkigal cried out, "Slay me not, my brother. I would say something to thee. Thou shalt be my husband, I will be thy wife. I will permit thee to hold sovereign sway in the Underworld. I will place the Tablet of Wisdom in thy hand. Thou shalt be Master, I will be Mistress." When Nergal heard these words he laid hold upon her and kissed her and dried her tears, and agreed to all she said. Nergal and Ereshkigal were married and have ruled the Underworld from that time. (For the texts *see* Meissner, *Babylonien*, Bd. ii, page 185.)

According to the Legend of Irra, Anu created seven devils and placed them under the authority of Irra to carry out his plan for the destruction of mankind. His minister Ishum tried to make him desist from his evil work. Nippur, Ur, Uruk (Erech), Dêr and Babylon were destroyed, and Irra in the form of a lion carried destruction wherever he went. Further, it was decreed that swamp land should be against swamp land, the Subarian against the Subarian, the Assyrian against the Assyrian, the Elamite against the Elamite, the Kassite against the Kassite, the Sutaean against the Sutaean, the Kutaean against the Kutaean, the Lullubaean against the Lullubaean, one land against another, one house against another, one man against another, brother against brother—all were to be killed. Then shall the Akkadian (i.e., Babylonian) rise up and overthrow them all. Irra next sent Ishum to Khiklu, where he levelled the mountains and cut down all the trees. Finally the wrath of Irra was appeased, and Babylon was rebuilt, and her king ruled the whole world. The last fragment of the Legend contains the Song of Irra, in which the god describes his triumphs and power, and says that the singer of this song, the king who honours the name of Irra, the scribe who writes down the song, and the house in which a copy of it is kept, will always be protected by the god. For summaries *see* Jastrow, *Bab.-Ass. Religion*, pages 528 ff., and Meissner, *op. cit.*, page 186.

The Legend of Adapa. Adapa, the son of Ea, and the first man, received wisdom from his father, but not immortality. He served as a priest in Eridu. Whilst fishing one day the south wind dashed his boat to pieces, and he was thrown into the sea; in revenge he broke the wings of the south wind. Seven days later Anu learned from his minister Il-abrat what had happened, and summoned Adapa to his presence. Ea, knowing Adapa's danger, told him to speak fair to the two doorkeepers of heaven, Tammuz and Gishzida, to put on the apparel of grief, and to express sorrow and regret for what had happened. Ea told Adapa that the doorkeepers would offer him the food and the water of death and a garment and unguent, and warned him neither to eat nor to drink; but he told him to accept the garment and to put it on, and the unguent and to anoint himself therewith. When Adapa appeared before Anu everything happened as Ea foretold. Anu was angry at first, but very soon told his doorkeepers to offer Adapa the food of life and the drink of life, and a garment and oil. When Anu saw that he would neither eat nor drink, he asked why he had not done so, and Adapa replied: "My lord Ea commanded, Eat not, drink not." Then said Anu, "Take him and carry him back to earth." Thus, apparently, through following Ea's commands, Adapa lost the gift of immortality which Anu was ready to bestow upon him. Ea, the Allwise, must have known that the food and the water of life would be offered to Adapa, and it would seem that he intentionally spoke of the food of death and the water of death in order to prevent Adapa becoming immortal like himself.

In the Legend of Etana we have a remarkable account of an attempt made by man to ascend to heaven on the back of an eagle. The first fragment of the Legend tells how the wife of Etana was unable to bring forth the child she had conceived, and describes his distress. He knows of the existence of a certain herb that will assist his wife if only he can get it, and he appeals to Shamash, the Sun-god, to help him to find it. Shamash advises him to consult a certain

eagle, perhaps his *totem* (?). Now the eagle had at one time a friend-
ship with a snake, but had broken with it, and had devoured the
snake's young ones. The snake found an opportunity for revenge
and stung the eagle and threw it into a pit. Shamash sent Etana up
the mountain both to help the eagle and to find the herb that
would help his wife to bring forth her child. Etana found the eagle,
and when he had helped it to recover its strength, the eagle promised to take him up to heaven, so that he might appeal to the
goddess of childbirth, and obtain the herb for his wife. Etana set his
breast against the breast of the eagle, and laid his hands on the
feathers of its wings, and the eagle began to fly up to heaven. After
two hours' flight the land below them looked like a hill and the sea
like a lake (or river). After another two hours' flight they arrived in
the heaven of Anu, but the herb was not to be found there, and
they continued their flight. After the third two hours' flight the
earth was invisible to them, and Etana could not see the sea at all.
Then Etana began to be exceedingly afraid, and he commanded
the eagle to stop and let him return to earth; and at that moment
he and the eagle fell to earth and were killed. The text of the Legend
comes to an end with this statement. Of the fate of the child, who
was presumably unborn, we know nothing.

A very ancient tradition in Babylonia states that the art of divining was invented by Enmeduranki, a king of Sippar, and the last but
two of the kings who reigned before the Flood, and the great mass
of Magical Literature that has been recovered from the ruins of the
ancient cities of Babylonia and Assyria proves that the Babylonians
were firm believers in the power of Magic from time immemorial.
There seems to be little doubt that with them Magic took the place
of Religion. We know that they had gods, great gods whom they
worshipped at festivals and on state occasions, but they thought that
they were too great, too far removed from them, to trouble about
the daily wants and affairs of men. But the imagination of the
Babylonians, both Sumerian and Semitic, had peopled earth, sky

and Underworld with a large number of spirits, some of which were benevolent and some malevolent. They accepted the kindly acts of the good spirits, about which they troubled little; but they passed their lives in deadly fear of the evil spirits, who were very numerous and very active. To counteract their evil doings the Babylonians had recourse to incantations and spells and magical ceremonies, and a considerable number of magicians and sorcerers and priests must have made a good living out of the fears of their ignorant and credulous neighbours. The art of divination was largely practised in the country, and the skill of the "Chaldeans" in this branch of magic has become proverbial throughout the world.

Many of the incantations and spells of which we have copies must have been composed in the prehistoric period, and they have survived because the beliefs that underlie them have never ceased to exist. The magical texts which we have show that at a very early period the professional magician began to collect and arrange his incantations, etc., in a definite order, according to the uses to which they were to be put and their contents. Each collection of magical texts had a special name. Thus the incantations directed against demons and devils filled a series of tablets, from sixteen to twenty in number, called "Evil Devil." Another series of nine tablets dealt with the diseases that devils caused in the head of a man. The Maklu Series, which treated of the burning of waxen images and added the necessary incantations in about 1,550 lines, contained eight tablets; the Shirpu Series contained nine tablets. The oldest centre of the cult of Magic apparently was Eridu, and it seems as if Ea in Babylonia, like Rā in Egypt, was the original author of the most potent of the incantations, or "words of power," which were in daily use. The general editing of the magical texts seems to have taken place in the third millennium BC, for in the time of Khammurabi Magic had developed into an important and complicated science. Originally the oldest texts were written in Sumerian, but at a later period it was found necessary to add Semitic translations of them on the tablets, probably because the priests were unable to read Sumerian. It is clear from the arrangement of the texts in groups of four rhythmic lines that they were sung or chanted by the priests.

The demons and devils that made the Babylonian's life a misery to him were many, but the forms of most of them and their evil powers were well known. Most of all he feared the Seven Evil Spirits, who were the creators of all evil. The first was the South Wind, the second a dragon, the third a leopard, the fourth a viper, the fifth a raging beast, the sixth a whirlwind, and the seventh a storm (hurricane). These evil spirits were created by Anu, and as Plague-gods they were the beloved sons of Bêl and the offspring of Ninkigal. They "rend in pieces on high, bringing destruction below; they are the children of the Underworld. Loudly roaring on high, gibbering below, they are the bitter venom of the gods . . . They pass through the highest walls, the thickest walls, like a flood; from house to house they break through. No door can shut them out, no bolt can turn them back, through the door like a snake they glide, through the hinge like the wind they blow, estranging the wife from the embrace of the husband, snatching the child from the loins of a man, sending the man forth from his home. They are the burning pain that bindeth itself upon the back of a man." As there were triads of gods, so there were triads of devils, e.g., Labartu, Labasu and Akhkhazu. The first harmed little children, the second caused the quaking sickness, and the third turned the face of a man yellow and black. Another triad comprised Lîlû, Lîlîtu and Ardat Lîlî. Lîlîtu was known to the Hebrews, and Rabbinic tradition makes her to be the beautiful wife of Adam, who roamed by night, and was a special danger to children. Besides these there were the Asakku, who caused the wasting sickness, the Namtaru, a plague-demon, the Alû, the Etimmu, the Utukku, the Gallû, many "gods" who had come to be regarded as devils, the Shêdu, the Khîmitu, etc. The demons who caused sicknesses seem to have formed a class by themselves, but each had its name, and a monstrous form of some kind was generally attributed to it. The Babylonians did not usually resort to prayer to the gods or appeal to the good spirits when afflicted by evil spirits, but went to the priest, who often assumed the character of a god, and who exorcised the devils by reciting incantations, of which the following are specimens: I. I am the priest of Ea. I am the magician of Eridu. Shamash is before me, Sin is behind me. Nergal is at my right hand, Enurta is at my left hand. When I draw near the sick man, when I lay my hand on his head, may a kindly Spirit, a kindly Guardian, stand at my side! Whether thou art evil Ghost, or evil Devil, or evil God, or evil Fiend, or sickness, or death, or a Phantom of Night, or a Wraith of the Night, or fever, or deadly pestilence, get thee gone from before me; go forth from the house. For I am the priest of Ea; it is I who recite the incantation for the sick man. Be thou evil Spirit, Demon, Ghost, Devil, evil God, Fiend, sickness, death, Night Phantom, Night Wraith, disease or pestilence, get thee far from me. Be exorcised by Heaven, be exorcised by Earth! Get thee hence. II. Seven are they, seven are they. In the Ocean Deep seven are they. . . . They were reared in their home, the Ocean Deep. Neither male nor female are they. They are as the roaming windblast. No wife have they, no son do they beget. They know neither mercy nor pity. They hearken not unto prayer or supplications. They are as the horses reared on the hills. The Evil Ones of Ea, throne-bearers of the gods are they. They stand in the highway to befoul the path. Evil are they, evil are they! Seven are they, seven are they. Twice seven are they. By Heaven be ye exorcised! By Earth be ye exorcised![1]

In some cases it was necessary to sprinkle the sick man with medicated water, or to plaster the door with bitumen, or to anoint him with medicated unguents, or to administer to him decoctions of herbs possessing magical qualities; and sometimes pictures or figures of the gods and devils and fabulous beasts and amulets were placed in the chamber. Sometimes it was necessary to use sympathetic or symbolic magic, and to imitate the actions of gods in their characters of creators and deliverers; sometimes the sacrifice of an animal, which was to be regarded as the substitute for the sick man, was made. In special cases a figure of the demon that was supposed to cause the sickness was burnt slowly in a fire whilst the incantation was being recited.

Sometimes the incantation took the form of a narrative of an act of some god. The Babylonians believed that toothache was caused by a worm gnawing at the root of the tooth, and the incantation which was supposed to cure the sufferer from toothache took the following form: "After Anu [had created] the Heavens, the Heavens created the Earth, the Earth created the Rivers, the Rivers created the Canals, the Canals created the Marshes, the Marshes created the Worm. Came the Worm [and] wept before Shamash, before Ea came her tears [and she said], What wilt thou give me for my food? What wilt thou give me for my drink? [Ea said], I will give thee dried bones [and] scented . . . wood.[2] [The Worm said], What are these dried bones to me and scented . . . wood? Let me drink among the teeth, and set me on the gums that I may devour the blood of the teeth and of their gums destroy the strength. Then shall I hold the bolt of the door.[3] So must thou say this: O Worm! May Ea smite thee with the might of his fist." When the sufferer had recited this three times he was to apply a mixture of beer and oil and the juice of a certain plant to the tooth. The "Toothache Tablet" was first published and translated by R. C. Thompson, *Cuneiform Texts*, Part xvii, plate 50, and *Devils and Evil Spirits*, vol. ii, page 161.

Another class of beings was greatly feared by the Babylonians, viz. warlocks and witches. These were usually men and women who were deformed, or who possessed some physical peculiarity which led their neighbours to believe that they were closely associated with devils, and that they sometimes served as dwelling-places for the powers of evil. As possessors of human intelligence, they were often considered to be more baneful than the devils themselves. They were specially masters of the Evil Eye and the Evil Spell,

Clay model of a sheep's liver, inscribed with omens and magical formulae used in divination. B.M. No. 92,668.

and they employed all the practices of the priests who exorcised devils, but with evil motives and the intent to do harm. The priests were masters of White Magic, and the warlocks and witches of Black Magic. The incantation, which in the mouth of a priest made a sick man well, in the mouth of the witch procured his death.

The section of Babylonian Literature dealing with Divination and Omens is very large, and can be little more than referred to here. The object of all divination was to find out about the future and the will of the god or goddess to whom a prayer, which was usually an incantation, was addressed; in fact, the suppliant wanted an answer to his prayer. This answer the priest had to give, and he could only do so by watching the behaviour of the figure he was burning, or the knots in a string which he was untying, or by the appearance of the entrails of the sacrifice which he had offered up on behalf of the suppliant. The omens derived from these enabled him to forecast the future. The priests kept a careful record of all omens, and the principal Omen Texts filled many scores of tablets. The omens tabulated number thousands. Besides the priests who used the cedar-wood staff and the bowl, there were many "prophets" in Babylonia who professed to be able to tell the future without reading the omens on the bodies of the birds or animals that were sacrificed. The use of the liver of an animal in divination dates from the earliest time, and it was believed that the science of reading the signs on it was the invention of Shamash. A fine example of an inscribed model, in clay, of a sheep's liver is preserved in the British Museum, and is reproduced on Plate IX. An interesting reference to the use of the liver in divination occurs in Ezek. xxi. 21, where it is said that "the King of Babylon stood . . . to use divination; he made his knives bright, he consulted with figures (i.e., models in wax or clay), he looked in the liver." Omens were derived from the Sun, Moon, Stars and Planets, celestial phenomena, and especially from eclipses, monstrosities, human and animal, the birth of children and animals, members of the body, the actions of animals, etc.

Very few texts containing Moral Aphorisms, or Admonitions as to a man's personal conduct, or his duty towards his neighbour, have hitherto been found, but some fragments of tablets in the Kuyûnjik Collection in the British Museum prove that, in the late period at least, collections of Moral Precepts formed a part of Babylonian and Assyrian Literature.

During his search for fragments of the Creation Epic, George Smith discovered a tablet (K. 3364) which he described as containing an address from a Deity to the newly-created man on his duties to his

God, and he thought that the text on the Reverse enumerated the duties of the woman to her partner. Several years later the late I.. W. King discovered a Babylonian tablet (No. 33,851) which contained the opening and concluding lines of the text on the Assyrian tablet. Later, other fragments were found which have added to the text, and finally Prof. S. Langdon collected the texts from all the fragments and showed that where complete the composition formed a Book of Wisdom of the kind familiar to us from the Book of Proverbs, the Wisdom of Jesus the son of Sirach, and other similar works. He published the texts with translations in the *Proceedings of the Society of Biblical Archaeology*, vol. xxxviii (1916), pages 105 ff., and added several interesting notes; and Meissner has translated extracts from the work in his *Babylonien*, Bd. ii, page 421. The following extracts illustrate the contents of this Babylonian Book of Wisdom:

> As a wise and discreet man thou shalt belittle thy knowledge
>   (or, capacity).
> Set a bridle in thy mouth; watch carefully thy speech.
> As the riches of men let thy lips be accounted rare.
> Let audacity for wickedness be an abomination unto thee.
> Utter not words of arrogance or lying counsel.
> The head of the man who worketh dissoluteness is dishonoured.
> Force not thyself into an assembly of men to tarry there; and
>   seek not out the place where there is contention,
> For in the strife they will compel thee to come to a decision
>   (i.e., to take a side),
> Thou wilt become involved in their seeking for testimony,
> And in a case with which thou hast nothing to do they will
>   drag thee forward as a witness.
> Harm not in any way thine adversary.
> Recompense the man who doeth evil to thee with good.
> Oppose thine enemy with righteous dealing.
>
> . . . .

Give food to eat and wine to drink.

Seek after the truth, nourish and honour [thy parents].

Over the man who acteth in this way his God will rejoice.

The god Shamash will rejoice and will requite him with good.

Marry not the strange woman whose lovers are many.

The maiden of Ishtar whose person is dedicated to the goddess,

The woman servant of the temple whose strength (?) is abundant,

Will never be a support to thee in thy misfortunes (or calamities).

In [thy] fighting she will exert herself against thee.

Reverence and obedience (or submission) exist not in her.

If she entereth [thy] house, lead her out,

For her mind is set upon the path of the stranger.

Finally, the house into which she setteth her foot is destroyed,
       and the man who hath married her will remain unhappy (?)

Utter no calumnies, say the thing that is fair.

Use not words of evil, speak that which is good.

He who uttereth calumnies speaketh that which is evil.

And as retribution for this Shamash will punish (?) him.

Open not thy mouth widely in chatter, set a watch on thy lips.

Give not utterance publicly to thine innermost thoughts.

If thou speakest in haste, later thou wilt have to withdraw
       thy words.

And to learn to hold thy peace thou shalt exert thy mind.

Thou shalt worship thy God daily

With offerings, prayer, and correct incense.

Mayest thou make thy heart to incline obediently to thy God,

For it is that that is acceptable unto God.

Prayer, weeping, and humble prostrations

Shalt thou offer unto Him daily.

Then shall thy power become mighty,

And thou shalt be fully guided on the right way by God.

With thine understanding observe [what is on] the tablet.

The fear of God begetteth prosperity.

Sacrifice prolongeth life,
And prayer looseth sin.
He who loveth the gods will not lightly esteem his God.
He who feareth the Anunnaki prolongeth his days.
Speak not that which is evil with a friend and acquaintance.
Utter not base things, speak that which is good.

As soon as the Kassites had taken possession of Babylonia they inaugurated a new system of land tenure, and under their rule the "Kudurru," or Boundary Stone, or Landmark, became an important title deed, or charter, and the inscriptions upon it often contain valuable historical information which cannot be obtained from any other source. The Kassite Boundary Stones usually record grants of land to favoured or deserving subjects by kings, and the earliest of them dates from about 1400 BC. The inscriptions mention the names of the kings, describe the boundaries of the lands granted, and sometimes tell us why they were granted. They usually end with a series of curses on the man who shall destroy or remove the landmark, and with figures and symbols of the gods who are invoked to make the curses effective. To give the reader an idea of the character of the inscriptions on such monuments, a summary of the texts on the *Kudurru* of Ritti-Marduk (*see* Plate X) is here given. The first paragraph gives the name and titles of Nebuchadnezzar I (1146–1123), the overthrower of the Lullubi, and the conqueror of the Amorites and the Kassites. The king determined to take vengeance on the Elamites, who had been raiding Babylonia, and under the protection of Marduk he set out on his campaign from Dêr, the frontier city of Anu. He marched continuously for 60 hours, and as the season was summer, "the metal axes burned like fire, and the heat of the stones on the roads blistered the feet. The wells were dried up by the heat, and no water to drink could be found. The spirit of the horses languished, and the legs of the mighty man trembled. Nevertheless, the king marched on, the gods aiding him; and Nebuchadnezzar, the

unrivalled king, continued to march on. He was not afraid of
the difficult road, and he urged on the drooping horses. Ritti-
Marduk, the chieftain of Bît-Karziabku, the captain of the chariots,
whose place was at the right hand of the king, did not fail his lord,
but drove on his chariot. The king made a forced march and came
to the river Ulâ (Eulaeus). The king of the Elamites formed up and
prepared to fight. Fire was kindled in their midst; the sun was dark-
ened by the cloud of dust which they made; they swept onward like
the whirlwind, raging like a storm. During the tempest of their
attack the warrior in his chariot could not see the soldier by his side.
Ritti-Marduk kept his place at the right hand of his lord and drove on
his chariot; fearlessly he attacked the enemy and drove his chariot
through the hosts of the foes of his lord. And by the decree of Ishtar
and Adad, who decide the outcome of battles, he brought about the
defeat of the King of Elam, who was overwhelmed with destruction.
Thus King Nebuchadnezzar triumphed over him, and conquered
the country of Elam, and plundered the country and sacked its cities,
and returned to Akkad in triumph and with gladness."

In return for this splendid service, Nebuchadnezzar granted a
Charter to Ritti-Marduk by which he freed all villages in Bît-
Karziabku from the jurisdiction of the neighbouring town of
Namar. This Charter freed Ritti-Marduk from taxes and dues
and contributions to local or public expenses of every kind; it
exempted all his people from the *corvée* on the canals, etc., and
secured him and his people from interference of every kind on the
part of the officials of Namar. The Charter was granted in the presence of thirteen of the highest officials of Nebuchadnezzar, and
the scribe who drafted it was Enlil-tabni-bullit, the prophet. The
last section reads: "Whensoever in after-time a son of Khabban, or
any other man who may be appointed governor of Namar or prefect
of Namar, whether he be small or great, whoever he may be, in
respect of the towns of Bît-Karziabku which the king has freed
from the jurisdiction of Namar, shall not fear the king or his gods,

and shall again assert the authority of Namar over them; or shall cut out the name of a god or of the king which is written down herein, and shall substitute another; or shall incite a simple man, or a deaf man, or a blind man, or an evilly-disposed man, to break in pieces this memorial with a stone, or shall destroy it by fire, or cast it into the river, or bury it in a field where it cannot be seen; may all the great gods whose names are invoked in heaven and upon earth curse that man with a curse of wrath; and may both king and god frown upon him in anger. May ENURTA, the king of heaven and earth, and Gula, the bride of E-sharra, destroy his land-mark and blot out his seed. May ADAD, the ruler of heaven and earth, the giver of springs and rain, block up his canals (i.e., irriga-tion channels) with mud. May he make him to be hungry and in want, may disaster, misfortune and calamity cling to his side by night and by day, and may ruin seize the inhabitants of his city. May the great gods SHUMALIA, the Lady of the shining mountain, who dwelleth in the heights and goeth by the water-springs, and ADAD, NERGAL and NANÂ, the gods of Namar, and SÎRU, the shining god, the son of the temple of Dêr, and SIN, and the Lady of Akkad, the gods of Bît-Khabban, in the wrath of their hearts bring calamity upon him. Let another possess the house which he hath built. With a dagger in his neck and a knife in his eye, let him cast himself upon his face before his conqueror, and let his adversary reject his supplication and cut off his life. Through the downfall of his house may his hands claw the mud. May he be bound to sorrow so long as his life lasteth, and as long as heaven and earth endure may his posterity be blotted out."[4] Sometimes the utterer of the curse prays that the destroyer of his landmark may be smitten with leprosy, or dropsy, or wasting of the bowels, and that he may wander like a starving dog through his city all night long, and lie down with the wild ass outside the city wall.

*Boundary stone inscribed with the charter of privileges granted to Ritti Marduk
by Nebuchadnezzar I about 1140 BC. B.M. No. 90,858.*

CHAPTER NINE

THE KING OF BABYLONIA AND HIS PEOPLE AND THEIR LIVES

AFTER THE GOD THE KING, IN THE EARLIEST TIMES, WAS ABSOLUTE lord and master of the country and of all who lived in it, and in some capacities he was held to be "like God." He and his governors and nobles formed a small class by themselves and possessed great power. There seems to be little doubt that in Sumerian times the population was divided into two (or three) classes, but it was not until the reign of Khammurabi that these classes were sharply defined. His Code recognizes three classes, viz., the Amelum (or Awelum), the Mushkînu, and the Wardum. The Amelum included the king, his governors and nobles, the landed proprietors, the priests and the educated class, the higher officers of the Government, and the highly skilled handicraftsmen. All of these were regarded as "free men." Among the nobles a certain number, probably by reason of their age and experience, formed a small class by themselves, and they possessed very great influence. The Amelum enjoyed many privileges, but on the other hand, if they were fined because of an accident which caused loss of life or limb to any man, their fine was heavier than that imposed on ordinary folk. The division between the highest class of the Amelum and the rest of the population was very sharply defined. From the texts belonging to the later period it is quite clear that the word

Amelum lost its original significance, and that it was used for "man," "any man," "any one," without the least regard to his position or property. The Mushkînu, or "serf" (?), lived in a special quarter of the city, and we know from the Code that he contributed less than the Amelum to the temples, and that all his fines and fees were on a lower scale than theirs. He was a free man, or partly so, and was, like the Amelum, compensated for property destroyed or for loss of limb. He was never put in the fighting line in war time, but served in the camps. Nothing is known as to his origin or mode of life in general, and it is difficult to find a word that will translate exactly the title *mushkînu*. In later times it lost its original significance, and its equivalent in Arabic, *maskîn*, whence it has passed into European languages, means "destitute," "poor man," and even mendicant. The Wardum, or slave, was the absolute property of his master, whether acquired by purchase or born on his land; his head was generally shaved in a peculiar way, and he was branded. He was fed and housed by his master, who provided him with a wife, whose offspring was the master's property. He could own property, and many slaves lived as tenants on their lords' estates. A slave might buy his freedom, or be freed by his master, to serve in the temple, or he might receive freedom by marrying a free woman, or on adoption by his own or another master. To harbour a runaway slave, or to help him to escape, or to refuse to give him up on demand was a serious offence against the Law, and entailed a heavy fine. The Wardum was in Babylonia what the *fallâh* was, and still is, in Egypt.[1] The King and the temples owned slaves in large numbers, and the women as well as the men had to do much hard work on the land, both in clearing out the water channels and canals, and in sowing and reaping. In addition to bringing up their families, they often had to attend to the cattle belonging to the temple, and to cook and to brew beer, etc. But, like the men, they were allowed to hold property and embark in business, and as has always been the case in the East, many of them showed themselves to be capable businesswomen. Among the women-slaves of the temples was a class who dedicated themselves to the god, and in many respects they were the equivalents in Babylonia of the Vestal Virgins in Rome. They were virgins vowed to chastity, and a special quarter in the temple was provided for them. The Code decreed that they should neither keep a wine-shop nor enter one. Nabonidus made his daughter the head and directress of the temple-virgins of Ur of the Chaldees.

A man was master of his house and family, and the full responsibility for the upkeep of the house and fields, and the maintenance of his wife and children and cattle and slaves was his. But the wife of a free man, or of any man, had considerable power, and enjoyed many rights and privileges. A wife was always mistress of the dowry that she had brought, and if she were so disposed could, in the event of her dying childless, arrange for that and her personal property to go back to her father's family. And she could spend her money in any way she pleased. The contract tablets and other documents prove that women invested their money in commercial undertakings, and bought and sold estates and slaves, and lent money on interest, and even went to law in their own names whenever it was necessary to do so. Women could, if they pleased, become scribes, and even members of judicial bodies, and many of them owned and managed large businesses. Sometimes a bride would stipulate that her husband should invest her dowry in some business undertaking, and that she should share with him the profit which accrued. In later times, if for some reason a wife could not, or would not, live in the same house as her husband, she could compel him to give her alimony. The Babylonian cynic railed at women, and said that "the wife is a well, a well, a pit, a pit, a sharp iron dagger which cuts a man's throat," but the fact remains that the tablets provide evidence that shows that the Babylonians owed much to their independent, business-like wives.

All over the East, from time immemorial, husbands and wives have wished and prayed for children, and as a rule boys were desired more than girls, because the boys were needed, when grown up, to defend the possessions of the family. Before the birth of a child both husband and wife used every means in their power to keep the demon Labartu out of the house; incantations were recited, and many magical rites performed to prevent her from working her evil will on the body of the woman. When the child was born the father addressed to him the words "My Son," which gave the boy the right to inherit his father's rank and property and to be reckoned as his legitimate son. The rich woman hired a nurse; the poor woman nursed her child herself for two or three years. Soon after he was weaned he was taken to a special place, a sort of playground, where he played with models of animals made of clay. The child was protected from the attacks of the gods and demons who harmed children by means of small amulets, or a written incantation, or the picture of the demon who was most feared, hung upon its body. From one of the laws in the Code of Khammurabi it seems certain that there was great infant mortality in Babylonia. In that country, as elsewhere in the East, girls and children who were not wanted, or who, for some reason, could not be reared by their parents, were cast into pits, or thrown out into the desert to be devoured by jackals and wild beasts, or, like Sargon of Agade, were laid in little reed-chests and committed to the river. In some cases the parents were able to pay for the keep of the child until it grew up, but it is clear from the law in the Code of Khammurabi that children were sometimes allowed to die, and the nurse substituted other children. That Khammurabi found it necessary to make such a law shows that baby-farming was common in Babylonia. Some of the boys who were farmed out were adopted by well-to-do but childless citizens who needed help on their farms or in their businesses, and some of the girls were taken under the protection of the temple-women, who brought them up and made them servants in the temples.

Hitherto no texts have been found to tell us what (if any) ceremonies of a religious character were performed after the birth of a child, though it seems that the town authorities registered its birth for military purposes. The reliefs on the monuments make it certain that circumcision was not practised, and it seems that the parents gave their children names when and as they pleased, and not necessarily soon after birth. The education of children varied according to the rank of their parents. The sons of the Amelum class accompanied their parents when they went on hunting, fowling, or fishing expeditions, and made themselves proficient in the use of weapons of war. Presumably they learned to read and to write cuneiform, and studied the ancient compositions and texts that would help them to occupy fittingly the position in life to which they were born. Boys intended to follow a trade were set to work as soon as they could be made useful to their parents or masters. The children of slaves went to work at a very early age, and helped to pasture the sheep, cattle, asses and other domestic animals. When boys reached a suitable age, probably when they were about fifteen years old, their parents arranged marriages for them. Usually each married a girl of his own class, who was then, as now, carefully chosen for him by his parents or the relatives who were rearing him. Owners found wives for their slaves willingly, for the children of slaves were the property of their masters. Domestic slavery was general and, though the lot of the slave was a hard one at all times and in any case, there is reason to believe that it was tolerable, for the Babylonians were not a naturally cruel people.

Children could not marry without their parents' consent, and they often lived with them for some years after marriage. The negotiations about the amount of the dowry were probably carried on by a professional intermediary, usually a woman, as at the present day, and the marriage contract was drawn up on strictly legal lines, the contracting parties being not the lovers, but their parents. In early times men often bought women for their wives, but in the later period, say about 600 BC, this custom was practically unknown. The marriage ceremony took place in the house of the bridegroom, to which the bride, closely veiled, had been brought. There, in the guest-chamber, in the presence of his chief relatives and friends, the bridegroom declared, "This woman is my wife." Whether the bride and bridegroom knelt down facing each other or stood up is not known. When the bridegroom had finished speaking, he took his wife's hand and embraced her, and the two then passed into the bridal chamber, where they remained for the greater part of a week. At the end of that time the bridegroom rejoined his friends and amused himself with them, and the young wife took up her duties as mistress of his house. During the week of marriage the kinsfolk and friends of the bride and bridegroom feasted and made merry, and gifts of food and drink were made to the poor. The childless wife had a difficult part to play when her husband kept concubines who had given him children, and much discord was caused by the slave-girl who had borne her master a son. Babylonian wives took no part in public affairs or meetings; their influence, which was very great, was exercised from their own houses. Polygamy was recognized and was common, but to all intents and purposes the Babylonian was a monogamist, and only took a concubine to give him children when his wife was unable to fulfil her duties. In early times Polyandry existed, probably on a small scale. A man could divorce his wife merely by saying "I have divorced thee," but in order to put the matter on a legal footing he usually employed a judge to make this declaration on his behalf, and paid him a substantial fee to write out the bill of divorcement. And to the wife whom he had divorced he was obliged to give a sum of money equal in value to the dowry that she had brought. According to the Code of Khammurabi, a wife could only be divorced for childlessness, adultery, roaming from home, and light and wanton behaviour. Adulterers were to be killed with the sword or drowned, and the wife who repudiated her husband was drowned, or hurled from a rock, or fined, or enslaved.

Household furniture was of a simple character and consisted chiefly of a bed, or couch, on which a man slept, or sat, or reclined at meals, stools, a small flat table at which to eat, the vessels necessary for cooking, which were made of clay or metal, bowls, water-pots and jars in clay, a corn-grinder, clay lamps, reed-mats, cushions, etc. The clothes of the family were kept in chests made of wood or clay. A large part of the population of Lower Babylonia lived, like Uta-Napishtim, the hero of the Story of the Flood, in reed huts or houses, which closely resembled the *tukuls* of the Sûdân at the present day. The dress of noblemen, priests, and high officials was comparatively simple, but it varied in quantity and thickness with the climate of the part of Babylonia in which they lived. In Sumerian times many people in the south went almost naked. Field labourers, fishermen, diggers, and cleaners of canals wore nothing at all, except a string tied round the loins. Men of the upper classes wore a sort of fringed tunic. Working women wore a narrow band round the loins; those of the upper classes wrapped themselves in a kind of shawl, but always left the right breast uncovered. Sandals and shoes, pointed and turned up at the toes, were worn by both men and women, and the men wore close-fitting caps, of the shape which resembled the turbans of later days. As time went on men began to wear long cloaks and capes, and sleeved garments were adopted by both men and women. Still later they wore a tunic or shirt next to the skin, and over this a second tunic with a belt, and a covering for the head and shoulders. The head-cloth worn by a woman was larger than that of a man, so that it might cover her face when she was in any public place or walking in the streets; both her head-cloth and her cloak were ornamented with decorated borders or fringes. The woman who went about unveiled was held in light esteem. In the temples and in their houses men went barefooted. The colour of the outer garments was of a sombre character, black, blackish brown or blue-black being the commonest; the innermost garment, which in later times was made of linen, was undyed and was probably cream-coloured. The apparel worn on high days and holy days was white. The well-to-do Babylonian, like all Orientals, loved a change of apparel, and enjoyed sitting in a clean place. His religion demanded cleanliness of person, and no man would dare to make supplication to his god in a dirty state or wearing dirty garments. The climate necessitated frequent ablutions, and when a man went dirty or wore filthy garments by choice his neighbours knew that he was in trouble or suffering mentally and physically. The custom of appearing before the god naked shows how difficult it was for a man to keep himself ceremonially clean. Originally the Sumerians, like the Semites, wore beards and did not shave the head, but at the time when the monuments we have were made they shaved both head and face. The women kept their hair, which they either wore loose and falling down over the shoulders, or twisted up in a knot, which rested on the back of the neck and was held in position by a bandlet. The Akkadians (Semites) gloried in their hair and beards, which they regarded as symbols of free men; some of them wore pointed or "squared" beards, like the early Egyptians, and some wore side-whiskers with them. Whether the Sumerians in the historic period shaved the whole body is not known, but when we remember the various kinds of insects which now infest the houses in Lower Babylonia, it seems probable that they would do so.

Next to ablutions and clean apparel for personal comfort and a feeling of well-being, the Babylonian required anointing with perfumed oils and unguents. The perfume of flowers or the odour of sweet incense was absolutely necessary for him, and a censer with incense to burn in it was found in most houses. The heat and glare compelled him to use eye-paint, and it is certain that his women employed both that and scented pomades and salves, not only to soften their skins and remove the ill-effects of sunburn and scorching winds, but to enhance their beauty. The house of every well-to-do man had a room set apart for ablutions—in fact, a sort of bathroom, containing a large flat vessel which served as the bath. A cleansing preparation made of oil and potash was used as soap,[2] and it seems that in some parts of Mesopotamia the use of depilatories was not unknown.

The fertility of the soil enabled the Babylonian generally to eat his fill, but he lived for the most part on a vegetable diet. His usual drink was water from one of the rivers or large canals, and on special occasions or days of festival he drank palm wine. In humble houses the family sat round the bowl or tray that held the food, and each person helped himself with his fingers, which were usually washed before the meal began. By way of grace the master or mistress mentioned the name of Ishtar or Shamash, just as the Arab today says "Bismillâh" (i.e., "In the Name of God"), when he dips his hand into the dish. The washing of the hands followed the meal, and the remains of the food were either eaten by the dogs of the house or thrown out into the street. In rich men's houses the guests sat after the meal and drank deeply of wine, probably fermented, ofttimes until they were drunk. The people in general took great delight in celebrating the births and marriages in their families, and in assisting in all public rejoicings and festivals of the gods. The miracle plays which were performed during the Festival of the New Year gave them great pleasure.

The Babylonians, both children and men, played a game with bones and pebbles on a plaque of clay something like a draught-board, and they must, it would seem, have had games of chance in which it was possible to gamble. From our point of view we must consider the Babylonians a very religious people, for there is no doubt that they frequented the temples and made their prayers and presented their offerings, according to their means, with regularity. Each man and woman went to the temple and employed the priest to help him or her to obtain what he or she prayed for, but there is no evidence that any system of public worship, in our sense of the word, existed. The suppliant stood up before his god and raised his open hands as he prayed; then he knelt down and bowed himself before the god, presumably until his forehead touched the earth, even as do the Muslims today. Sometimes he kissed the feet of the god or touched his robes with his hands, and sometimes he wept bitterly and made loud lamentations over his sin, or folly, or misfortune. The offerings presented to the gods were of many kinds, food, drink, oil, incense, clothing, etc., being the commonest. The most important and most significant offering the suppliant gave was the animal, usually a sheep, which was killed before the god, and was intended to be a substitute for the suppliant himself, or for one or all of his family. By the sacrifice of the animal he intended to show the god that he recognized his divinity, and acknowledged his own wickedness, which merited death.

The early Sumerian temples were comparatively small buildings, but those that existed in Babylon in the time of Nebuchadnezzar II were very large, and contained many chapels which were built round a spacious hall. A large statue of the chief god of the temple was placed in the forefront of the sanctuary; sometimes he was represented standing upright and sometimes seated on a richly decorated throne. The statues of the gods who were associated with him stood either in the hall itself, or in the side-chapels, and in some temples the statues of kings and of prominent noblemen and warriors found a place. At the sides of the entrance stood colossal figures of lions, or bulls, or many-formed fabulous monsters, which were to prevent the entry of fiends and devils into the temple. The god was supposed to require a couch on which to recline or rest, and in great temples this couch was made of gold inlaid with semi-precious stones, or of wood plated with gold and inlaid with ivory. Its exact shape is unknown, but it probably resembled the Arab *dîwân*. Theoretically, the god travelled about the country, and as all Babylonia was enclosed by rivers and intersected by arms of rivers and canals, a boat or barge was provided for him, as well as a char-iot. The boats of the gods were made of metal or of a special kind of wood inlaid with precious stones. Some gods appear to have had two boats, the one being a large, serviceable craft which was used when the god journeyed by water, and the other a small boat which rested on its sledge in the temple or sanctuary. The latter was probably the equivalent of the Hennu Boat in sanctuaries in Egypt. The god's state chariot was usually made of ebony and inlaid with many kinds of semi-precious stones, and in very early times it was thought that the chariot, with the god in it, was drawn across the sky by two fabulous animals, for which, after the Kassite conquest of the country, horses were substituted.

The most important object in early temples was the low, rectangular mass of brickwork on which the offerings were laid, and which served as an altar. This was originally quite flat, but when the animals brought as sacrifices were to be slaughtered upon it, it had slightly raised edges and a kind of spout through which the blood flowed out. Sometimes, especially during the late period, a square pillar stood in the middle of it, and on this the animal was lifted up and slain. At a still later period the pillar-altar was provided with a step on which, as the monuments show, the stand in which incense was burnt was placed; on the altar itself, i.e., the higher part, fruits, flowers, vegetables, joints of meat, etc., were laid. In the courtyard of every temple was a small lake, or "sea," and from this the water-pots and bowls used in the temple were filled. Every temple was provided with many small instruments that were used in slaying and cutting up the sacrifices, and performing ceremonies in connection with the recital of incantations, and magical rituals in general. As many magical ceremonies were performed in the temples at certain hours of the night, artificial light was necessary, and a number of lamps, both large and small, must have been included among the temple furniture. On days of festival the pleasure of the people was enhanced by the music which was sung and played by the temple staff. Among the musical instruments may be mentioned the reed-flute, both single and double; the trumpet;

the large harp, which stood on the ground and was played with the right hand; the small harp of from ten to fifteen strings, which was portable and was played with both hands; the lyre; the large squat round drum which either stood on the ground or was fastened to the front of the player, who struck it with both hands; the small drum with a long, narrow tapering body, also played with the hands; cymbals, bells and tambourines. The singing of the temple men and women, the clapping of hands of the children, and the playing of these instruments must have produced a very considerable noise. Of Babylonian musical notation little or nothing is known, but it is probable that, to the copies of the rhythmical compositions sung by temple choirs, signs were added which indicated to the singer how certain passages were to be sung.

The priests attached to a great temple were very numerous, and might probably be counted by the score. All the important priests lived in the precincts, and were maintained out of the revenues of the temple, and, since the Babylonians had no metal currency, were paid in kind. Many of them possessed private means, and "pluralists" were not unknown in Babylonia. There were several orders of priests, and each performed specific duties. The Shangu and Makhkhu were the heads of the priesthood. The Urigallu performed very important functions at the New Year Festival. Clad in white, he entered the sanctuary alone and remained there reciting prayers for many days. He recited the Story of the Creation, and superintended the preparation of the scenes for the miracle play which was performed during the festival, and he confirmed the king in his sovereignty annually, and on certain occasions acted as his Commissioner or Deputy. The "Stewards" acted as personal attendants on the gods, and dressed their statues, and bore their emblems. Other special orders dealt with water ceremonies, the music of the temple, incantation services, the interpretation of dreams, divination and the reading of omens, funerary ceremonies, etc. The business of the temple and the management of its estates and properties were conducted by a staff of educated men, who were assisted by a large number of handicraftsmen of all kinds. The priestesses of the temple were presided over by the High Priestess, whose duty it was to direct and control as far as possible the women servants of the temple, and the "Ishtar Maidens," who dedicated themselves to the service of the goddess.

From time immemorial a large part of the population of Babylonia devoted itself to commerce, and the thousands of business and contract tablets which exist in Museums proclaim alike the activities and the variety of the operations of the Babylonian merchant and trader. The rivers and canals gave him easy transport by water, and in very early times he was able to build ships capable of sailing from Eridu to Dilmun, i.e., the Islands of Bahrên. Caravans of asses carried his exports into Elam and other countries to the east of the Tigris, and northwards into Armenia, Syria, and the neighbouring countries. Westwards the caravans traded with Southern Arabia, the Peninsula of Sinai and Egypt, and in every important foreign market, and every place where barter went on, the Babylonian merchant had his representative. The caravan-master was as much a government courier and postman as a trader, for he carried the king's despatches and private letters as well as business documents.

In business transactions, as in all the other affairs of life, magic entered, and the wise man enquired of the gods and, by the help of the priest, put himself under their protection before he set out on his journey. The kings of the countries through which the caravans passed were expected to allow them free and undisturbed passage through their dominions, and the king whose subjects plundered a caravan was expected to make good the loss sustained. In very early times the importance of Mesopotamia as a connecting link between the West and the East was clearly understood; and before Egypt through the power and ability of its kings became the clearing house of the world, the city of Babylon occupied that position, and even in late times was always a formidable rival to Egypt. The traffic between Europe and Persia passed through the country of Northern Mesopotamia, but the Euphrates and its banks formed the highway by which the products of India and Arabia and the east coast of Africa made their way into Europe and the large islands of the Mediterranean.

The chief exports of Babylonia were grain, skins, oil, dates, pottery, and reeds for making mats, baskets, sandals, etc. Its imports were gold, which was brought from Nubia and the coasts of the Red Sea in the form of rings and bags of alluvial gold dust; silver, which came from the Taurus mountains, and was bartered in the form of rings and ingots; copper from Cyprus and Makan (Sinai); rock-salt, which was the purest known, from Northern Assyria; iron from the neighbourhood of the Black Sea, etc. Lead and tin were separated from silver by smelting. The Sumerians discovered that copper alloyed with tin or antimony increased in hardness, and both these substances were important imports. As there was no stone in Babylonia and very little wood, both had to be imported; hard stones, porphyry, diorite, quartzite, and sandstone were brought from Sinai and Egypt, limestone and basalt from Armenia and Northern Assyria, and marble from countries near the Mediterranean Sea. Large quantities of lapis-lazuli came from Persia, and from powdered lapis-lazuli a paste for inlaying in jewellery was made, which became an important article of commerce, both in Babylonia and Egypt. Pearls and mother-of-pearl were exported to Europe and Egypt. Horses came from the highlands east of the Tigris, camels from Arabia, ivory and elephant-hides from the south, peacocks from India. The Babylonian merchants, like many other Oriental peoples, dealt largely in slaves, and the slave trade must have yielded them large profits. The slave, both male and female, was regarded as a chattel, and as a beast of burden like the ox, or ass, or camel; Khammurabi valued the slave at twenty shekels. Whether the trade was organized, as it was in modern times by Arab dealers, cannot be said, but it is very probable that Africans were shipped to the Persian Gulf, and that the leaders of caravans purchased them from dealers in the Bahrên Islands and imported them into Babylonia, where they were either sold or let out on hire. But the Babylonian was, on the whole, a humane man, and there is every reason to believe that the lot of his slave was better than is ordinarily supposed.

In the paragraphs above we have seen how the ordinary Babylonian was born and brought up, how he married, how he worshipped his gods, and how he lived and earned his bread; it now remains to see what happened to him when he died. The wise man, when he felt old age coming upon him, set his house in order, made his son his heir, made arrangements as to the division of his goods among his family and kinsfolk, provided for his children by slave-women and for their mothers, and then waited for death to come. Though he knew where he was to be buried he built no tomb for himself and hewed no sarcophagus, even if he was a wealthy man, but was content to think of being laid in the clay, the dampness of which rotted everything quickly. He loved life, and hated death because he believed that the life he would live after death would be sad and dreary, and perhaps painful. In the next world he believed he would sit in darkness with the shades of other departed beings about him, and be clothed in feathers like a bird, and eat dust and feed upon clay. There is no definite statement on the subject in the texts, but it seems that the Babylonians and Akkadians thought that any good or virtuous actions performed in this world were rewarded by long life and prosperity in this world, and not by a life of bliss in the next. Therefore they made the most of their life in this world, and thought with sorrow of the time when they would be obliged to leave the "warm precincts of the cheerful day." But every man wished to be properly buried in the earth, for it was believed that the spirit of the unburied man wandered about his village by night, eating whatever it could find to satisfy its hunger, and drinking dirty water to slake its thirst. The Underworld must therefore have provided food and drink for the spirits of the dead which dwelt there.

Of the fate of the spirits of those who were drowned in the rivers and canals or killed and eaten by wild beasts the texts tell us nothing. When a Babylonian died it was the bounden duty of his family to ensure a proper burial. In the case of the poor man the ceremonies attending the burial of his body were short and simple; it was either buried naked or wrapped in a mat or cloth of some kind, and was laid in the earth within a few hours of his death. He who died during the night was buried at sunrise; he who died during the day, at sunset. This has been the custom from time immemorial in Mesopotamia, and is still. Many slaves and outcasts were probably thrown out into the desert, and the jackals and hyenas disposed of their bodies; and some were cast into the rivers. In the case of the "master of a house," or a person of rank and position, a crowd of professional "wailers," or "mourners," who had been waiting for his breath to leave his body, surrounded the house and began to wail at the top of their voices and to chant compositions of a stereotyped character, in which the virtues of the deceased were proclaimed. The "wailers" sang their laments to the accompaniment of flutes and other instruments of music; the number and intensity of their dirges varied according to the social position of the deceased and the generosity of the paymaster of the funeral. The women mourners uncovered their heads and faces and smote their breasts as they wailed, and men shaved their heads and beards, rent their ordinary apparel and then arrayed themselves in sackcloth. Occasionally they cut themselves with knives and cast themselves on the ground in agonizing attitudes to show the intensity of their grief. We may assume that the professional undertaker provided all that was necessary for the funeral, including the mourners. As the Babylonians made no attempt to mummify their dead, the period of mourning was comparatively short, perhaps two or three days, or a week at most. The body was sometimes rubbed with salt, as in Egypt, or with oil, but whether evisceration was ever performed is not known.

Remains of graves have been found, both in Babylonia and Assyria, which prove that the bodies of the dead were sometimes burnt, but cremation can never have been practised generally because of the scarcity of wood or other materials of the kind for burning. It is true that reeds and bitumen may have been used for forming the funeral pyre, but even so the burning of the dead can never have been general. Some bodies were buried in the houses which they had inhabited, and it is possible that the houses were set on fire after the burial of their owners. The sculptured monuments found at Shûsh (Susa) show that after a battle the dead were collected into heaps and earth was thrown over them. In Lower Babylonia the body was sometimes buried in a sort of large baked clay box, bowl, or coffin, usually oval or round in shape, and resembling somewhat the primitive coffins of Egypt. In these the skeletons show that the deceased was laid upon his side, and that his legs were bent up, with his knees near his chin, as in many of the pre-dynastic graves in Egypt. Sometimes the body was covered over with a large inverted baked clay pot or bowl, the equivalent of which is also found in Egypt. In late Babylonian and Parthian times the dead were buried in baked-clay coffins, glazed or unglazed, which are, because of their shape, commonly known as "slipper coffins"; some fine examples of these are to be seen in the British Museum. Kings were often buried in their palaces, and noblemen in chambers specially set apart for this purpose in their houses.

Whether any religious service was performed when the dead man was laid in his grave is not known, but in the case of well-to-do folk a great feast was made, in which all those who were invited to share in it were supposed to take a final meal with the deceased. The remains of the feast were, as at the present day, distributed among the poor and needy. This last meal had its significance, for by it the spirit of the deceased was placed in communion with the gods and the spirits of his kinsmen and friends likewise; as they all ate the same food and drank the same drink, they became one body, according to an ancient and well-nigh universal belief. And it was important for the welfare of the spirit of the dead that offerings of food and drink should be placed in or at his tomb at regular intervals. The great need in the Underworld was pure water, therefore must the living pour out libations of pure water, so that some of it might trickle through and quench the thirst of the spirit confined below. Food, oil and scented unguents were also offered, so that the spirits of these substances might be absorbed by the spirit of the departed. The tears of the living comforted the dead, and their lamentations and dirges consoled them. To satisfy the cravings of the dead these offerings were sometimes made by priests who devoted their lives to the cult of the dead, and the kinsmen of the dead often employed them to recite incantations that would have the effect of bettering the lot of the dead in the dread kingdom of Ereshkigal. The priests also recited at stated intervals commemorative formulas, which probably much resembled the *zikars* that the Arabs recite for the benefit of the dead at the present day.

The chief object of all such pious acts was to benefit the dead, but underneath it all was the fervent desire of the living to keep the dead in the Underworld. The living were afraid lest the dead should return to this world, and it was necessary to avoid such a calamity at all costs. In a learned paper, Wiedemann has proved that in all ages men have believed in the existence of Vampires, and he has described the various methods which were employed in ancient and modern times to keep the dead in their graves. To this desire, he believes, is due the care that the Egyptians took to bury their dead in tombs deep in the ground and in the sides of the mountains. The massive stone and wooden sarcophagi, the bandages of the mummy, the double and triple coffins, the walled-up doors of the tomb, the long shaft filled with earth and stones, etc., all were devised with the idea of making it impossible for the dead to reappear upon earth. In very early times the body was decapitated and the limbs were hacked asunder, and in later times the viscera were removed from the body and placed in hermetically sealed jars (*see* A. Wiedemann, *Der Lebende Leichnam,* Elberfeld, 1917). So far as we know, the Babylonians did none of these things to their dead, but the fact that the priests were employed by the relatives of the dead to recite incantations in the tombs suggests that the living believed in the possibility of a spirit returning to this world in the form of an evil Utukku, and that the belief in Vampires existed among the Babylonians as well as among other early peoples.

CHAPTER TEN

Babylonian Writing and Learning

The babylonians and chaldeans were masters of the arts of astrology, divination, the weaving of spells, the reading of omens, and of every branch of magic, and their fame as magicians and sorcerers and authors of incantations has gone out into all the world. A native tradition says that the art of divination was practised by them before the Flood, but whether it was of indigenous or foreign origin is not known. They taught the rest of the world many things, and their wisdom was proverbial at a very early period, but, curiously enough, they have received little credit or thanks for the greatest of all their gifts to mankind, viz. the art of writing. The Akkadians, i.e., Semitic Babylonians, borrowed that art from the Sumerians, and transmitted it to many nations of Western Asia, and along with it went much of the Sumerian knowledge and the wisdom that the Babylonians were believed to possess. The earliest form of Sumerian writing was pictorial, as will be seen later, but the pictures passed from that form at a very early period into conventional representations of them, which were formed by groups of wedges arranged in various ways. It was this wedge-writing, now commonly called Cuneiform (from the Latin *cuneus*, "a wedge"), which the Akkadians adopted and passed on to their neighbours. The Sumerians brought their system of writing with them when they occupied Babylonia, but they were not the only people who used pictorial writing. The Elamites employed pictorial characters that were like the Sumerian, but their forms were more primitive still. Examples of this writing were found by J. de Morgan at Shûsh (Susa), and have been published by Scheil in the volumes of the great French work, *Délégation en Perse*. The discoveries of Sir John Marshall at Harappa in the Panjab and at Mohenjo-Daro in Sind prove that peoples in India during the Sumerian period also used a system of pictorial writing. Two instructive tables in the Indian and Sumerian forms of several pictographs, arranged in parallel columns by C. J. Gadd and Sidney Smith, of the British Museum, will be found in the *Illustrated London News* for October 4, 1924.

Early writers and travellers in Persia and Mesopotamia knew of the existence of cuneiform inscriptions at various places in these countries, but no one could read them, and the information they contained was not revealed until the first half of the nineteenth century. The first good copies of the inscriptions at Takht-i-Jamshîd (Persepolis) were made and published by Niebuhr about 1778. About ten years later Silvestre de Sacy succeeded in translating the Pehlevi inscriptions of the Sassanian kings, and suggested that the earlier Persian cuneiform inscriptions were drawn up in the same form. Profiting by this suggestion, Grotefend guessed that the most frequently occurring royal names mentioned in the Persepolitan inscriptions were those of Darius, Xerxes and Hystaspes, and applied phonetic values to the cuneiform signs which represented them. His first efforts to decipher the Persian cuneiform inscriptions were published in 1802. In 1837 Colonel (later Sir) Henry Rawlinson, who was on active service in Persia, deciphered and translated correctly the first two lines of the Persian Version of the great trilingual inscription of Darius I on the Rock of Bihistûn, and his paper on them was read at a meeting of the Société Asiatique in Paris. Niebuhr had never seen this inscription, and knew nothing of the trilingual inscriptions of Darius I and Xerxes on Mount Elvend. In 1842 Rawlinson returned to the Rock and, with the help of a certain "Kurdish boy," succeeded in copying, at considerable personal risk, the whole of the Persian Version, and three years later he published the text with a complete translation. His translation of the first part of the Susian Version, which was completed by Edwin Norris, and his translation of the Babylonian Version appeared before the close of 1856. Thus to Rawlinson is due the decipherment of the cuneiform inscriptions. The greater part of his work was done without the help of books, for for many years he was stationed in places where there were none. The work of Hincks was most valuable in respect of details as to the exact values of the syllabic characters, and without the help of Norris as a copyist Rawlinson could never have published for the Trustees of the British Museum his great *Corpus* of texts, *The Cuneiform Inscriptions of Western Asia,* 5 vols., folio, 1860–1884. He possessed naturally the ability to decipher texts, and almost unconsciously gave the correct values to the Persian alphabetic characters, and also to the syllabic Susian and Akkadian characters. And he owed his triumph in translating the Bihistûn Inscriptions for the first time entirely to his faculty of grasping the general meaning of an inscription almost at a glance. With the exception of George Smith, who first translated the "Deluge Tablet," no other Assyriologist has ever possessed the ability to do this to any considerable degree.

As already said, the Sumerians brought with them into Babylonia a pictographic script, but they soon found that they were obliged to modify it. It is possible that in their home country they wrote upon skin or parchment, or upon some kind of material of a vegetable character like papyrus; but in their new country these writing materials were evidently not forthcoming, for they began to write on stone and clay. The later Babylonians and Assyrians wrote on stone and clay, but they also used *kushshu,* "skin" and *niâru,* "papyrus."

Now it was easy enough to draw figures of objects, animate and inanimate, on skin or papyrus, but very difficult to do so on stone or clay. Cutting figures on stone was a slow process, and on clay it was difficult to make accurate drawings with clean lines, because the clay worked up under the drawing tool and blurred the lines of the figures. Very few examples of actual pictures drawn on clay exist, and they may, perhaps, be limited to two; on one, a clay plaque in the British Museum, is the figure of a man drawn in outline, and on the other, also a clay plaque (found by Prof. Langdon at Kish), is what seems to be a series of pictographs. The choice of clay as a writing material made it necessary to draw the pictorial characters in

modified outline, thus: 1. , represents a man standing

upright; 2. , a woman standing upright; 3. , a man standing

upright, with a crown on his head, i.e., king; 4. , the sun;

5. , a plant or tree; 6. , a star or god; 7. , a house;

8. , garden or plot of irrigated land; and so on. But the engraver found it a difficult and tedious task to cut these and other "line" characters on stone, and the scribe found the same when he outlined them on clay. Several examples of "line" pictographs, both on stone and on clay, are known, and from some of these in the British Museum the following specimens are taken.

In A, which contains an extract from an inscription cut upon a flat slab of stone, we see that the engraver made no attempt to reproduce the early pictographs, and that all his characters consist of perpendicular, or horizontal, or diagonal lines. It is not at

A

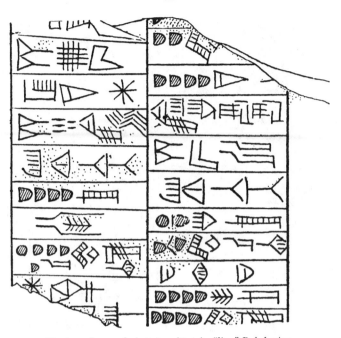

Portion of an archaic text written in "line" Babylonian.
From Cuneiform Texts, Pt. V, pl. 3. B.M. No. 22,506.

present possible to assign an exact date to this inscription, but it was probably engraved at the beginning of the third millennium BC. It and other inscriptions show that the original pictographs had, even at that early date, already lost their original forms, and that conventional linear forms of them were already in use.

The Babylonians and Assyrians never forgot that their cuneiform characters were derived from the Sumerian pictographs, and some of Ashurbanipal's scribes tried to find out exactly how they had come into being. Thus in B we have an extract from a tablet in which the scribe has set down several cuneiform characters in one column and the pictographs from which he thought they

B

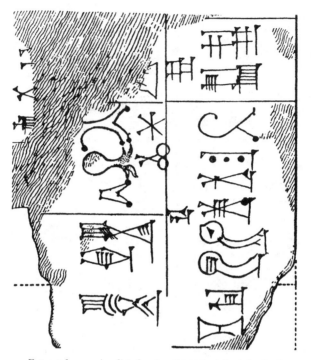

*Extract from a sign-list showing the pictorial originals of
certain cuneiform characters.
From Cuneiform Texts, Pt. V, pl. 7. B.M. 81–7–27, 49.*

might be derived in another. The conventional linear representations of the pictographs were more easily impressed on clay than cut on stone, as the two inscriptions (C and D) taken from bricks of Ur-Nammu, King of Ur about 2300 BC, show. But we see that whilst the characters cut upon stone are made up of lines, the characters on the bricks are made up in some cases of lines pure and simple, e.g., ▦, and ▷, and in others of lines which are broadened at one end, and have in fact become wedges, e.g.,

C

Brick of Ur-Nammu recording the erection of a temple to Nannar, the Moon-god,
and the building of the wall of the city of Ur.
From Cuneiform Texts, Pt. XXI, pl. 2. B.M. No. 90,004.

has become , has become and so on. In E we see
that all the characters are composed of wedges. At a later
period the Babylonian and Assyrian scribes dropped the linear
forms of the pictographs, and characters built up entirely of wedges
were impressed upon clay tablets and bricks, and cut with elaborate precision on stone. And not content with the number of
wedges that were sufficient to give meanings to the characters,
the scribes often added a number of wholly unnecessary
wedges to them, perhaps with the view of adorning them or
mystifying the unlettered.[1]

The scribe, when making these linear semi-pictorial characters,
used a stilus, which at first was probably a small stick, or a piece of
some kind of reed. Later it became a little broader at the top, and
the impression made by it in the clay instead of being a line, ———

or ▌, became a wedge ▌. Thus the character ⊞ or became , i.e., a character composed of wedges. But it was impossible to represent curved or circular objects exactly with such a stilus, and

thus the character ⌢ or ⟨≡, which represents rain falling from

the vaulted heaven, became ⟨≡≡, and ◊, the sun, became ◇. All these characters, composed of groups of wedges, in process of

time became simplified, and for ✳ we have ⊷, and

becomes ⊯, and ⟨≡≡ becomes ⟨≈, and so on. Gradually the pictorial character of nearly all the signs used in Sumerian writing

D

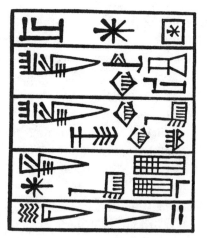

Brick of Ur-Nammu recording the building of a temple to Enlil (Bêl) in Nippur. From Cuneiform Texts, Pt. XXI, pl. 4. B.M. No. 90,802.

disappeared, and No. 3 (page 147) became first ,
then , and finally . The wedge-shaped, or cuneiform,
characters cut upon stone did not change greatly as time went on.
Cuneiform writing was adopted by the Assyrians and by the
peoples who lived to the north and west of Assyria, and for a short
period its use was general in Syria and Palestine. About 750 BC the
Urartians near Lake Wan (Van) adopted the simplified form of
cuneiform writing then in use among the Assyrians, and two
centuries later the Old Persian language was written in cuneiform.
The Persians invented a cuneiform alphabet, the characters of
which were derived from Babylonian originals.

E

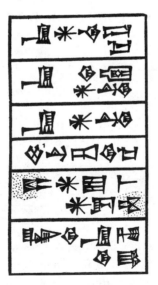

Inscription from a brick of Enannaduma, son of Ishme-Dagan,
recording his names and titles.
From Cuneiform Texts, Pt. XXI, pl. 21. B.M. No. 90,166.

The Persian version of the Inscription of Darius I at Bihistûn begins thus:

a - da - m   Da - a - ra - ya - v - u - sh
I am   *Darius,*

kh - sh - a - ya - th - i - ya   va - z - ra - ka
the King   *great,*

kh - sh - a - ya - th - i - ya   kh - sh - a - ya - th - i - ya
the king of   *kings*

a - na - m   kh - sh - a - ya - th - i - ya
            king of

p - a - r - sa - i - ya   kh - sh - a - ya - th - i - ya
Persia,   *king of the*

da - h - ya - u - na - a - m   V - sh - ta - a - s-
provinces,   *of Hystaspes*

pa - h - ya - a   p - u - tr   A - r - sh - a - ma - h - ya - a
     the son,   *of Arsames*

na - pa - a   Ha - kh - a - ma - n - i - sh - i - ya
the grandson,   *the Achaemenian.*

The oldest Sumerian documents known to us were written, according to some, in the fourth millennium BC, or, according to others, in the fifth millennium; but whichever view be accepted, they prove that the art of writing was established among the Sumerians at a very early period. In other words, they had at that time learned to use pictographs solely for the *sound* of the word which expressed the idea they represent, without any actual reference to the object depicted. When the use of the cuneiform script died out in Mesopotamia is not known, but it is certain that it was used in Babylon until the end of the first century BC.

A comparatively small proportion of the population of Babylonia learned to read and to write cuneiform, and those who were masters of the art were usually the priests, the high officials, and the scribes who kept the accounts of the palace and temples, and made copies of the religious and magical works used by the priests. A school or college was attached to each large temple, and both boys and girls, or young women, were admitted as pupils. The master's method of teaching was probably the same then as now. The pupils sat on the ground, at the teacher's feet, learned their texts by frequent repetition, asked their teacher questions and were questioned by him, and learned to write on tablets of moist clay. Among other work the pupil would learn by heart and copy lists of objects, countries, cities, rivers, stars, gods, trees, stones, plants, woods, fish, birds, cattle, clothes, synonyms of words, verbal forms, etc., from the store of tablets that the teacher kept for this purpose. The Ancient Egyptian mother took bread and beer to her boy when he was at school, but whether the Babylonian mother did so is not known.

The instruction of boys intended for the priesthood continued for a period of several years, and the studies of those who determined to become great scribes never ended. Of the character of the education of the male performers on musical instruments nothing is known; the maidens who were to lead the songs in the temple, and chorus girls, and tambourine players, were taught by the inferior orders of priestesses in chambers set apart for the purpose.

When a pupil had learned to read and write correctly in the elementary school, and the teacher had formed a good idea of his ability, the question as to his future had to be decided. If he was to be a physician, or a lawyer, or an estate agent and surveyor, a special training was necessary, and he was placed under the tuition of expert teachers of Medicine, or the Law, or Land Surveying. All such expert teachers were employed of necessity in the temples. If it was decided that the pupil should study the various branches of Magical or Theological Literature he would do so under the priests. The education of the Babylonians was entirely in the hands of the priests, who derived their knowledge from Nabû, the inventor of writing, and letters, and every kind of learning, and the Lord of "Houses of Tablets" (or Books), i.e., Libraries. The temple certainly possessed a chamber containing a collection of tablets, or what might be called a "school library," for the use of the pupils of the priests, and besides this there was a larger chamber where the great Series of tablets inscribed with incantations, oracles, omens and miscellaneous religious and magical texts were stored. Within the temple precincts also was what might be called the Record Office, in which all documents relating to the business transactions of the temple were kept, that is to say, lists of the estates owned by the temple, lists of the produce of certain farms, lists of slaves, etc. Here, too, were probably kept copies of royal edicts, and decrees, and correspondence with foreign kings, lists of taxes, and records of legal decisions and official documents of all kinds. Whether in early times each king maintained a private library is uncertain. The Assyrian king Ashurbanipal either added to or founded a large library, although the great Library of the Temple of Nabû already existed in his city. Some important documents were kept in boxes made of baked clay, as is known from the inscriptions of Nebuchadnezzar II, and either he or Nabonidus provided the baked clay box for the "Sun-god Tablet," which is now in the British Museum. Boxes made of reeds were also used, as the excavations at Abû Habbah showed. Great mercantile firms like those of Murashu and Sons and Egibi and Sons kept their less important documents on their business premises, or perhaps in their houses, but many of the important contract tablets were deposited in the Record Office attached to the local temple. At Dêr and at Abû Habbah many hundreds of "case-tablets," i.e., tablets enclosed in clay envelopes inscribed with duplicate texts of the contracts, and bearing the impressions of many cylinder seals, were found in rows on stone shelves, and thousands of the smaller tablets were in large baked-clay jars. Private individuals kept their business documents buried in the ground under their houses, and very large numbers of small contract tablets have been recovered by the natives, who systematically dig through every part of the site of an ancient town.

The Keeper of the Temple Library, the Rab Girginakki, was probably a priest, and it was his duty to preserve carefully the tablets under his charge, and to replace all illegible or broken tablets by new ones. It was his duty, too, like a Librarian in modern times, to add to his Library, and we know that he acquired copies of ancient documents from other Libraries, and sometimes sent scribes to distant cities to make copies of tablets and bring them back to him. Some of the archetypes of which he wanted copies were so much damaged, or parts of them so illegible, that he could not make out the text. Though the Babylonians were lovers of learning, there is no evidence that they formed private libraries; but the Assyrians seem to have done so, for among the tablets of Ashurbanipal's Palace Library are several that belonged to private individuals. It is impossible to say how many tablets were preserved in any of the great temple Libraries of Babylonia. The excavations at Shirpurla (Lagash), Nippur and Abû Habbah showed that the tablets stored in the Library of each of these cities were to be counted by many tens of thousands, but unfortunately the greater number were business and commercial documents. The most valuable "finds," both historically and philologically, were made at Nippur. Naturally one asks, Where are the Libraries that must have existed at Babylon and Kûthâh, to which Ashurbanipal sent his scribes to copy ancient works? As regards Assyria, nearly all that is left of the Royal Library of Ashurbanipal and the Library of Nebo is in the British Museum, and the remains of the Library of the "City of Asshur" are in Berlin; as for the Library that existed at Nimrûd, there is, alas, only too good reason to fear that the greater number of its tablets were broken and destroyed when excavations were first made there.

We may now enumerate the various branches of learning that the Babylonians studied. One of the most important of these was Grammar. Under this heading must be included the lists of words and signs used in schools and other places of instruction. In Sumerian times all works of this kind were drawn up in the Sumerian language, but when under Khammurabi the Akkadians, or Semitic Babylonians, conquered the country, it became necessary to prepare grammatical works in the two languages, the non-Semitic Sumerian and the Semitic Akkadian. It is from bilingual texts of this class that our knowledge of Sumerian is chiefly derived. Very few bilingual texts of the period of Khammurabi's dynasty exist, but we have many that were copied during the reigns of the kings of the last Assyrian Kingdom, and especially under Ashurbanipal. All these were copied from Babylonian originals, and we may assume that the Assyrian scribes copied not only the signs and words of the old lists, but used the general arrangement of them adopted by their Babylonian predecessors. Lists of signs, or syllabaries, were of three classes: 1. Syllabary in three columns. In the middle column is the sign to be explained, in the column to the left is the phonetic value of the sign as a Sumerian value, and in the column to the right is the Assyrian name of the sign, thus:

| | te - ir | | | ki - ish - tum | |

Babylonian Syllabary written 455 BC. B.M. No. 92,693.

From this we learn that the sign 𒀀𒅊, which had the Sumerian value of *te-ir,* was called in Assyrian *ki ish tum.* 2. In the second the same arrangement is followed, but the right-hand column gives the meaning of the sign or group in the middle column, thus:

𒀀 𒀀	𒀀	𒀀 𒀀
gi - ig		mar - su

From this we learn that the sign in the middle column, which had the Sumerian value of *gi-ig,* had the meaning of *mar-su,* i.e., "sick" or "ill" in Assyrian. 3. In a syllabary of this class there are four columns. In the second column is the sign to be explained, in the first is the Sumerian value, in the third is the Assyrian name of the sign, and in the fourth is the Assyrian meaning, thus:

𒀀 𒀀	𒀀	𒀀 𒀀 𒀀	𒀀 𒀀 𒀀
na - am		na - am - mu	shi - im - tu

From this we learn that the sign in the second column, 𒀀, which had the Sumerian value of *na-am,* had the name *na-am-mu,* and the meaning of "destiny" or "fate" in Assyrian. Some syllabaries contained indications of dialectic variations in Sumerian, and notes of a more or less explanatory character. As the number of cuneiform signs known is about 420, it follows that a complete syllabary of any one of these three classes must have filled many tablets.

Lists of objects, the names of gods, etc., were drawn up in double columns in Sumerian and Akkadian, and also words and phrases from archaic literary compositions; in incantation texts, hymns, etc., the Sumerian original is written in lines across the tablet, and the Semitic translation is given below. In later times, when the knowledge of the Sumerian language began to die out, and the Babylonians found it difficult to understand passages in the archaic literary compositions, the scribes wrote commentaries and explanatory lists which were of the first importance for the Babylonians themselves; and for the foreign peoples like the Hittites, who adopted the cuneiform script, and quoted Sumerian and Semitic words and phrases in their texts, they were invaluable. The Hittites also copied the Babylonians in drawing up bilingual lists of words and phrases, and a trilingual list is known, in which the Sumerian and Akkadian words are explained or translated in Hittite; and the scribes and learned men in Babylon compiled bilingual lists of words in the language of the Kassites and Semitic Babylonians.

Chronology. The Sumerians dated their years by events, and the system of dating by the years of kings' reigns did not become general until after the conquest of Babylonia by the Kassites; in Assyria the lists of the Eponyms, each of whom ruled for one year, were the principal authorities for chronology. The following are examples of the manner in which documents were dated: "Year when the country of Anshan was laid waste"; "Year in which Khammurabi restored the temple of Eturkalamma for Anu, Ishtar and Nannai." Tablets containing lists of events by which Babylonian kings dated their reigns may be seen in the British Museum (Nos. 92,702,16,924). The scribes also drew up Lists of Kings, with lengths of their reigns, which were later grouped into Dynasties, and it is now possible to compile from these a list of the kings who reigned before and after the Flood, and from about 2000 BC to assign exact dates to their reigns. The reader will find useful lists of the kings of Babylonia in Gadd, *Early Dynasties of Sumer and Akkad,* London, 1921, and in the *Guide to the Babylonian Antiquities,* 3rd edition, London, 1922, issued by the British Museum. The next step taken by the scribes was to add to the lists of kings' names and the years of their reigns short notices of important events, i.e., to write Chronicles; such notices are often of the greatest value historically. Thus we learn from a chronicle in the British Museum (No. 21,001) that, in the 14th year of the reign of Nabopolassar,

Junction was effected between Babylonians,
Medes, and Scythians.
In the months of Sivan—Ab. Siege of
Nineveh pressed; three battles.
In the month of Ab (day wanting). Capture
of Nineveh. Death of Sinsharishkun and
many commanders. The city plundered and
destroyed. Escape of a contingent of the
defaulters, etc.

Now, the 14th year of Nabopolassar was the year 612 BC, and from
the important statements quoted above, Mr. C. J. Gadd was able
to prove that Nineveh fell 612 BC and not 606 BC, as was commonly
supposed. *See* his *Fall of Nineveh,* London, 1923. Many important
facts concerning Babylonian History are given in the Chronicles
published by L. W. King (*Chronicles concerning Early Babylonian Kings,*
London, 2 vols., 1907) and Sidney Smith (*Babylonian Historical
Texts,* London, 1924). The Dynastic Chronicles are not always
trustworthy, for they give the Dynasties one after the other as if
they succeeded each other, but we know now that several of them
were contemporaneous. Such Chronicles as these were the
sources from which Berossos drew his information, and for this
reason many of his statements are not to be trusted, especially as
no one date can be fixed with certainty. With the Eponym Lists
the case is different, for one of them states that an eclipse of the
sun took place in the month of Sivan in the eponymy of Par-
Sagale. As astronomers have shown that an eclipse of the sun did
actually take place on June 15, 763, we have a fixed point from
which to reckon forwards and backwards.

The Babylonians and Assyrians found their Dynastic Chronicles
unsatisfactory, and as a result compiled tablets of Synchronous
History. The writing of History began with the chronicling of the
deeds of kings. At first the historical inscriptions merely give us
the names of the kings and of the temples they built and the number

of the canals or wells they dug. Later they added short descriptions of the wars they fought, the number of the enemy slain, and some account of their loot. In the battle that Rimush, King of Kish, fought against the people of Kizallu he killed, according to his inscription, 12,650 men and took 5,864 prisoners! Alike to Khammurabi and Nebuchadnezzar II the great and universal conquests seemed as of no importance, and each dismissed them in a few brief lines. But the descriptions of their building operations and the work they had done for the gods fill several columns. The Assyrian historical inscriptions are very different in character, for they enumerate the campaigns undertaken by the kings, and summarize the results of the various wars in such a way as to suggest that the great inscriptions on the baked clay prisms and cylinders, obelisks, bas-reliefs, etc., were drafted by scribes who had the reports of eyewitnesses of the deeds recorded to work from.

For information about the political events and the general condition of the country and its people our best sources are the Letters and Dispatches written by kings and governors, and private letters sent by heads of business houses to their agents and clients. The opening lines of these show that the bearers of government dispatches or private letters read the documents they carried to the persons to whom they were addressed. The Tall al-Amârnah Tablets, which are inscribed with royal dispatches from kings and governors of cities and towns in Mesopotamia, Syria, and Palestine to Amenhetep III and his son Amenhetep IV, are far more important than the ordinary royal narratives of wars and the building of temples. The information supplied by them is invaluable for the history of Mesopotamia for about one hundred years (1450–1350 BC).

The Law formed an important study in early Sumerian times, and fragments of various Codes of Law have come down to us. Many of these Codes were drawn up before the reign of Khammurabi, and extracts from them were incorporated by him in his own great Code, which has already been described. The Assyrians also drew up Codes of Law, and the punishments meted out to wrongdoers by them were far more severe than those ordered by the old Babylonian Codes. Like most Orientals, the Babylonians quarrelled frequently about the ownership of land, cattle and slaves, and appealed to the Law on every possible occasion. The ordeal of trial by water was frequently employed in finding out the truth, and the accused or the defendant was thrown into the river to sink or float according as he was guilty or innocent; the drinking of water from a divining bowl does not seem to have been common until the late period of Babylonian History. In important cases the decisions or judgments of the King or the Courts were accepted generally as laws. Much light is thrown upon the working of Commercial Law by the contracts concerning the sale and hiring of lands, houses, slaves and cattle, the transport of merchandise by land and water, and the everyday transactions of life.

Mathematics. The numerals 1 to 9 were expressed by wedges, thus ⟙ = 1, 𝗠 = 3, 𝗪 = 7; the sign for 10 was ⟨, and numbers 11 to 19 were expressed by ⟨ plus a number of wedges; thus ⟨𝗬 = 14, ⟨𝗪 = 19. The numbers 20 to 50 were expressed by repetitions of the signs for 10: thus ⟨⟨⟨ = 30, 𝗫 = 50. The number 60 was expressed also by a single wedge, ⟙, the *soss*, which the Sumerians employed in making their mathematical calculations. The numbers 70, 80, 90 were expressed by ⟙⟨, ⟙⟨⟨, and ⟙⟨⟨⟨ respectively. The sign for 100 is ⟙⟌, and that for 1,000 is ⟨⟙⟌, i.e., 10 x 100. The obelisks (?) that Ashurbanipal carried off from Thebes weighed ⟙⟙ ⟨⟙⟌ 𝗪 ⟙⟌, 2,500 talents. When the sign ⟙ was intended to represent multiples of 60, and ⟨ multiples often, some distinguishing mark was probably added to each. Subtraction was expressed by the sign ⟙⟌; thus ⟨⟨⟨⟨ ⟙⟌ ⟙⟙ = 40 – 2 = 38. Division was expressed by the sign ⟨⟙⟌. Fractions were: ✚ = ½, 𝗠 = ⅓, 𝗬𝗬 = ⅔, 𝗬𝗬 = ⅙, and these and others were based on the sexagesimal system. The tablets dating from about 2300 BC show that the mathematicians of Ur understood Arithmetic and Geometrical Progression and the extraction of the square and cube roots. The Babylonians of the later period adopted something like a decimal system, for they had special signs for 100 and 1,000. In an agricultural country like Mesopotamia the art of land-measuring, or Geometry, played a very important part, and there, as in Egypt, the surveyors were able to calculate the areas of fields and estates with considerable accuracy. A handy list of land and other measures will be found in the *Guide to the Babylonian Collections in the British Museum,* pages 24, 25. Many tablets that were intended to be studied by those who wished to become surveyors have come down to us, and the problems set out on them have been solved. A typical example in the British Museum has been published by Mr. C. J. Gadd in the *Revue d'Assyriologie,* tom. xix, pages 149 ff.

Astronomy. The astronomers of Babylonia were regular and systematic observers of the heavens, and Greek and Latin writers asserted that the records of such observations extended over a period of many tens of thousands of years (Diodorus says 470,000 years, and Pliny 720,000 years). Their importance for the fixing of the Calendar is obvious. The astronomer usually made the day to begin at sunset or midnight; he divided it into six parts, each containing two hours, and each two-hours period was divided into thirty parts. The year contained at first 360 days, which were divided roughly into twelve months, each containing thirty days. The Babylonians used water-clocks and sun-clocks in measuring time during the night and day. The Babylonians soon found out that their year, which consisted of twelve lunar months, differed considerably from the solar year of 365 2422 days, and in order to make the lunar and solar years to coincide they added from time to time an intercalary month called the Second Adar, and later a Second Elul. Before the reign of Khammurabi many of the City-States had their own calendars, in which the order of the months varied, but from about 2050 BC the months were arranged in the following order:

I.		*Nisannu*	..	Nisan
2.		*Airu*	..	Iyyar
3.		*Simānu*	..	Siwan
4.		*Du'ûzu*	..	Tammuz
5.		*Abu*	..	Ab
6.		*Ulûlu*	..	Elul
7.		*Tishrîtu*	..	Tisri
8.		*Arahsamna*		Marchesvan
9.		*Kislimu*	..	Kislev
10.		*Tebîtu*	..	Tebet
11.		*Shabâtu*	..	Sebat
12.		*Addâru*	..	Adar
			..	IInd Adar

The year began with the month of Nisan, i.e., some time near the Vernal Equinox, but at one period the month of Tishrîtu, in which the Equinox of September 21 took place, was held to be the first month of the year. The Era of Alexander began at this time; and the Copts and Abyssinians begin their year on August 29.

The Babylonians made observations of the five Planets, Mercury, Venus, Mars, Jupiter and Saturn, and they were well acquainted with the twelve Signs of the Zodiac and the thirty-six Dekans; and they compiled lists of the fixed stars, and according to Diodorus, they knew that an eclipse of the moon was caused by the shadow of the earth falling on it. A handy list of the Signs of the Zodiac will be found in *Babylonian Legends of the Creation,* page 68 (British Museum). The Babylonians studied the heavens diligently, not so much to increase their knowledge of astronomy as to learn from the stars, which they regarded as gods, the will of heaven in respect of their king, their country, and themselves, and so became the founders of the science of Astrology. They possessed a very real knowledge of the elementary facts of astronomy, but they were not in all periods such great astronomers as some think. Such knowledge as they had travelled eastwards to China, and northwards to the land of the Hittites, and westwards into Eastern Europe and Egypt. About the time of Nebuchadnezzar II (604–561 BC), perhaps under Western influence, the character of Babylonian astronomy gradually changed, and astronomers began to pay less attention to the astrological side of their science. The astronomical texts that have come down to us show that about the end of the fourth century BC the observers of the heavens were able to compile lists of observations of the moon, etc., which are admitted to possess scientific value. Among the founders of the new school of astronomy in Babylon was, as Schnabel has shown, Nabu-rimannu, who flourished in the second half of the fifth century BC. The Director of the Astronomical School at Sippar was Kidinnu, who flourished in the first quarter of the third century BC (Schnabel, *Berossos,* page 211).

Chemistry. The Babylonians were at no time scientific chemists, but both they and the Sumerians well understood the art of working in metals, and they made alloys and carried out many semi-scientific processes, which they learned by experiment, connected with it. They had also learned the art of debasing metals by means of artfully compounded alloys, and were able to make imitations of precious stones. They probably found out how to make fluxes for glazes and enamels by accident, but the market for such things must always have been limited and not very lucrative.

Geography. Physical geography in our sense of the word was unknown to the Babylonians. The priests had decided how the heavens, the earth, and the Underworld had been made, and how they were situated in respect to each other, and the position of the World-Ocean, and in the opinion of the pious Sumerian or Babylonian there was no more to be said. The scribes drew up lists of the countries and cities which paid tribute to their king, and seem to have invented some kind of classification. And caravan Guides and Government Envoys were provided with Itineraries, which probably resembled those that we find in the works of Ibn Hawkal, Ibn Jubayr, Mukaddasî and other Arab geographers. Distances were reckoned by "hours" then, as by caravan men now.

Fragments of Babylonian maps, drawn on clay, may be seen in the British Museum. One of the most interesting of these is the Map of the World reproduced here. Here the earth is represented as a round flat surface. The towns and cities are marked by circles, some of which contain names, e.g., Babylon, 𒀭 𒈗 𒆤, which stands near the large central black dot, and close by, in the right, is the "country of Ashshur." The double lines running from north to south represent the Euphrates, which empties itself in a region full of swamps and marshes; the rectangle lying across these lines represents Babylon. The city Dûrilu is mentioned and the district of Bît Ya'kinu, 𒂍 𒁹 𒀀 𒆤 𒀫. The world is surrounded by the "Bitter River," 𒀭 𒆷 𒁷 𒄿 𒊒, and conical projections mark the positions of eight (?) districts; in one of these "the sun cannot be seen," 𒌓 𒀀 𒀫 𒆤 𒉿.

Medicine. The earliest inhabitants of Mesopotamia of whom we have any knowledge believed that the sickness and diseases of the human body were caused by malignant spirits and devils, and tried to overcome their powers by the use of incantations and spells. Naturally the priests became the physicians. They soon discovered that incantations were not always effective, and then began to employ various substances, both vegetable and mineral, in their attempts to heal their sicknesses, and thus the Sumerian and Babylonian science of medicine came into being. They did not, however, abandon the use of incantations and spells, and it is doubtful if, even in the latest period of their history, they ever succeeded in separating magic from their system of medicine. The art of healing was taught to mankind by Ea, the lord of wisdom, the centre of whose cult was Eridu, and we may therefore

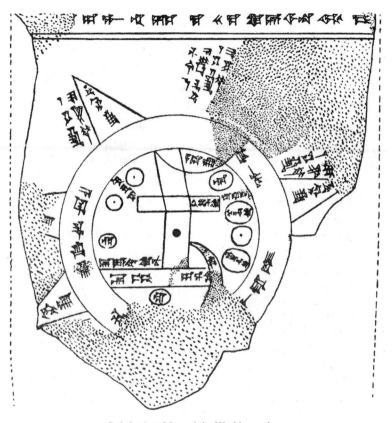

Babylonian Map of the World, on clay.
It was made to show the countries in which Sargon of Agade carried on wars.
The position of Babylon on the Euphrates is shown.
From Cuneiform Texts, Pt. XXII, pl. 48. B.M. No. 92,687.

assume that it was the Sumerians who introduced the science of medicine into Mesopotamia. The use of medicines and the manner of applying them were taught to men by the goddess Ninkharsag and the eight gods whom she created to heal special diseases. Other gods of medicine were Ninurta and his wife Gula, and Ninazu, the patron of physicians, and his son Ningishzida. The symbol of this last-named god was a staff round which a double-sexed, two-headed serpent called Sachan was coiled, and a form of this is the recognized mark of the craft of the physician at the present day. The serpent was chosen as the symbol of renewed youth and immortality because it cast its skin and so renewed its youth, and because of its longevity. Pausanius says (ii. 27) that the statue of Aesculapius at Epidaurus represented the god holding a staff in one hand, while his other hand rested on the head of a snake; and that by his side lay a dog. We may note that the emblem of the Babylonian goddess Gula, who made the dead to live, was a dog.

In process of time the surgeon as well as the physician came into being, and the Code of Khammurabi shows that in his time surgeons performed operations on the eyes and hands, and perhaps also on other members of the body. But the surgeons' knowledge of anatomy must have been very limited; and, as dissection was apparently unknown to them, they were incapable of performing internal operations. Of the functions of the various organs of the body, such as the heart and the liver, Babylonian physicians had no real knowledge; curiously enough, each member of the body was identified with a god, as in Egypt (*Book of the Dead*, chap. 42). Few remains of Sumerian medical texts have come down to us, and therefore little is known of the early history of medicine in Mesopotamia. But the texts we have of the later Babylonian and Assyrian times show that the physicians made lists of all the diseases that attack the organs and members of the body, and wrote diagnoses of them, and indicated the prescriptions to be used and the general treatment to be followed. The medicaments used were chiefly vegetable, animal and mineral, and in many respects the prescriptions resemble those of the Egyptians as found in the Ebers Papyrus. Decoctions and tinctures were made from herbs and plants, mineral substances were reduced to powder either by heating or pounding in a mortar, roots were macerated, and it is quite clear that the "making up" of many prescriptions was a serious business. Quantities were measured apparently by "rule of thumb," and probably each physician decided for himself the times of the day or night when medicines were to be taken. The value of heat in certain cases was well understood, and the benefits of massage and kneading of members of the body were discovered at an early period. Medicated oils and unguents were applied to the body direct, or were smeared on pieces of linen which were kept in position on the body by bandages. To introduce medicines into the eyes, ears, etc., the physician used a reed or a metal tube, and for lancing abscesses, etc., he employed a copper knife, as the Code of Khammurabi informs us. To what extent the medical knowledge of the Babylonians may be regarded as scientific cannot be said until all the medical tablets have been published and translated. Several Assyriologists, e.g., Boissier, Dumon, Kuechler, Oefele, Virolleaud, Zehnpfund, and Ebeling, have studied Babylonian Medicine, and published books thereon, but the first really comprehensive work on the subject we owe to our fellow-countryman, R. Campbell Thompson, who has published a *Corpus* of Medical Texts from the Kuyûnjik Collection in the British Museum. This *Corpus* contains copies of the texts on 660 tablets and fragments, and places in the hands of the student for the first time a mass of new material, the value of which, from a medical point of view, it is difficult to overestimate. Thompson has already identified a large number of medicines, both vegetable and mineral, and the information that he is printing in a companion work to his *Corpus* shows that much of what has already been said on the subject is inaccurate. The special value of his work is that he has had free access to the tablets for many years past, and had collated his texts over and over again with the originals.

Hand in hand with the science of medicine went the science of Botany, for lists of plants had to be compiled for the use of the physician and magician. The plants were grouped and classified, and the names are often given by which they were known, not only in Babylonia, but in foreign countries. The interest of the Babylonians in Mineralogy and Zoology is shown by the lists of stones, birds, fishes and insects that have been recovered from Babylonia and Assyria.

CHAPTER ELEVEN

BRITISH MUSEUM EXCAVATIONS IN BABYLONIA BY R. C. THOMPSON, H. R. HALL, AND C. L. WOOLLEY

SO SOON AS THE MILITARY OPERATIONS WHICH THE BRITISH were carrying on in Babylonia made it possible, the Trustees of the British Museum decided to re-open the work of excavating the ancient historic sites in Lower Babylonia. The ruins at Mukayyar, i.e., Ur of the Chaldees, had been examined by W. Kennett Loftus whilst engaged on the Turco-Persian Frontier Commission in 1849–52, and in the following year he made excavations for the British Museum at Abû Shahrên (Eridu), Warka (Erech), Sankarah (Larsa) and Tall Sifr, or the "Copper Hill" (so called because of the numerous copper objects found there). His excavations were described by him in his work, *Travels and Researches in Chaldea and Susiana,* London, 1857. In 1854 Mr. J. E. Taylor, working under the direction of Sir Henry Rawlinson, carried on excavations at Abû Shahrên, Mukayyar (Ur of the Chaldees) and Tall al-Lahm, and published papers on them in the *Journal of the Royal Asiatic Society,* vol. XV, pages 260–276 and pages 405–415. Mr. Haynes, in 1899, excavated a very small part of Mukayyar on behalf of the University of Pennsylvania, but until 1918 no further work of excavation was done on the sites mentioned above. In March of that year, R. C. Thompson, then serving with the Intelligence

Department of the G.H.Q. Staff in Mesopotamia, was ordered to re-open the excavations of the sites to the south and south-east of Nâsirîyah for the British Museum. He first examined all the mounds in the "protected area" of Nâsirîyah, and then directed his attention to Abû Shahrên, which lies far out in the desert, and was then outside the "protected area." Labour was very difficult to obtain, all the water required for the camp had to be brought from the Euphrates, a distance of between 20 and 30 miles, and the unsettled state of the country made the probability of successful excavation very doubtful. The feeding of the workmen was a matter of extreme difficulty, and for four weeks Thompson and his men worked at considerable personal risk under the ever-present dread of attacks by marauding Arab tribes.

Abû Shahrên marks the site of Eridu, which the Babylonians and Assyrians believed to be one of the oldest cities in their land. It came into being from out of the World-Ocean, and it was the seat of the god Enki, the father of Marduk, who subsequently, as Bêl-Marduk, became the chief god of the Babylonians. Its priests were, from the earliest times, renowned for their skill in working magic and for their learning. One of its oldest known kings was Adapa, who, owing to misdirection on the part of a god, lost the chance of becoming immortal. Of the city in early historic times nothing is known, and the oldest inscriptions found by Thompson were made by Ur-Nammu and Bur-Sin, Kings of Ur 2300–2220 BC. The latter calls himself "High Priest of Eridu"; he restored the burnt brick facing of the *zikkurat,* or temple-tower, which Thompson found to be about 84 feet high, and to have a core of unburnt bricks. The stairway which led up the side was discovered by Taylor, who says that it was 15 feet broad and its inclined plane 70 feet long, and that the brick steps, which were covered with marble, were each 4 feet wide. E-Apsû, the temple of Eridu, is mentioned by Khammurabi in the introductory paragraph of his Code (Col. 1), but he only says that he "restored E-Apsû to its place."

According to Thompson, Eridu and Ur and the neighbouring cities were occupied in pre-Sumerian times by a people who were entirely different from the Sumerians, but who were the same as those whose remains were found by de Morgan at Shûsh (Susa, "Shushan the palace") and Musyân. Their original home seems to have been the Pamirs of the Hindu Kûsh. They made thin pottery, artistically painted (though it is doubtful if they were acquainted with the potter's wheel), similar to that found by de Morgan at Shûsh. They were an agricultural people, they tilled the ground with stone hoes, reaped their crops with clay sickles, and ground their corn on stone querns. The art of weaving was known to them, and their weapons consisted of bows and arrows, slings and stone axes. They used obsidian pins, and their women wore beads of carnelian (?) They could neither write nor carve stone. They lived, like the modern Arabs, in reed-huts or in mud-brick houses. Eridu did not stand on the sea shore, but on the margin of the tidal waters of the Euphrates lagoons, perhaps on one of the mouths of the Euphrates. It was not occupied generally by any people after the time of Khammurabi, not even by the Parthians; no tablets were found there, but the place was filled only with Sumerian graves, which suggest that the site had ceased to be inhabited when they were made. The body was laid naked in the ground, with a few pots about it; it may have been dismembered, as sometimes in Egypt. Neither burial mats nor coffins were found. The burials were made in the sand at the depth of three or four feet. Thompson is convinced that the pots, both with a spout and without a spout, are Sumerian.

The inscriptions on bricks are in Sumerian. The inscription on Ur-Nammu bricks on the facing of the *zikkurat* reads: "Ur-Nammu, King of Ur, who hath built the Temple of Enki, ➤╂ ➤𒌋 ⟨𒂍, of Eridu." The inscription on the bricks of Bur-Sin reads: "Bur-Sin, proclaimed by Enlil in Nippur as SAG-USH of the Temple of Enlil, the powerful king, the King of Ur, the king of the four regions, unto

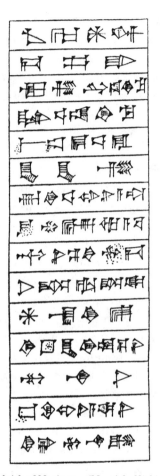

Inscription from a brick of Nurimmer (Nur-Adad?) king of Larsa, about 2027 BC, discovered by R. C. Thompson at Abu-Shahrên.

Enki, his beloved king, hath built his beloved Apsû (i.e., 'Ocean')." The most important brick inscription is that of Nurimmer (Nur-Adad?), King of Larsa (2027–2012 BC), which reads: "Nur-Immer, the mighty man, the true irrigator of Ur, the King of Larsa, the priest who hath cleansed the Temple of E-babbara: Eridu from of old having been destroyed, for his happy reign he erected, its building he renewed; for Enki, the pure abode, his beloved place, he built; the oracle (?) as it was before he restored to its place." The remains of the foundation sacrifice, i.e., the skeleton of a bull, were found close to the foot of the *zikkurat*. Red, burnt, plano-convex bricks, to join which thick layers of bitumen were used as mortar, were found both by Taylor and Thompson, and they may be regarded as the oldest Sumerian bricks known.

Among the remains of the predecessors of the Sumerians at Eridu may be mentioned buff or greenish pottery painted in black with geometric designs, and (rarely) with animal forms; well-knapped hoes of flint and chert, ground stone axe heads, stone flakes, knives, etc., flint borers, fish-hooks, arrow-heads, barbed arrow-heads, bone tools or implements; corn grinders and querns; egg-shaped missiles for slings; obsidian and crystal pins; baked clay sickles of various sizes, both right-handed and left-handed; clay nails, with convex heads, turned up at the points, spindle-wheels, beads, clay figures of animals, a painter's pot, etc. A full account of Thompson's excavations at Abû Shahrên, and his trial diggings at Mukayyar, Tall Tawaiyil, Murajib, Abû Rasên, Tall al-Lahm, Tall al-Jabarah and Tall al-Judedah, with maps, plans, drawings of objects, etc., will be found in *Archaeologia*, vol. LXX, pp. 101–144.

One of the most important results of Thompson's work at Eridu (Abû Shahrên) was the discovery that Eridu was not situated on the sea-shore, but that it stood sufficiently near the sea to be regarded and called a sea-port. The fresh-water shells found in the neighbourhood prove that the water which lay near it was fresh water from the Euphrates. It has been thought, and probably rightly, that the chief trade of the city in early times was in stone. The masses of granite and other hard stones which lie on the mounds round about were never found in Babylonia, but were brought there for stone merchants from Sinai and the western shore of the Red Sea, probably from some place near Berenice

Troglodytica. Thompson has rendered Assyriology another service in showing exactly where Eridu stood and in correcting the mistakes made by Delitzsch and Hilprecht and others, who even placed it on the wrong side of the Euphrates! Indeed, Hilprecht's description of the site has suggested to some that he wrote about the ruins without seeing them.

In 1918 Thompson returned to England on leave, and the Trustees of the British Museum decided to send out Dr. H. R. Hall to continue his work. Hall was transferred from the Intelligence Branch of the Army in England to Mesopotamia, and was attached by Lieut.-Col. (now Sir) A. T. Wilson to the Political Service for archaeological duty. He began to work at Ur, meaning to carry on the excavations at Abû Shahrên a little later, but he made a remarkable discovery at Tall al-'Ubêd, near Ur, and he practically confined his labours to these two sites. His chief work at Ur was the excavation of a large burnt-brick building, which has been identi-fied with E-kharsag, and was erected by Ur-nammu, the father of Dungi (or Shulgi), a king of the third Dynasty of Ur (2276–2231 BC). Hall next excavated a section of the temenos-wall of the temple, which was made of unbaked bricks and was 38 feet thick, with chambers 48 feet by 14 feet in its thickness. This work was followed by the excavation of a part of the outer wall of the city east of the *zikkurat,* and the discovery of several tombs, in which the bodies lay on their left sides with their knees drawn up to their chins. During the short time that Hall could devote to Abû Shahrên he cleared out five blocks of houses and two streets, and found pottery vases, wall-cones, spindle-wheels, gilt-headed copper nails, etc.; these houses were built before the reign of Bur-Sin I (or Amar-Sin) (2230–2222 BC). He examined the stone bastions of the wall of Eridu, and found in the brick bastions plano-convex Sumerian bricks of the pre-Sargonic type, and rectangular bricks dating from about 2250 BC. Some of the latter had stamped upon them two crescents, back to back, similar to those which he found at Tall al-'Ubêd. The signification of these crescents is still under discussion. For further details and discussion, *see* Hall's papers in the *Journal* of the Society of Antiquaries, December 1919, *Journal of Egyptian Archaeology*, vols. viii and ix, and the *Centenary Supplement* of the Royal Asiatic Society, October, 1924.

We now come to the fine discovery that Hall made at a place called Tall al-'Ubêd[1] and Tall al-'Abd (i.e., "Hill of the Servant," or "Hill of the Little Servant"), which lies about four and a half miles from the *zikkurat* at Ur. Here he found, and partly excavated, a little temple, and obtained important results. From the inscribed foundation, tablet which was found in the ruins by Mr. C. L. Woolley during the winter of 1923–24 we now know that this temple was dedicated to Nin-kharsag by a king, hitherto unknown, called *A-an-ni-pad-da,* 𒀉 𒀭 𒈗 𒉺𒆳 𒂗, the son of Mes-an-ni-pad-da, 𒈩 𒀭 𒈗 𒉺𒆳 𒂗, a king of the 1st dynasty of Ur, who flourished about 3300 BC (?). It is now known that later kings of Ur carried out works on the site, and later still Dungi (or Shulgi) set up a building there. It has been said that A-an-ni-pad-da lived about 4300 BC, but no evidence exists that justifies us in assigning so early a date to the building; until further information about early Sumerian chronology is forthcoming, such dates as 4300 and 4700 BC when attributed to antiquities must be regarded as improbable. But this view in no way detracts from the importance of Hall's discovery, for the temple is probably the oldest Sumerian temple known, and is in any case far older than the temples at Tall Lôh. In the course of his excavations at Tall al-'Ubêd, Hall found two panther heads in copper with bitumen cores; a copper stag's head from a relief representing Imgig; the lion-headed emblem of the god Ningirsu grasping two stags by their tails; four lions' heads of bitumen, with portions of their copper coverings, and with their original tongues, teeth, and eyes of jasper, shell and schist; a bull's head in copper, a gold horn, and plano-convex Sumerian bricks. Besides these he found many fragments of painted pottery of the pre-historic Period and of the same type as that found by de Morgan at Shûsh and at Tepé Musyân in Persia, and generally associated with the early Elamites. More important still is the portrait figure in tufa stone, probably of a priestly official named Kur-lil (?), a fine example of Sumerian art of the Ur-Ninâ period, about 3000 BC (*see* Plate II). All these objects are exhibited in the British Museum and, with many others from Hall's "find," are described in the official *Guide*, page 57 f. No attempt is made here to describe these objects at length, or to estimate the archaeological value of the information that they supply as to the high state of the civilization of the Sumerians in the second half of the fourth millennium BC, for many questions connected with them are still being discussed by Assyriologists and archaeologists. And it is unnecessary to make such an attempt, for Hall is writing a book on his season's work at Abû Shahrên, Ur and Tall al-'Ubêd, and in it we shall find his discovery discussed in the light of the results obtained by Mr. C. L. Woolley, who has completed the excavation of the temple and the other buildings of a later date. Al-'Ubêd is a very small mound, being only about 150 feet long, but the objects found in it are, from their antiquity and peculiar character, perhaps the most instructive and important of all the antiquities hitherto unearthed in Babylonia, for they place the Sumerians and their civilization in an entirely new light.

The exigencies of the public service of the British Museum made it impossible for Hall to continue his work at Tall al-'Ubêd, and the excavation of the temple was completed by Mr. C. L. Woolley in the winter of 1923–24. Hall's work at Ur revealed the fact that the complete work of excavation of the *zikkurat* there and of the site generally would occupy many years, and, whilst the question of ways and means was being considered, Dr. George Byron Gordon, the Director of the Museum of the University of Pennsylvania, expressed a wish to take part in the proposed work.[2] An arrangement was made, and the excavations at Ur and Tall al-'Ubêd in 1923–25, which will be briefly described later, were carried out at the joint expense of the Trustees of the British Museum and the Trustees of the University of Pennsylvania.

In 1922–23 Mr. C. L. Woolley and Mr. F. G. Newton, architect, and Mr. Sidney Smith, of the British Museum, Assyriologist, began work at Ur. Three sides of the rectangular temenos enclosure, which measures 400 metres by 240, were traced, and work was done on the girdle wall, which has a total width of 11.70 metres. This consists of two parallel walls of mud brick connected by cross-walls forming intramural chambers. The temenos wall had six gates, and was originally built by Ur-Nammu 2294–2277 BC; it remained in use until the fifth century BC. Work was done in connection with parts of it by Nebuchadnezzar II, Nabonidus and Cyrus. The excavations of this season made it possible to trace the history of the great temple of the Moon-god, E-nin-makh. It was founded in prehistoric times, and its plan remained substantially the same until the reign of Nebuchadnezzar II, who introduced radical changes; the works of the later king, Nabonidus, were modified greatly by Cyrus. Repairs were carried out in parts of the temple by Amar-Sin and Ibi-Sin, kings of the third dynasty of Ur, and by later kings, and fallen bricks bearing the name of Kudur-Mabug were found in the upper portion. Nebuchadnezzar II did not restore the temple, for he re-made it and completely changed its ancient character. He laid down new brick pavements, put an altar in each of the two central rooms, and built a platform, probably to hold an image of the god. His alterations of the surroundings of the sanctuary were of a drastic character, and in the place of a mass of chambers, where only a private ritual was possible, he substituted an open temple suitable for public worship. According to Mr. Woolley, "Nebuchadnezzar introduced a new plan of building to accommodate a new form of worship."

It is possible that an allusion to this radical change in the Babylonian method of worship is referred to in the third chapter of Daniel. There we read of an "image of gold," 60 cubits high and 6 cubits wide, which the king set up "in the plain of Dura, in the province of Babylon" for all men to worship. When Nebuchadnezzar II remodelled the temple at Ur there can be no doubt that he provided a statue of Bêl-Marduk, the great god of Babylon, and had it set up in the open court of the temple where all worshippers could see it. The issuing of the edict compelling all men to bow down before the "image of gold" suggests that he wished the Babylonians to worship in a manner to which they had not hitherto been accustomed. The dimensions given of the "image" (60 cubits by 6 cubits, i.e., 90 feet by 9 feet, or 110 feet by 11 feet) suggest that more than those of the statue of the god is included in them.

Among the antiquities found were: A hoard of gold, jewellery, silver, bronze vessels and beads of the sixth century BC; the hair pins, lockets, bracelets, etc., are set with carnelian, agate,

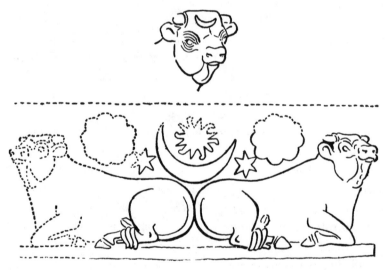

The "Bull of Heaven." From a relief on a steatite bowl.
The head of the Bull, full face, drawn above shows the crescent on his forehead.
Found in the temple of the Moon-god at Ur.
From The Museum Journal, Philadelphia, Vol. XV, No. 1, p. 27.

amethyst, sardonyx, crystal, malachite, feldspar, lapis-lazuli, chalcedony, etc. In the gate built by Nabonidus was discovered a headless diorite statue of Entemena, a king of Lagash, about 2800 BC, who is represented with his hands crossed over his chest in the attitude of prayer. It was probably brought from Lagash to Ur as a war-trophy. Other "finds" were fragments of bowls on which are carved figures of bulls and a figure of the "Bull of Heaven," and one fragment bears the name of Rimush, a king of Agade, about 2700 BC. Many fine examples of native pottery were obtained, and a number of vessels which were either imported from Egypt under the first Dynasty, or were copied from Egyptian models. Small terra-cotta figures of animals, men, etc., of the Sumerian period were found in large numbers, and when they have been studied they will, no doubt, cast much new light on the primitive beliefs of the people during the third millennium BC, and perhaps even earlier. For Mr. Woolley's article on the season's work, with plans and illustrations, *see* the *Antiquaries Journal*, No. 4, October, 1923.

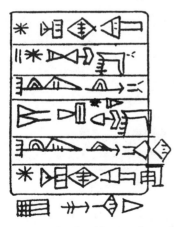

"Nin-kharsag,

A-an-ni-pad-da,

King of Ur,
Son of Mes-an-ni-pad-da,

King of Ur,

to Nin-kharsag

a temple has built."

From The Museum Journal of the University of Pennsylvania,
Vol. XV, No. 3, p. 152.

EXCAVATIONS AT UR OF THE CHALDEES BY THE TRUSTEES
OF THE BRITISH MUSEUM AND THE TRUSTEES MUSEUM
OF THE UNIVERSITY OF PENNSYLVANIA

In 1923–24, Mr. Woolley, assisted by F. G. Newton (whose death from sleepy sickness at Asyût in Upper Egypt on December 25, 1924, is greatly deplored), C. J. Gadd and G. M. FitzGerald completed the excavation of the temple at Tall al-'Ubêd, discovered by H. R. Hall in 1919. Mr. Woolley describes the mound as small and isolated and lying four miles W.N.W. of Ur, on the line of the old canal. The site was occupied at different periods by three different structures, of which the earliest is today the best preserved. The temple was set upon a solid platform with foundations of stone, a core of unbaked brick, and walls built of baked and unbaked bricks. A flight of steps led up to it, and on the S.W. side was a smaller platform of unbaked bricks, with another flight of steps. The temple is now a complete ruin. The foundation tablet, made of white marble and shaped like a plano-convex brick, was found about 8 metres away from the façade, where it was thrown when the wall in which it had been placed was destroyed. The inscription on it reads: A-an-ni-pad-da was the son of the first king of the third dyansty of Ur, which contained five kings (the last three being Meskem-Nannar, Elulu I and Balulu) and lasted about 177 years. There is no evidence that justifies us in assigning 4000 BC as the date when the reign of Mes-an-ni-pad-da began, but, as already said, he probably reigned towards the close of the first half of the fourth millennium BC, say 3600 BC. One thing seems to be quite certain so far as the objects found at Tall al-'Ubêd are concerned: we know nothing older than they in Babylonia, and the temple itself was the oldest in that country. The temple was destroyed at an early date, probably by some enemy king, who, not content with pulling down the walls, tried to destroy the platform on which it stood. Of the builder of the second temple on this site we know nothing, and nothing belonging to it has been found. He built a large brick platform over the mound, and its terraces came down to the old canal, along one side of which he made a burnt brick wall; the part of the wall that ran along the terrace is still more than two metres high. Of the third building on the site, only the foundations of a small corner remain; the burnt bricks here bear the usual inscription of Dungi (or Shulgi). Dungi was the last king to build at Tall al-'Ubêd, and after his reign the site was left desolate.

The platform of the temple of A-an-ni-pad-da was rectangular, and its corners were oriented to the cardinal points of the compass. Among the ruins were found many fragments of rounded timber, sheathed with copper plates held in position by large-headed copper rivets. Some of these are probably the remains of the columns of the porch which stood before the main door, others are parts of the roofing beams and of the shrine itself. The inscriptions of later kings, e.g., Nebuchadnezzar II, prove that the wooden rafters of temples were often plated with metal. On the floor, lying together in front of the platform, were two wooden columns covered with tesserae of red sandstone, black paste and mother-of-pearl inlaid in a deep layer of bitumen; they were 2.30 metres long and 0.90 metres in circumference. They belonged to the main door of the shrine. Other objects found were: Remains of four wooden bulls, covered with copper plates, made in the round; two of these, one headless, were brought away. They are 0.60 metres high and 0.70 metres long. The copper plates were held in position by copper nails, and tail, horns and ears were attached after the plating was done. The pasture in which the bulls were supposed to be feeding was represented by a large number (over 50 were found) of artificial flowers, the stems and calices being of baked clay, and the petals and corollae being of white limestone, red sandstone and black paste. They varied in height from 0.18 metres to 0.37 metres. Higher up on the façade of the shrine was a continuous frieze of copper bulls, the heads of which are turned towards the spectator.

The bodies are in low relief, and the heads are in the round. The head of each bull was cast hollow and filled with bitumen, and the body is formed of carved wood covered with a plate of copper. The total height of the frieze was 0.22 metres, and the average length of each animal was 0.60 metres. Above the frieze of bulls was a frieze of inlay work. The inlaid design was made of white limestone or shell, and the background was formed of tesserae of black paste; the design was inlaid in a thick layer of bitumen spread over a board (now perished), and was framed in a copper border nailed on wood. The design shows us two men milking two cows, each with her calf before her. Behind them is a byre, from which issue two heifers, and over its door is a crescent on its back ⌣, placed there probably to keep off the "evil eye," much as an inverted horse-shoe is placed over the door of a farm building, etc., in England with the same object. To the left of the byre we see two men engaged in making and pouring butter milk into a vessel with a spout. In the "milking panel" the figures are cut in limestone, and it is possible that they were covered with a thin layer of plaster and painted. On one small plaque was carved in relief the figure of a man-headed bull with a lion-headed eagle perched on its back; it had some relation to one of the panels, but was not attached to it. Other friezes were decorated with human figures, the god, the ibex, etc., and one panel, probably placed above the others, contained figures of birds.

As a striking contrast to all these examples of art work may be mentioned the old well-head of the temple, which was probably the one dedicated "for the life of the king" by one Ur-Nannar. It is decorated with figures of men, animals, etc. Of peculiar interest is the gold bead, in the form of a scaraboid, inscribed with the name of A-an-ni-pad-da; it is probably the oldest piece of Sumerian jewellery known. To the south of the temple is a very ancient prehistoric settlement, where, among the ruins of daub and wattle huts, were found stone door sockets, rough stone querns and grinding stones, painted hand-made pottery, incised ware, flakes of flint and obsidian, clay sickles, etc. Many graves of the same early period were found, as well as graves of a later time, which shows that a part of the mound was always used as a cemetery. The objects found in the later graves were wheel-made pottery, flint implements, and tools and weapons of copper. All these belong to a date anterior to 2500 BC. In some of the graves here the bodies had been buried in the contracted position, in others the bodies were laid at full length; in some the graves had the form of trenches lined with bricks, and in others they were oval or round. A very large number of miscellaneous objects were found in these graves, which, when carefully examined, will throw great light on the lives and religious beliefs of people who lived at a period about which nothing has hitherto been known. They prove that the people buried there believed in another world, and renewed life, or resurrection, and, as the later Babylonians and Kassites buried their dead at Tall al-'Ubêd and in its neighbourhood, it seems as if the goddess Nin-kharsag was at all times in some way associated with the doctrine of re-birth. As the expenses of the excavations made by Mr. C. L. Woolley were defrayed by the British Museum and the Museum of the University of Pennsylvania, the objects found were divided between the British Museum and the University Museum in Philadelphia. Those that fell to the share of the Trustees are, or will be, exhibited in the British Museum. For a detailed account of the excavations, *see* Mr. Woolley's paper in the *Journal* of the Society of Antiquaries for October, 1924, pages 329–346. *See* also *The Museum Journal,* Philadelphia, December, 1924, pages 237 ff.

The works carried out at Ur during the season 1923–24 may now be mentioned; of these the principal was the clearing of the great *zikkurat,* the building of which was begun by Ur-Nammu (2294–2277 BC) and his son Dungi, or Shulgi, and finished (as we know from the inscribed cylinders which Taylor took from it in 1854) by Nabonidus (555–538 BC). The Sumerians brought the knowledge of the temple-tower with them from the country to

Drawing from stone reliefs for inlaying from the Temple of Nin-kharsag at Tall al-'Ubéd (Ur of the Chaldees).

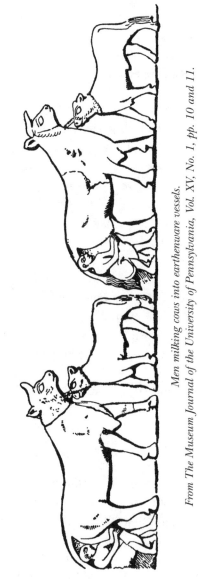

Men milking cows into earthenware vessels.

From The Museum Journal of the University of Pennsylvania, Vol. XV, No. 1, pp. 10 and 11.

Drawing from stone reliefs for inlaying from the Temple of Nin-kharsag at Tall al-'Ubéd (Ur of the Chaldees).

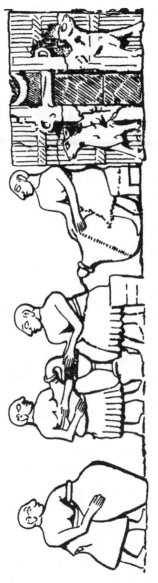

Four Sumerians engaged in straining some liquid.
Reed cow-byre with cattle emerging.

the east or north-east, whence they came, and this knowledge seems to have passed into Egypt, where it is represented by the "Pyramid" of Mêdûm. The idea of the "stepped tower" is, in my opinion, not a native Egyptian conception, otherwise we should find several later examples of it. There is no reason to doubt that a temple stood on the top of the "Pyramid" of Mêdûm, and also one on the top of the "Pyramid" of Sakkârah. We know that one stood on the top of the *zikkurat* attached to E-zida, and it is therefore probable that one stood on the *zikkurat* at Ur. In any case the *zikkurat*, whether it had four or seven stages, was no mere artificial hill, but a symbol of the various heavens of early Sumerian theology, and the statue in its temple, or shrine, on the top represented Enlil (later Bêl-Marduk), seated in the "heaven of heavens," or the highest heaven. The clearing of the *zikkurat* at Ur is a fine piece of work, for now we know what a *zikkurat* was like, and it justifies the importance attached to it by Rawlinson and Taylor, whose preliminary excavations showed later workers what was most worth excavating at Ur.

The *zikkurat* at Ur is a rectangular structure measuring at its base 65 metres by 43 metres, and its angles, not its sides, are oriented to the cardinal points of the compass. It has a solid core of unbaked brick with a thick facing of burnt brick, and its walls had an inward batter. To make a good bond, reed-mats dipped in pitch were laid between the brick courses at regular intervals. The surface is relieved by shallow buttresses, and provision is made for drainage in the form of perforations made in the brick facing. Similar perforations were observed by Rawlinson in the buildings at Babylon and Birs-i-Nimrûd. The *zikkurat* was built in stages, which diminished in area; the first was 9.75 metres high, the second 2.50 metres, the third 2.30 metres, and the fourth 4 metres. At the S.E. end there were four stages, at the N.W. end only three. A temple, now destroyed, stood on the top stage. On the N.E. side are the three stairways leading to the summit, and each has 100 steps; the two side stairways start at the two corners and converge at the top of the central stairway, where there is a wide gateway through the parapet of the second stage. The two bottom stages were the work of Ur-Nammu and his son, and many of their successors repaired parts of it. Except in the matter of repairing the stairways, Nabonidus left the old building untouched, but he built three new stages on the top, and on the topmost of these he set a shrine. The courtyard was 100 yards long and 60 yards wide; "the bounding wall was decorated with attached half columns fronted by a colonnade; the whole was whitewashed. Above this rose the terrace on which stood the *zikkurat,* isolated and huge. The lower part was all painted black . . . over the black parapet showed the upper terrace of bright red brick, and on the top of all the shrine built of glazed bricks of brilliant sky blue" (*Museum Journal,* June, 1924). The stages and the shrine built by Nabonidus are in ruins. Among the objects found during the work were fragments of the inscribed foundation cylinders of Nabonidus; a fragmentary inscription dealing with contracts for the demolition of existing buildings at Ur, and the erection of new ones in their places; door-sockets of Ur-Nammu, Bur-Sin, Gimil-Sin, Kuri-Galzu and Nabonidus; foundation cones of Sinbalatsu-ikbi, and cones of Ur-Nammu, Nur-Adad, Warad-Sin; a part of the face of a diorite statue of a man, fragments of sculpture, small models of boats in bronze, etc. (*see* the *Journal* of the Society of Antiquaries for January, 1925).

During the winter of 1923–24 the Joint Mission excavated the cemetery of Dikdikkah, which lies about 1½ miles to the north-east of the *zikkurat,* and obtained a very interesting collection of objects, all of which date from the period of the third Dynasty of Ur. Among these were several cylinder seals and a large group of terracotta figures. These represent gods and their adorers, animals, boats, chariots, household furniture, etc. The nude female figures represent temple-women. The figures of goddesses have horned crowns and are draped, and those of women wear very elaborate headgear and several garments, some pleated and flounced. The figures of men are either beardless and have shaven heads, or wear beards curled and trimmed and have long curls hanging down on their shoulders. Figures of gods have their characteristic symbols, maces, flails, etc. Lions, pigs, monkeys, horses, tortoises, are represented. The chairs have woven seats and high backs decorated with patterns in which buds, trees, crescents, stars, etc., are represented. The chariots have solid wheels with cogged rims, and a pole for two horses. Pots and beads were found in abundance.

The excavation of the House of Princess Bêl-shalti-Nannar, the daughter of Nabonidus, who was high priestess of the Moon-god at Ur, and of the Hall of Justice, has been described by Mr. C. L. Woolley in his letters to *The Times* (January 7, March 11, 1925), and he has given much information about the ruins generally in his letters of February 1 and February 10, 1925.

In *The Museum Journal* (Philadelphia, March, 1925), Woolley published an account of the season's work at Ur, and in *The Times* of April 16 he described the great *zikkurat*, and the portions of the great memorial stele of Ur-Nammu, its builder, which he had the good fortune to find among the ruins round about the *zikkurat*. From these publications and from a draft of his detailed *Report* which, by the courtesy of the Trustees of the British Museum and the Trustees of the Museum of the University of Pennsylvania at Philadelphia, I was permitted to see, the following brief statement about his work at Ur during the past season (1924–25) has been compiled.

During the winter of 1923–24 the *zikkurat*, which stands in the west corner of the Temenos enclosure, had been cleared, but nothing had been done to bring to light any of its immediate surroundings. On the N.E. side the floor level of the courtyard, which dates from about 1400 BC, was about 10 feet below the foundations of the *zikkurat*, a fact showing that the great temple-tower was probably built upon one or more terraces, which raised its lowest storey well above the surrounding plain. The first thing to be done was to see if this were so or not, and work was started in the area between the N.E. face and the western angle of the Temenos wall. Almost at once remains of the Persian Period were found, and beneath these were the ruins of buildings, layer upon layer, which represented the building operations of nearly two thousand years. Below these the crude brick wall of the terrace built by Ur-Nammu was discovered, with the foundation cones still fixed in the face of it. On the S.E. side the temple of NIN-GAL, the wife of the Moon-god NANNAR, built about 700 BC, was excavated, and below that were the remains of an earlier temple built by Kuri-Galzu about 1400 BC. The net result of the work in this part of the field is that we have—(1) a complete plan of the *zikkurat* and its surroundings in the Neo-Babylonian Period, after the wholesale reconstructions of Nebuchadnezzar II and Nabonidus; (2) the plan of the Kassite Period for three sides of the *zikkurat;* (3) a good part of the plan of the buildings of the Larsa Period (2000 BC); (4) the plan of Ur-Nammu's work on one side of the tower; and (5) a good general idea of its lines on two of the other sides. On the S.E. of NIN-GAL's temple was a street, but that and the entrance to another temple, built by one of the kings of Larsa and rebuilt by Kuri-Galzu, have not been yet completely excavated.

A small mound which had been worked in by Taylor in 1854 was then attacked, and was found to contain the sanctuary of a temple built by Nabonidus (555–538 BC) for his daughter Bêl-shalti-Nannar, whom he made high priestess of Ur. Below this was a large temple of Kuri-Galzu, built on the ruins of a temple nearly seven hundred years older, and below that was a temple built by a king of Ur several hundred years before that. Further work showed that the *zikkurat* was built on a terrace, nearly 6 feet high, of crude mud bricks, and the baked clay cones driven into them record the dedication to Nannar, by Ur-Nammu, of the terrace called E-temen-ni-il. These cones form a regular pattern on the slopes and buttresses of the wall, and it is the first time they have been found in position. The inscriptions show that "E-temen-ni-il" was the name of the terrace or terraces of the *zikkurat,* and "E-gish-shir-gal" the name of the whole group of buildings which we commonly call the Temenos. The terrace contained many fragments of the painted "pre-historic" pottery of the kind found at Tall al-'Ubêd and 'Abû Shahrên. From a shaft sunk on the line of the terrace wall came a very interesting shell plaque on which two human figures are engraved. There is little doubt that it was made early in the third millennium BC. Its importance as a work illustrating early Sumerian Art is very great. About 2000 BC the old terrace wall was refaced with a *kisu,* or revetment of brick, nearly 12 feet wide; this was probably the work of Sin-idinnam (2011–2006 BC). Later another king added a bastion-tower, which projected about 28 feet, and in the brickwork near were found cones or bricks of Warad Sin, Enannatum of Isin, Gungunu of Larsa, Sumu-ilum, Silli-Adad, and Kudur-Mabug.

Of the Kassite kings, the only one who did much work at Ur was Kuri-Galzu, who only claims to have "restored" or "rebuilt" the temple of the older Sumerian kings. After his time the buildings at Ur were allowed to fall into decay for about seven hundred years. By digging through the ruined temples, etc., it was found that the lowest pavement of the Temenos was made of plano-convex bricks dating from the time of the first Dynasty of Ur, about 3000 BC. Bricks of Ur-Nammu and Shulgi (Dungi) found here prove that they had built on, or perhaps mended, the old pavement. The Assyrian governor of Ur, Sin-balatsu-ikbi, about 700 BC, carried out some repairs, and then nothing was done until Nebuchadnezzar II (604–562 BC) practically rebuilt the city. The work of the Persian Period at Ur was insignificant. The excavations made on the other sides of the *zikkurat* revealed many important facts about the temples of Nin-gal, E-nin-makh, and E-dublal-makh, but it seems pretty certain that many more remain to be discovered. Woolley's identification of E-Gig-Par with the convent which Nabonidus built at Ur for his daughter is interesting, and the tablets inscribed with "school exercises" for children found in some of the chambers lend support to his view. Princess Bêl-shalti-Nannar seems not only to have kept a school in her convent, but also a children's Museum, which contained many interesting "exhibits." Thus Woolley found in one of the rooms a part of an inscribed statue of Shulgi (Dungi 2276–2231 BC), a cone of Kudur-Mabug (2070 BC), tablets dating from 2200 BC, a granite mace-head, a boundary stone of the Kassite Period, and a clay pedestal inscribed in Sumerian (with a label in the Semitic language of the country) with texts from bricks of Amar-Sin, king of Ur, about 2230 BC. Under one of the floors a large collection of unbaked inscribed tablets (dating from about 2000 BC) was found; all are contracts dealing with the business affairs of the temple.

The greatest and most important "finds" of the season 1924–25 were the broken stele of Ur-Nammu, the builder of the *zikkurat* of Ur, and the broken statue of the scribe Dada-ilum, who is represented as seated cross-legged and wearing a flounced garment which reaches from his waist to his feet. The latter probably dates from about 2800 BC. A fragment of a statue or stele mentions Utuhegal, King of Erech (2301–2295 BC). The portions of the great limestone stele of Ur-Nammu which have been preserved are of very great interest, for nothing resembling them has hitherto been found. When complete the stele was about 15 feet high and 5 feet wide. It was sculptured on both sides with reliefs arranged in bands separated by raised borders, each band containing a distinct scene, which commemorated some act of Ur-Nammu, the founder of the third Dynasty of Ur. The monument bore an inscription, of which only fragments have been recovered; these merely record the names of the canals which the King dug. The best-preserved scene, part of which is reproduced in the Frontispiece of this book, represents the Moon-god Nannar seated on a throne. He holds in his outstretched right hand a reed or rod, a loop of cord, and a circular object made of cords or reeds, which are tied round with a cord. What this object was is not known. In his left hand the god holds a digging tool or a builder's adze, the head of which was made of copper, or perhaps bronze. The rod and cord recall the "line of flax" and the "measuring reed," which Ezekiel saw in the hand of the "man, whose appearance was like the appearance of brass" (Ezekiel xl, 3), and suggest that Nannar was regarded as the architect of the temple and *zikkurat* which Ur-Nammu built at Ur. Before the god stands a vessel containing a date-palm, with a cluster of dates hanging down on each side of the vessel. To the left of the palm is the neck of a vase with water flowing on to the roots of the palm; this vase was held by the king, who, in performing the ceremonial watering of the palm, was accompanied by an attendant goddess. In the register below another scene of worship is represented. Behind the seated figure of the god we see the king Ur-Nammu carrying on his shoulders the tools used in building operations, viz., a digging tool, a basket for carrying away the earth, a pair of compasses, a trowel or mortar spreader, and a tool at present unidentified.

Other fragments of the stele contain representations of Ur-Nammu receiving from Nannar the command to build the temple and *zikkurat,* and workmen carrying baskets of earth or mortar up ladders and doing the work. A row of prisoners of war show that the military triumphs of the king were recorded on the stele, and elsewhere we see figures of two men beating a drum (?), the sacrifice of an ox and a goat, the pouring out of libations, and figures of celestial beings of some kind (angels?) who fly round the head of the king carrying vases of water to pour into the canals which he dug. How long Ur-Nammu's great stele remained intact at Ur cannot be said, but we may assume that it was broken by the Elamites, who invaded Babylonia and captured Ur about 2150 BC. But for its size and weight they would probably have carried it off as a trophy to Shûsh (Susa); as they could not do this they hewed it in pieces.

The Kingdom of Osiris in the Tuat (VIth Division).

1. The wicked tied to stakes of torture in the Tuat.

2. The field labourers of Osiris tending and reaping the wheat plant in the fields of the Tuat, being provided with grain, tcheser beer and cool water.

3. The blessed carrying the bread of Maāt, or the substance of Osiris, on their heads.

NOTE ON THE PLANT SCULPTURED ON
THE STELE OF UR-NAMMU.

According to Mr. Woolley's description of the Stele of Ur-Nammu published in *The Times* and the *Journal* of the Philadelphia Museum, the little tree (?) which is seen growing in the vase placed before Nannar the Moon-god is a palm. The two bunches of fruit which hang over the sides of the vase may be intended to represent clusters of dates, but I cannot think that they have anything to do with the tree (?). It seems to me that it represents some grain-producing plant, perhaps wheat, which was grown in the country and supplied both gods and men with food. It is clearly a plant closely associated with, and sacred to, the god. The Egyptians associated the Maāt plant with Osiris, as we see from the scenes and texts which are here reproduced from the alabaster coffin of Seti I preserved in Sir John Soane's Museum. In the middle register we see the wicked tied to the jackal-headed standards ⌐ of Rā Khepera, Shu and other gods. In the register below we see figures of men who are engaged in tending a plant very much like the plant sculptured on the Ur-Nammu Stele, and one figure has a scythe, which indicates that he was a reaper of the plant. In the register above we see some men carrying on their heads a loaf, ⊖, and others a feather, ∫, symbolic of Maāt, the goddess of Truth. The former group of beings (Second Register) are the blessed whose "Kau (i.e., dispositions) have been washed clean," and who have been chosen by Osiris to live with him in the house of "holy souls." The latter group of beings (Third Register) are the "labourers in the wheat-fields of the Tuat" (i.e., Other World), and the plants they tended and reaped are said to be "the members of Osiris." The plant was Osiris, and Osiris was the plant, and the blessed in eating "the bread of everlastingness" which was made from the grain of the plant ate Osiris. But Osiris was Maāt, i.e.,

Truth ══════ , therefore in eating that bread they ate Truth. In eating his body they became one with him and therefore eternal, and they were "called to the enjoyment of the land of the House of Life and to its truth." Those who have seen wheat growing in Mesopotamia, whether by the Great Zâb or on the fields of Babylonia, cannot fail to see in the plant on the Ur-Nammu Stele a colossal ear of wheat. And the ancient belief about connection of the Moon-god with the growth of crops and vegetation generally is too well known to need pointing out.

The Director of the Joint Mission, Mr. C. L. Woolley, has had, during his first and second seasons, the benefit of the services of the Assyriological experts, C. J. Gadd and Sidney Smith, of the British Museum, and of the architect, the late lamented F. G. Newton, whose plans, drawings and reconstructions have done so much to make us understand what the *zikkurat* and the buildings clustered about it were like. Mr. Woolley has proved once and for all that every archaeological mission should be accompanied by an architect. During his third season, Dr. L. Legrain, of the University Museum, Philadelphia, served the expedition as Assyriologist. It is greatly to be hoped that means will be forthcoming for the continuance of the work at Ur, for somewhere in the ruins around the *zikkurat*, i.e., in the Temenos, must be hidden the great Library of the Temple. And if Mr. Woolley does not find it, the native antica hunters will.

The excavations at Tall al-'Ubêd and Mukayyar ("Ur of the Chaldees") have added largely to our knowledge of the Sumerians and their civilization, and it is to be hoped that the Assyriologists will get to work and tell us as soon as possible exactly what the objects recovered prove or suggest.

After reading the reports on the excavations, archaeologists will naturally ask, What steps will the Baghdâd Government take to preserve the *zikkurat* at Mukayyar, and the buildings at Ukhêmar which they have allowed to be excavated? The natives have now no need to dig in the ruins for bricks and stones with which to build their houses, for the European scientists have uncovered them, and they are ready for their use, and unless the ruins are properly guarded, such valuable building materials will rapidly disappear. Many limestone man-headed bulls and countless square yards of bas-reliefs have been burnt and turned into mortar with which to build houses in Mosul, and the houses of the towns of Hillah, Kûfah, Kifl, Karbalah, and other places are built of bricks taken from Babylon. And the burnt brick facings of most of the *zikkurats* have been carried away by the natives and used for building purposes.

CHAPTER TWELVE

THE EXCAVATIONS AT KISH, NEAR BABYLON

DURING THE PAST THREE WINTERS (1922–24) THE HERBERT WELD and Field Museum Expedition has carried out a series of important excavations at Kish, the site of which is marked by the mound of Ukhêmar, which lies 8 miles due east of Babylon. Herbert Weld represents the University of Oxford, and the Field Museum the University of Chicago. The Director of the Expedition is Dr. Stephen Langdon, Professor of Assyriology in the University of Oxford, and he has been assisted by Messrs. E. Mackay, Hesketh, D. Talbot Rice, Colonel Lane, and Father Burroughs, S.J. The mound of Ukhêmar has been visited and described by many travellers, including Buckingham and Ker Porter, but the first who made any serious attempt to excavate it was Oppert. He found a large quantity of pottery, terra-cotta figures, an inscribed basalt slab, and many miscellaneous antiquities. All these were despatched in boats to Basrah, but all were lost in the Tigris near Kurnah in May, 1855. Rawlinson, Layard, and Rassam examined the mound, and each assumed that Oppert had taken all that was worth having from it, and left it severely alone. In 1912, the Abbé H. de Genouillac excavated there for a few months, and a description of his work is given by him in his recently published book.[1] In 1922, Herbert Weld visited Ukhêmar, and was so much impressed by its general appearance, and the fact that the site had not been completely excavated, that he determined to begin work there, and directed Langdon to make the necessary arrangements. As already said, Ukhêmar marks the site of Kish, which, according to ancient Babylonian tradition, is the oldest city in Babylonia. It was thought that Kish was the first city built after the Flood, and the first dynasty of kings who ruled immediately after the Flood were, according to the King-Lists that have been recovered, kings of Kish. But as these Lists say that Etana the Shepherd and Barsalnunna and Iltasadum reigned for 1,500, 1,200 and 1,200 years respectively, and as the whole dynasty consisted of twenty-three kings, who are said to have reigned for 24,510 years, 3 months and 3½ days, it is quite clear that the 1st Dynasty of Kish is somewhat mythical or fabulous in character. The same must be said of the 1st Dynasty of Uruk (Erech, or Warka); but there is no good reason for doubting that Kish was a very ancient city.

The first mention of Kish is found in an inscription of Mesilim, ⌐ ⟨⊫, cut on a mace head dedicated to the god Ningirsu at Lagash, in the time of Lugal-shag-engur, Patesi of that city; at that time Kish was a powerful City, and apparently its king was the paramount lord in Babylonia. It is not possible at present to assign an exact date to the reign of Mesilim, and of his works at Kish nothing is known; Langdon is inclined to think that he flourished before the reign of Ur-Ninâ (about 2900 BC). Of the four early rulers of Kish he has found no remains during his excavations, though the name of the fifth king, Lugaltarsi, is preserved on a lapis-lazuli tablet. And the evidence which Langdon has collected proves, he thinks, that Kish was the oldest capital of Sumer and Akkad, and that it maintained control of the entire land for longer periods, and more often, than any other City-State before the coming of Sargon, who removed his seat of royalty from Kish to Agade. The founders of Kish were undoubtedly Sumerians. Sargon, the Semite, became king of Kish because the god Enlil slew "Kish like the bull of heaven." Sargon, whose date is given as about 2752 BC (Weidner says 2637–2582 BC), is said to have been a gardener at Kish and a cupbearer of Ur-Ilbaba, the second king of the last Dynasty of Kish. Sargon's capital lay near Sippar (Abû Habbah), but where exactly is not known. The Semites held predominant positions in Kish, and many of the names of the kings of its last dynasty are Semitic; the founder of that dynasty was Queen Kug-bau (or Ku-Bau), who kept an inn and sold wine. Among the skulls found at Kish is one which is dolicocephalic, and belonged, according to Mr. Buxton, to a Semite; another, of the mesocephalic type, he thinks is Sumerian. In the reign of Sargon a mixed population of Semites and Sumerians inhabited the city, but, curiously enough, Sargon and two of his successors were proud to call themselves kings of Kish.

It is difficult to trace the history of Kish after the downfall of the dynasty of Sargon, but, in spite of all the attempts made to destroy it utterly by the kings of neighbouring City-States, it seems to have retained a certain amount of its old importance, as a trading centre at the least. Khammurabi (1955–1913 BC) restored Emete-ursag, the temple of Ilbaba and Ishtar, and repaired the *zikkurat* attached to it, in the 35th year of his reign, and his son Samsu-iluna (1912–1875 BC) had the top of the *zikkurat* Unirkidur-makh "made high, like heaven." Of the works of the kings Langdon has discovered many remains, and it is greatly to be hoped that he will find all the fragments of the stele of the Code of Laws which Khammurabi set up in the temple of Ilbaba. Of the domination of the Kassites, who also were proud to call themselves kings of Kish, few remains have been found. The Assyrians in the eighth century BC made themselves masters of Kish and the neighbouring City-States, and Tiglath Pileser III made offerings to the gods in Khar-sag-kalamma, the great temple of Kish. On the plain by Kish Sennacherib fought a great battle against Merodach-baladan, and the Babylonian usurper and his Elamite allies were routed with great slaughter; the rebel fled to Babylon, leaving his horses and mules and wagons on the battle field. From an inscription recently published by Sidney Smith (*The First Campaign of Sennacherib*, London, 1922), it is quite clear that the people of Kish were adherents of Merodach-baladan. Under the kings of the Neo-Babylonian Empire a period of renewed prosperity began for Kish. Nebuchadnezzar II restored the temples in the eastern and western parts of Kish, and made the city one of the defences of Babylon. He built a great wall and a moat, which ran from Kish to some point on the Euphrates about 12 miles to the north of Babylon. Langdon calculates that this wall was about 15 miles in length, and a long line of mounds, which are probably the remains of it, can still be seen stretching in a north-westerly direction from Ukhêmar to the Euphrates. Kish prospered, like many other cities, under the rule of the Persians, but it never recovered its old political power. It was occupied by the Parthians, and a remnant of the people continued to live there for probably a century or two later. Its final decay was brought about by the results that followed the change of the course of the Euphrates, which left Babylon and made a new bed for itself to the west of the city.

The mound of Ukhemar marks the site of Western Kish, and it derives its names of the "little red [hill]" from the reddish colour of the *zikkurat* there; this name suggests that there was another *zikkurat* in the neighbourhood, as indeed there was, viz. the twin *zikkurat* of Khar-sag-kalamma, or Eastern Kish. The ruins of the temple Emete-ursag lie to the east of the *zikkurat*. The height of the *zikkurat* is about 90 feet, and the S.W. and N.E. sides of its base are each 190 feet long, and the S.E. and N.W. sides each 180 feet long. The city ruins cover an area of about 120 acres, and in them letters of the period of Khammurabi, a bone stilus, pottery, and copper implements of the first Dynasty have been found. Western Kish was separated in late times from Eastern Kish, or Khar-sag-kalamma, by the Euphrates. Eastern Kish was the oldest and most important part of the early city. The two *zikkurats* were united by their temples, and the larger is about 75 feet high. The object of the building Tall al-Bandar, which is about 60 feet high, is not clear; it is undoubtedly a very interesting ruin, though Langdon does not think that it was a temple; it is to be hoped that he will dig through it and also through the other mounds that lie round about Ukhêmar and Inghara (spelling doubtful). The ruins that lead to the two *zikkurats* are half a mile long, and a magnificent palace, built of plano-convex bricks, was discovered by Langdon near the temple of Khar-sag-kalamma. It seems that the antiquities found there and elsewhere in Eastern Kish belong to the Sumerian period, whilst those excavated at Ukhêmar date from about 2000 BC and later. The principal deity of the whole city was Innini-Ishtar, and her temple and special sanctuary were called Khar-sag-kalamma and E-tur-kalamma, and are mentioned together in liturgies. She seems to have been a mother-goddess or a goddess of child-birth, and to have possessed attributes similar to those of Nintud, Nin-kharsag and Aruru.

In 1923 work was begun on the S.E. side of the *zikkurat;* a part of the temenos wall was traced, a great bastion excavated, and many important facts connected with the building of the temple were ascertained. A corridor runs round the entire base of the *zikkurat,* and is connected with rooms built in the temenos wall. This wall at Ur is 38 feet thick, and its rectangular chambers measure 48 feet by 14 feet. The walls of the court of the temple Emete-Ursag have been traced to a depth of 4 feet, and the court is 142 feet long and 123 feet wide. At a depth of 25 feet below its pavement pre-Sargonic bricks were found, and also black and white incised pottery of the period about 3000 BC. Fragments of painted pottery similar to those found at Abû Shahrên and Tall al-'Ubêd, a model of the war-chariot of Ishtar, and many other models were unearthed. A description of the antiquities which Langdon has excavated at Kish, and a series of chapters in which he has discussed their historical and archaeological importance, will be found in his recently published volume on his work and researches at Kish. It is to be hoped that he will be able to continue the excavation of this ancient City and ultimately to give us a complete history of its rulers.

The most important architectural discovery was made in a low mound which covers an area of three acres, and here were found the plaque on which the return of the victorious King of Kish is represented and the mother-of-pearl objects for inlaying. The Sumerian palace here is built of plano-convex bricks. The walls are not panelled, but have shallow alcoves; the original palace of Kish is probably earlier than 4000 BC. On the long low wall were found "four huge low round pillars" in a perfect state of preservation, and Langdon believes that no other example of this feature of Sumerian architecture is known. De Sarzec discovered at Tall Lôh "a curious construction consisting of four round pillars built together into one huge pillar, on a platform"; this dates from the time of Gudea, and its object is unknown, unless it formed one of a series of composite pillars in a "hall of pillars." In a chamber in the southern wall, Messrs. Mackay and Lane found many beautiful white limestone figures of women, animals, etc., for inlaying in friezes. It is impossible to reconstruct the scenes, for the framework and the base in which they were inlaid are wanting. These figures reveal a decorative design of "supreme elegance," and there is no doubt that the artistic genius of the Sumerians has been underestimated.

The graves excavated by Mackay belong to the pre-Sargonic period, but were made after the site was abandoned. No cist graves were found. In some the bodies had been wrapped in matting, and all the bodies lay parallel with the walls. In graves of the mat-burial type two unique types of pottery were found: 1. The water jar, with wide handles, high collar, "keeled" lip, and short foot; on each handle is a representation of the head and breasts of the mother-goddess, Innini, or Ishtar, goddess of childbirth, of Emete-Ursag. She created man out of clay, and sorrowed with him and for him, and made intercession on his behalf before Enlil. 2. The red, coarse clay vessel made in two pieces the base and stem forming the one piece and the dish the other. In the base are four holes through which air entered to the stem; it is thought that such vessels were bowls for food, which was kept hot by charcoal burning in the stem. In one grave a pestle and mortar were found. In the pre-Sargonic graves were found copper implements, copper and silver ornaments, arrow-heads, spear-heads, two forks, dagger-blades, a chop-ping-knife, copper hairpin with lapis-lazuli knobs, a flat sword, a scythe, chisels, double-headed axes, hatchets, battle-axes, etc. Cylinder-seals were found in the graves of men.

The Bît Akkil, or Library, lies below the ruins of great buildings of the Neo-Babylonian period, and dates from the time of Khammurabi. The tablets found here are entirely grammatical and philological, and the number of sign-lists and school texts was very large. The tablets were kept in pots arranged on shelves, and the tablets in each pot dealt with one subject only. Many syllabaries and religious texts were found. About nine out of every ten tablets were unbaked. In one room two clay figures of Papsukhal, messenger of the gods, and three figures of dogs were found; the names of two of the dogs are inscribed on them, viz., "Biter of his enemy" and "Consumer of his life." Near the doorway a fine bronze stag with a clay core was found.

In the Sumerian palace Mackay was so fortunate as to discover the oldest known specimen of Sumerian writing, from which Langdon argues that the earliest writing known is not earlier than 3500 BC, and that the tablet of A-an-ni-pad-da is not older than 3200 BC. This and many other questions cannot be settled off-hand, and we must wait for final decisions until all the antiquities discovered by Thompson, Hall, Woolley and Langdon have been thoroughly examined and compared and discussed. Though up to the present Fate has not allowed Langdon to reap so rich a harvest of antiquities from Kish as Hall reaped from Tall al-'Ubêd, there is no doubt that Langdon's discoveries have thrown much light, and will throw more, on Sumerian civilization and on the problems of early Sumerian chronology and history. It is all-important to have plans of all the great buildings which he and his colleagues have excavated and copies of the texts of the tablets they have found as soon as possible; and it is greatly to be hoped that funds will be forthcoming so that they may continue their work. To Prof. S. Langdon Assyriologists are indebted for another fine piece of pioneer work.

LIST OF THE PRINCIPAL KINGS
OF BABYLONIA

THE FOLLOWING LIST IS BASED UPON THE NATIVE LISTS OF
Dynasties which have been published by C. J. Gadd and E. F.
Weidner (*see* Meissner, *Babylonien*, Bd. II, pp. 439 ff.) and others.
The dating followed is that of Weidner, but it can only be regarded
as approximate; exact dates cannot be given before the reign of
Nabonassar (Nabû-Nâsir) 747–735 BC.

At Kish,

Dynasty I . . . Galibum, Kalumumu, Duggagib, Atab (?), Atabba,
Arpium, Etana the Shepherd, Balih, Enmenunna, Melam-Kish,
Barsalnunna, Dubzah (?), Tisqar, Ilkû, Iltasadum, Enmenbargigur,
Agga. Twenty-three Kings reigned 24,510 years 3 months and 3½ days.

Dynasty II . . . Dadasig, Mamagal, Kalbum, Umushe (?), Ur (?)
nunna, Ibinish (?), Lugalmu. Eight Kings reigned 3,195 years.

Dynasty III . . . A Queen called Ku-Ba'u, who reigned one
hundred years.

Dynasty IV.—Puzur-Sin I, Ur-Zababa, Zimudar, Usiwatar,
Ashdarmuti Ish. . . . Shamash (?), Naniyah. Seven Kings reigned
ninety-seven years and eight months.

211

At Erech,

Dynasty I.—Meskemgasher, Enmerkar, Lugalbanda, Dumuzi, Gilgamesh, Ur-Nungal, Ugukalamma, Labasher, Ennunnadanna, Ur (?) hede, Melamanna Lugalkigin (?). Twelve Kings reigned 2,310 years.

Dynasty II.—Enshakush-anna, Lugal-kigubni-dudu, Lugal-kisalsi. Three Kings reigned 480 years.

Dynasty III.—One King, Lugalzaggisi, 2662–2638 BC.

Dynasty IV.—Five Kings reigned thirty years (2456–2427 BC).

At Ur,

Dynasty I.—Mesanni-padda, Meskem-Nannar, Elulu I, Balulu. Four Kings reigned 177 years.

Dynasty II.—Four Kings reigned 108 years.

At Awan.—Three Kings reigned 356 years.

At Khamasi.—One King reigned 360 years.

At Adab.—One King reigned ninety years.

At Mari.—Six Kings reigned 136 years.

At Lagash (about 3000 BC)—Lugal-shag-engur, Ur-Ninâ, Akurgal, Eannadu, Enannadu I, Entemena, Enannadu II, Enetarzi, Enlitarri, Lugal-anda, Urukagina (2700 BC) (?), Engilsa (2650 BC) (?).

At Umma.—Surush-kin, E-abzu, Ush, Enakalli, Urlumma, Illi (about 2900–2800 BC).

At Akshak.—Unzi, Undalulu, Urur, Puzur-Sakhan, Ishu'îl, Shu-Sin I. Six Kings reigned ninety-three years (2900–2800 BC) (?).

At Agade (Akkad):

Sargon	2637 BC
Rimush	2581 BC
Manishtusu	2572 BC
Narâm-Sin	2557 BC
Shar-gali-sharri	2519 BC
Igigi	2495 BC
Imi	2495 BC
Nani	2495 BC
Elulu II	2495 BC
Dudu	2492 BC
Shudurul	2471 BC

Eleven Kings reigned 181 years.

Kings of Gutium:

Imbia	2426 BC
Inkishu	2389 BC
Nikillagab	2383 BC
Shulmê	2377 BC
Elulumesh	2371 BC
Inimabakesh	2365 BC
Igeshaush	2360 BC
Yarlagab	2354 BC
Ibate	2339 BC
Yarla	2336 BC
Kurum	2333 BC
. . . nedin	2332 BC
. . . rabum	2329 BC
Irarum	2327 BC
Ibranum	2325 BC
Hablum	2324 BC
Puzur-Sin II	2322 BC

Yarlaganda	2315 BC
. . .	2305 BC
Tiriga	2302 BC

Twenty Kings reigned 125 years and 40 days.

At Lagash (about 2400–2300 BC).—Lugal-ushumgal, Ur-e, Puzurmama, Ugme, Ur-mama, Ur-Bau, Nammakhni, Ur-gar, Darazag, Lu-Bau, Lu-gula, Gudea, Ur-Ningirsu, Ur-Lama.

At Ur:

Ur-Nammu	2294 BC
Shulgi (Dungi)	2276 BC
Ibi-Sin	2212 BC
Bur-Sin I	2230 BC
Gimil (Shu)-Sin II	2221 BC

Five Kings reigned 108 years.

At Isin:

Ishbi-Irra	2186 BC
Gimil-ilishu	2153 BC
Idin-Dagan	2143 BC
Ishme-Dagan	2122 BC
Libit-Ishtar	2102 BC
Ur-Ninurta	2091 BC
Bur-Sin II	2063 BC
Libit-Ellil	2042 BC
Irra-imitti	2037 BC
Ellil-bâni	2029 BC
Zambiya	2005 BC
Iter-pisha	2002 BC
Ur-Dukugga	1998 BC
Sin-mâgir	1994 BC
Damik-ilishu I	1983 BC

Fifteen Kings reigned 226 years.

At Larsa:

Naplânum	2187 BC
Emisum	2166 BC
Samûm	2138 BC
Zabâi	2103 BC
Gungunum	2094 BC
Abisarê	2067 BC
Sumu-ilu	2056 BC
Nûr-Adad	2027 BC
Sin-idinnam	2011 BC
Sin-eribam	2055 BC
Sin-iqishâm	2003 BC
Silli-Adad	1998 BC
Warad-Sin	1997 BC
Rîm-Sin	1985 BC
Khammurabi	1924 BC
Samsuiluna	1912 BC

Sixteen Kings reigned 287 years.

At Babylon, Dynasty I.—From Amurru:

Sumuabum	2057 BC
Sumulailu	2043 BC
Sâbum	2007 BC
Awêl-Sin	1993 BC
Sin-muballit	1975 BC
Khammurabi	1955 BC
Samsuiluna	1912 BC
Abi'êshuh	1874 BC
Ammiditana	1846 BC
Ainmizaduga	1809 BC
Samsuditana	1788 BC

Eleven Kings reigned 300 years.

At Babylon, Dynasty II.—Kings from the Sea-Coast:

Iluma-ilu	1884 BC
Itti-ili-nibi	1824 BC
Dâmik-ilishu II	1768 BC
Ishkibal	1732 BC
Shushshi	1717 BC
Gulkishar	1690 BC
. . . -ri-en	? BC
Pesgaldaramash	1635 BC
Aidarakalamma	1585 BC
Ekurulanna	1557 BC
Melamkurkurra	1531 BC
Êa-gâmil	1525 BC

Eleven Kings reigned 368 years.

At Babylon, Dynasty III.—Kassite Kings:

Gandash	1746 BC
Agum I	1730 BC
Kashtiliash I	1708 BC
Ushshi	1686 BC
Abirattash	1678 BC
Tazzigurumash	1658 BC
Kharba-Shipak	1638 BC
[8th King]	1618 BC
Agum II	1598 BC
Kurigalzu I	1578 BC

At Babylon, Dynasty III.—*Contd.*

Meli-Shipak I	1559 BC
Nazi-Maruttash I	1540 BC
Burnaburiash I	1521 BC
Kashtiliash II	1502 BC
Agum III	1483 BC
[16th King]	1464 BC
Karaindash	1445 BC

Kadashman-Kharbe I	1426 BC
Kurigalzu II	1407 BC
Kadashman-Ellil I	1388 BC
Burnaburiash II	1369 BC
Kurigalzu III	1344 BC
Nazi-Maruttash II	1319 BC
Kadashman-Turgu	1293 BC
Kadashman-Ellil II	1276 BC
Kudur-Ellil	1270 BC
Shagaraktishuriash	1262 BC
Kashtiliash III	1249 BC
Ellil-nâdin-shumi	1241 BC
Kadashman-Kharbe II	1240 BC
Rammân-shumiddin	1238 BC
Rammân-shumnâsir	1232 BC
Meli-Shipak II	1202 BC
Marduk-apal-iddin I	1187 BC
Zababa-shumiddin	1174 BC
Ellil-nâdin-ahê	1173 BC

Thirty-six Kings reigned 576 years.

At Babylon, Dynasty IV.—Kings from Isin:

Marduk-shâpikzeri	1170 BC
Ninurta-nâdin-shumi	1152 BC
Nebuchadnezzar I	1146 BC
Ellil-nâdin-apli	1122 BC
Marduk-nâdinahi	1116 BC
Itti-Marduk-balâtsu	1100 BC
Marduk-shâpik-zêr-mâti	1091 BC
Rammân-apal-iddin	1083 BC
Marduk-ahê-erîba (?)	1061 BC
Marduk-zêr-	1060 BC
Nabû-shumlîbur	1047 BC

Eleven Kings reigned 132 years.

At Babylon, Dynasty V.—Kings from the Sea-Coast:

Simmash-Shipak	1038 BC
Ea-mukin-shumi	1020 BC
Kashshu-nâdin-ahê	1019 BC

At Babylon, Dynasty VI.—Kings from Basu:

E-ulmash-shakin-shumi	1016 BC
Ninurta-Kudurri-usur I	999 BC
Shiriktum-Shukamuna	996 BC

At Babylon, Dynasty VII.—King from Elam:

Mârbîti-apal-usur	996–991 BC

At Babylon, Dynasty VIII:

Nabû-mukîn-apli	990 BC
Ninurta-Kudurri-usur	954 BC
Mârbîti-ahê-iddin	953 BC
Shamash-mudammik	941 BC
Nabû-shum-ukîn I	900 BC
Nabu-apal-iddin	885 BC
Marduk-zakir-shumi I	851 BC
Marduk-balâtsu-ikbi	827 BC
Bâu-ahê-iddin	814 BC
[Five names wanting]	811–806 BC
Marduk Bêl-zêri	805 BC
Marduk-apal-usur	804 BC
Eriba Marduk	802 BC
Nabû-shum-ishkun	762 BC
Nabû-nâsir	747 BC
Nabû-nâdin-zêri	734 BC
Nabû-shum-ukîn II	732 BC

Twenty-two Kings reigned 258 (?) years

Assyrian Kings ruling in Babylon:

Ukîn-zer	732 BC
Pûlu	729 BC
Ulûlâi	727 BC
Marduk-apal-iddin II	722 BC
Sargon II	710 BC
Sennacherib	705 BC
Marduk-zâkir-shumi II	703 BC
Marduk-apal-iddin II	703 BC
Bêl-ibni	702 BC
Ashur-nâdin-shumi	699 BC
Nergal-usêzib	693 BC
Mushêzib-Marduk	692 BC
Sennacherib	688 BC
Esarhaddon	681 BC
Shamash-shum-ukîn	668–648 BC
Kandalânu	647–626 BC

At Babylon, Dynasty of Chaldeans:

Nabopolassar	625 BC
Nebuchad-nezzar II	604 BC
Awêl-Marduk	561 BC
Neriglissar	559 BC
Labashi-Marduk	556 BC
Nabonidus	555–538 BC

At Babylon.—Persian Kings:

Cyrus	538 BC
Cambyses	529 BC
Darius I	521 BC
Xerxes I	485 BC
Artaxerxes I	465 BC
Xerxes II	424 BC

Darius II	424 BC
Artaxerxes II	404 BC
Artaxerxes III	359 BC
Arses	338 BC
Darius III	336–331 BC

ENDNOTES

PREFACE

[1] "Ich für meine Person lebe des Glaubens, dass das althebräische Schrifttum, auch wenn es seinen Charakter als 'offenbarter' oder von 'offenbartem' Geist durchwehter Schriften verliert, dennoch seine hohe Bedeutung immer behaupten wird, insonderheit als ein einzigartiges Denkmal eines grossen, bis in unsre Zeit hineinragenden religionsgeschichtlichen Prozesses," *Babel und Bibel.* Zweiter Vortrag, Stuttgart, 1903, pp. 38, 39.

[2] *Zum babylonischen Neujahrsfest*, Zweiter Beitrag, Leipzig, 1918.

[3]

See Ledrain, *Monuments Égyptiens*, pl. xxii ff.; and Budge, *First Steps*, p. 186.

CHAPTER I

[1] The more correct reading is SHUMER, and the original meaning of the word seems to have been "land."

[2] The Sumerian form of the name is AGADE.

[3] The reader who wishes to gain an idea of the character of the language will obtain much help in the *Sumerian Reading Book*, by C. J. Gadd of the British Museum. Here he will find a syllabary and a series of texts transliterated and translated.

CHAPTER II

[1] We owe this reading to Mr. C. J. Gadd.

[2] This sign means "god" and is prefixed to the names of gods and kings and divine personages and things.

[3] A sign placed after the names of countries and cities.

CHAPTER III

[1] For a discussion on this point, *see* my *Nile and Tigris*, vol. i. pages 297 ff.

CHAPTER IV

[1] For an account of their discovery and translation *see* G. Smith, *Chaldean Account of Genesis*, London, 1876. For the texts *see* King, *Cuneiform Texts*, Part xiv, and Langdon, *Epic of Creation*, Oxford, 1923.

CHAPTER VI

[1] The "kuffah" is a large basket made of willows and coated with bitumen inside and out. It is perfectly circular, and resembles a large bowl floating on the stream; its sides curve inwards at the top. It is made in all sizes, and some are large enough to hold three horses and several men.

CHAPTER VIII

[1] For these and other incantations *see* R. C. Thompson, *Devils and Evil* Spirits, London, 1903.

[2] Meissner, "a ripe fig and an apple with a sweet smell."

[3] Meissner, "Den Pflock richte auf, ergreif den Fuss" (*Babylonien*, page 234). According to this authority the priest says, "Because thou hast said this, O Worm, may Ea smite thee with his strong hand."

[4] The cuneiform text and a complete translation of it will be found in King, *Babylonian Boundary Stones in the British Museum*, London, 1912.

CHAPTER IX

[1] The Egyptians mention three classes of men: the Henmemt, 𓀀𓀀 𓀀 𓀀𓀀, the Rekhit, 𓅐𓏤𓃀𓏤𓀀, and the Pat, 𓂧𓏤𓀀𓀀

[2] In the later period of their history the Egyptians used in washing their bodies a material called antchir, 𓃟𓈖𓈗𓏭𓏭𓂝𓏤𓏤 . This word, which is found in Demotic papyri, was borrowed by the Copts who wrote it ⲁ ⲛ ⲭ ⲓ ⲣ , and it is usually translated "soap."

CHAPTER X

[1] Lists of the cuneiform characters in the various stages of their development will be found in AMIAUD and MECHINEAU, *Tableau comparé des écritures babylonienne et assyrienne archaïques et modernes avec dassement des signes d'après*

leur forme archaïque, Paris, 1902; in BARTON, *The Origin and Development of Babylonian 'Writing,* Leipzig, 1913; and in SCHEIL, *Recueil de signes archaïques de l'écriture cunéiforme,* Paris, 1898.
[2] ⟨ or ⟨ is a sign of division between words.
[3] This sign means "month."

CHAPTER XI

[1] 'Ubêd is probably a diminutive of 'Abd, for diminutives are very common in names of places in Lower Babylonia.
[2] Dr. Gordon is a trained anthropologist and archaeologist, and has had great experience in directing archaeological excavations both in his own country and in the East. He was chief of the Harvard University Expedition to Central America, 1894–1900, and is the author of many works, among them being: *The Prehistoric Ruins of Copan* (1896), *Researches in the Uloa Valley* (1898), *The Hieroglyphic Stairway at Copan* (1902), *The Book of Chilam Balam of Chumayel* (1913), *Baalbek* (1919), *The Walls of Constantinople* (1921), and two delightful books on London, *Ancient London* (1923), and *Rambles in Old London* (1924).

CHAPTER XII

[1] *Fouilles françaises d'El-Akhymer,* Tome Ier, Paris, 1824. Reviewed in *Revue d'Assyriologie,* vol. xxii, p. 39.

INDEX

A-an-ni-pad-da, 181, 185, 187
Ab, month of, 164
Abiêshu', 30
Ablutions, 135
Abu, 87
Abû Habbah (Sippar), 7, 86, 158, 205
Abû Hatab, 7, 86
Abû Rasên, 179
Abû Shahrên (Eridu), 6; excavations
   at, 175 f.
Abû-shu-namur, 112
Adab (Bismya), 7
Adad, 86, 125, 126
Adad-Nirari I, 33
Adam, his demon wife, 117
Adapa, 84, 114, 171; Legend of, 114
Adar, 167
'Adhem, river, 9
Adonis, 86
Adultery, 101, 133
Adze, 198
Aesculapius, 172
Africans, 142
Agade, 7, 17, 19, 55, 171, 185, 204
Agate, 184
Agum, 32
Agum-kakrime, 30
Aia, 86
Aiburshabu, 61
Akhkhazu, 117
Akkad, 6, 7, 125; language of, 14,
   163; limit of, 6

Akkadians, 10
Akki, the irrigator, 18
Akurgal, 12
Al-Basrah, 4
Alexander the Great, 48, 55, 58, 93
Aliens, rights of, 97
Alimony, 130
Al-'Irâk, 2
Al-Jazîrah, 2
Allatu, 81, 87
Alloys, use of, 169
Alluvium, 1, 5
Al-Madain, 48
Alphabet, the cuneiform, 155
Altar, 138
Alû, 89, 117
Amar-Sin (Bur-Sin), 23, 180, 183,
   197
Amasis II, 42
Amelum, the, 128
Amenhetep III, 23
Amenhetep IV, 32
Amethyst, 185
Amiaud, A., chap. x 222n[1]
Ammiditana, 30
Ammisaduga, 30, 70
Amorites, 124
Amrâm-ibn-'Alî, 54
Amraphel, 27
Amulets, 118
Amurru, 43, 86
Anatomy, 172

Anbar, 2
Angels (?), water-carrying, 198
Animals, clay models of, 131
Animism, 81
Annihilation, 93
Anointing, medical, 135
Anshan, 45, 47, 163
Anshar, 65, 66
Antimony, 141
Antu, goddess, 73, 83, 86
Anu, 65, 66, 73, 83, 113, 114, 163;
    heaven of, 80, 114; hymn to, 106
Anunitu, 86
Anunnaki, 63, 69, 88, 92, 93, 106,
    124; the six hundred, 81
Apadânâ, 53
Aphorisms, Moral, 121
Apil-Sin, 27
Apirak, 20
Apparel, priests, 135; various colours
    of, 135
Apries, 42
Apsû, 64, 81, 84, 178
Arabia, 141
Arabians, 22
Arabs, 48; neglect of canal-system, 4
Arali, 81
Arallû, 91
Arantu flower, 107
Ardat Lîlî, 117
Area of Babylonia, 9; calculations of,
    167
Arioch, 27, 28
Arithmetic, 167
Arits, the Seven, 91
Ark, the; building of the, 72
Armenia, 140, 141
Arrian, 58
Arrow-heads, 179, 209
Arsacidae, Era of, 48
Arsames, 156
Aruru, goddess, 64, 72, 207

Asakku, 89, 117
Asâs Amîr, 3
Ashshur, 88, 170
Ashur, 82, 88; city of, 33, 88; Library
    of, 219
Ashurbanipal, 151, 158, 160, 166;
    Library of, 158; takes Babylon, 39
Ashur-dân, 33
Ashur-nadin-shumi, 38
Ashur-nasir-pal, 36
Ashur-rêsh-ishi, 34
Ashur-uballit, 33
Ass, the wild, 126
Ass-caravans, 140
Assault, 103
Assyria, 2, 32, 86
Astrology, 147, 168
Astronomy, 167
Atrakhasis, 71
Awan, 11
Awêl-Marduk, 219
Awêl-Sin, 27
Awelum, 128
Axes, 177; double-headed, 209
Azupirâni, 18

Babbar, 12, 85
Bâbil, 52
Bâbil Street, 52
Bâbilu, 51
Baby-farming, xi
Babylon, 23, 33, 42, 113, 140;
    captured by Assyrians, 33; by
    Cyrus, 44–47; dynasties of, 27 ff.;
    founding of, 48; moat of, 54; site
    of, 7; towers of, 54; walls of, 53, 54
Babylon, the Second, 57
Babylon Castle, 50
Babylonia, 2, 4, 9; area and popula-
    tion of; 9; limits of, 2
Babylonians, 5
Baghdâd, 9, 48

Bahrên, Islands of, 140, 142
Balulu, 186
Bandages, medical, 173
Barakhsu, 19
Barsalnunna, 204
Barton, G.A., chap. x 223n[1]
Basalt, 141
Basin system of irrigation, 13
Baskets, 141; for earth, 198
Basrah, 203
Bath room, 136
Battle-axes, 209
Ba'u, 87
Bead, gold, 188
Beads, 177
Beards, 135, 194
Beatus Odoricus, 51
Beauchamps, L'Abbê J., 52, 57
Bed, 134
Beer (tcheser), 199
Bêl (Enlil), 43, 47, 83, 99, 117;
    heaven of, 79; Tomb of, 54
Bêl-ibni, 38
Bêlit-Sêri, 87,92
Bêl-kudur-usur, 33
Bells, 139
Bêl-Marduk, 54, 57, 93, 176, 184; his
    death and resurrection, 89
Bêl-Shalti-Nannar, 44, 194–197
Bêl-shar-usur, 43
Belshazzar, 44, 53
Belt, 134
Beltis, 60
Benjamin of Tudela, 51, 58
Berenice Troglodytica, 179
Berossos, 11, 71, 93, 164
Bihistûn (Behistûn) Rock of, 148,
    149, 156
Bilingual texts, 160
Birs-i-Nimrûd, 35, 54, 57, 85, 192
Birth, registration of, 131; rejoicings
    at, 136

Birtu, 87
Bismâya, 7
Bismillah, 136
Bît Akkil, 209
Bît Bazi, 35
Bît Gipari, 44, 53
Bît Karkar, 86
Bît Karziabku, 125
Bît Khabban, 126
Bitter River, 170
Bitumen, 118, 144
Bit Yakin, 38
Black Heads, 45, 99
Black Sea, 141
Blinding a man or animal, 126
Boat of the god, 137
Boat of Marduk, 59
Boat of Nabû, 60
Boatman, fee of, 104
Boats, 193
Boissier, A., 173
Bolbi, 51
Borsippa, 57, 60, 61, 85, 86
Book of Proverbs, 122
Book of the Dead, 87, 91
Book of Wisdom, 122
Botany, 174
Bottle, leather, 112
Boundary Stones, 124, 197
Bowls, divining, 121, 166
Bows and arrows, 177
Boxes for tablets, clay and reed, 158
Bracelets, 184
Branding, 103
Bread of everlasting, 199
Breasts, beating of the, 143; cutting
    off of the, 102
Bribes, 109
Bricks, 6; made by gods, 69; plano-
    convex, 176, 192; wall of glazed,
    52
Bridge of Babylon, 54, 56

Buckingham, J. Silk, 203
Bull, fire-breathing, 73; skeleton of, 179
Bull of Heaven, 184, 185
Bulls, bronze, 61; colossal, 137; man-headed, 89, 185; wooden, 185
Bunene, 85
Buranun, 2
Burial, the Babylonian, 143
Burnaburiash, 32
Burning the dead, 144
Burroughs, Father, 203
Bur-Sin, 24, 176, 177, 193
Butcher, 110
Butter-milk, 188
Buxton, Mr., 10, 205

Calah (Nimrûd), 3, 83, 85
Calendar, 167
Calumny, 122
Cambyses, 47
Camels, 141
Canals, 1; system of, 4, 12
Capes, 134
Caps, 134
Caravan-master, 140
Carchemish, 40
Carnelian, 177
Case-tablets, 159
Cattle breeder, 4
Cedars, Forest of, 73; of Lebanon, 60
Cedar-wood, magician's staff of, 121
Cemetery, 189, 193
Censer, 135
Centaurus, 87
Chairs, 194
Chalcedony, 185
Chaldeans, 34, 36, 116, 147; land of the, 2
Chariot, of the god, 137; of the sun, 85

Chariots, 193
Charters, Babylonian, 124
Chastity, 130
Chedorlaomer, 28
Chemistry, 169
Childbirth, 115; goddess of, 208
Childlessness, 133
Children, custody of, 102; exposure of, 131; substitution of, 102
China, 169
Chinese, 9
Choirs in temples, 139
Choppers, 209
Chorus girls, 157
Chronicles, 163, 164
Chronology, 11, 163
Cicero, 93
Circumcision, 132
Citadel of Babylon, 52
City of Abraham, 7
City-States, 96
Clapping of hands, 139
Cleanliness, personal, 135
Climate, 134
Cloaks, 134
Clothes, 134; chests for, 157
Code of Laws, 96 ff.; of Khammurabi, 16, 27; of Urukagina, 16
Coffins, 144, 177; pottery, 53; slipper, 144
Colchis, 3
Colleges, 157
Columns, wooden, at Kish, 187
Commemorations, 145
Commentaries, 162
Commerce, 140
Communion of living and dead, 145
Compasses, 198
Concubine, the status of, 102
Concubines, 133
Cones, inscribed clay, 15, 193

Constantinople, 48
Contract tablets, 30
Convent of Bêl-shalti-Nannar, 196, 197
Copper, 141; figures of animals in, 180
Corn-grinder, 134
Corvee, 125
Cosseans, 84
Couch of the god, 137
Cow-byre, 191
Cows, milking of, 188
Creation, the, 80, 139; Story of the, 63 ff., 80, 110; Seven Tablets of, 63
Crescents on bricks, 180
Croesus, 44
Crops, 4
Crown, the horned, 106
Crystal, 179, 185
Ctesiphon, 48
Cube root, 167
Cuneiform, 147, 148, 152
Cushions, 134
Cyaxares, 40
Cylinders, inscribed baked clay, 165
Cylinder seals, 159, 209
Cymbals, 139
Cyprus, 18, 141
Cyrus I, 47
Cyrus II, 44, 45, 183

Dada-ilum, 197
Dagon, 83
Damgalnunna, 84
Damkina, 84
Daniel, Book of, 183
Darius I, 148, 156
Darius III, 48
Dates, 141; clusters of, 194
Dating of documents, 31, 70, 163
Day and Night, divisions of, 167

Dead, cult of the, 145; disposal of the, 143; positions of in grave, 144; the unburied, 110
Death, 91, 118
Decimal system, 167
Decorations, medical, 172
Deification of Kings, 24
Dekans, the Thirty-Six, 68, 168
Delitzsch, F., 180
Della Valle, Pietro, 51
Delta, 2
Depilatories, 136
Dêr, 7, 113, 124, 126, 159
Dêr on Tigris, 38
Desertion, husband's or wife's, 102
Diadin, 3
Dialects, 162
Diarbakr, 20
Diet , 136
Dikdikkah, Cemetery of, 193
Dilbat, 87
Dilmun, 140
Diodorus quoted, 52, 80, 93, 167, 168
Diorite, 141
Dirges, 143
Diseases caused by devils, 170
Dissection of bodies, 172
Distich, 106
Divination, 116, 120, 147
Diviners, 109
Divorce, 102, 133
Divorcement, Bill of, 133
Dîyâlâ river, 3
Doctor, penalties of the unskilful, 103
Dog of Aesculapius, 172
Dogs, models of, 209
Door of the Underworld, 91
Dove, 77
Dowry, 130, 132
Dragon, 117; of Babylon, 52

Dragon-goddess, 94
Draught-board, 136
Dreams, interpretation of, 139
Dress of priests and others, 134
Drowning, 100
Drums, 139, 198
Dudu, 21
Duku, 81
Dumon, R., 173
Dumuzi, 86
Dungi (Shulgi), 23, 24, 180, 181, 187, 189, 196
Dura, plain of, 184
Dûr-ilu, 100, 170
Dûr Kuri-galzu, 33
Dûr Papsukal, 36
Dykes, 6
Dynasties of kings, 163

Ea, 20, 54, 65, 77, 84, 90, 111, 116, 118, 170; author of magic, 114; the heaven of, 80
Eabani (Enkidu), 73
Eagle of Etana, 114
Eagle, lion-headed, 188
E-Anna of Erech, 64, 72, 83
Eannadu, 12
E-Apsû, 84, 176
E-babbara, 178
Ebers Papyrus, 172
Eclipse, 43, 121, 164, 168
Edfu, 85
E-dublal-makh, 196
Education of children, 132
Egibi and Sons, 158
E-Gig-Par, 196
E-gish-shir-gal, 85, 196
Egypt, 2, 167; Ashur-banipal's conquest of, 40
Egyptians in Palestine, 40
E-hul-hul, 43
E-kharsag, 180

E-kharsag-kurkurru, 88
E-khul-khul, 85
E-Kur of Nippur, 64, 81, 100
Elam, 5, 10, 140
Elamites, 13, 19, 22, 25, 38, 39, 124, 182, 198; writing of the, 148
Eldred, J., 51
Elephants, hides of, 141
Ellasar, 28
Elul, 186; the Second, 167
Elvend, Mount, 149
E-makh, 56
E-mete-ur-sag, 87, 181, 205, 206
E-mutbalum, 28
Enakalli, 12, 14
Enannadu I, 14
Enannadu II, 15
Enannaduma, 155
Enannatum, 196
En-anum, 87
En-dagga, 87
Enedôrachos, 71
Enetarzi, 15
E-nin-makh, 183, 196
E-ninnû, 21
Enki, 20, 23, 84, 99, 176
Enkidu, 73, 74, 79, 93; spirit of returns to earth, 79
Enlil (Bêl), 12, 16, 20, 49, 63, 74, 76, 81, 110, 177, 192, 204
Enlil-tabni-bullit, 125
Enlitarzi, 15
Enmeduranki, 71, 115
Enmesharra, 92
Ennugi, 74
Entemena, 15, 185
Entrails, omens from, 168
Enurta, 54, 56, 79, 94, 118, 126
Enzu, 85, 93
Epidaurus, 172
Eponyms, 163
Equator, 83

Equinoxes, 168
Era of Alexander the Great, 168
Era of Abyssinians, 168
Era of Copts, 168
Erech, 13, 21, 63, 72, 78, 107, 113, 197
Ereshkigal, 81, 87, 111, 112, 145
Eridu (Abû Shahrên), 6, 23, 49, 63, 84, 114, 116, 118, 140, 170, 175; seaport of, 175
Eridu, excavations at, 175
Erua, 108
E-sagila, 49, 54, 57, 59, 63, 85
Esarhaddon, 38
E-sharra, 88, 126
E-shumedu, 83
Etana, 92, 204; Legend of, 115
E-temen-an-ki, 53, 60
E-temen-ni-il, 195
Etimmu, 89, 117
E-tur-ka-lamma, 163, 207
Eulaeus, 125
E-Ulmash, 86
E-ulmash-shakin-shumi, 35
Euphrates, 2, 64; change of course of the, 4, 56, 206
Europe, 169
E-uru-gal, 87
Evil-Eye, 119
Evil spell, 119
Evil-Merodach, 42
Evil-speaking, 123
Excavations in Babylonia: By J. E. Taylor (1854), 175; by R. C.Thompson (1918), 176 f.; by H.R. Hall (1919), 180 f.; by C. L. Woolley (1921–25), 181 f.; by S. Langdon (1923–25), 203
Exorcists, 118
Exports, 140
Eye for an eye, 102
Eye paint, 135

Ezekiel quoted, 198
E-zida, 23, 48, 57, 60, 192
E-zu-ab, 100

Face behind him, 91
Fallâh, 129; fallâhîn, 16
Fârah, 7
Feast, the funeral, 144
Federigo, Cesare, 51
Feldspar, 185
Fennerley, Mr., 53
Ferry in the Underworld, 91
Fever, 118
Field-labourers, 199
Figures, magical, 118
Fire-god, 94
Fisherman, 110
Fitch, R., 51
Fitzgerald, G. M., 186
Flint, weapons of, 179
Flood, the, 11, 83, 93; Kings before the, 163; Story of the, 70 ff. Flowers in stone, 187
Fluxes, 169
Forks, 209
Four Quarters of the World, 20, 99
Fowler, 110
Frât Su, 3
Freemen, 128
Frieze of bulls, 187
Fringe, 134
Furniture, 134

Gadd, C.J., 40, 72, 148, 163, 164, 167, 186
Gallû, 89, 117
Games of chance, 136
Gandash, 31
Garden, Hanging, the, 52
Gate, Upper, of Babylon, 61
Gate of Beltis, 60
Gate of God, 49

Gates of Hell, the Seven, 87
Gatumdug, 13
Genouillac, H. de, 203
Genuflections, 136
Geography, 169
Geometrical Progression, 167
Geometry, 167
Geshtin, 86
Geuljik, 3
Ghost, 118
Gibil, 83, 93
Gilgamish, 93; Epic of, 70 ff., 110;
    seeks immortality, 78
Gimillum, 28, 96
Gimil-Sin, 24, 193
Gishzida, 114
Glazes for pottery, 176
Glazing on bricks, 52
Gobryas, 44
God, daily worship of, 123
Gods, early, 6; list of, 86; the 3,600,
    88
Gods of healing, the Eight, 170
Gods and goddesses, 81, 92
Gold, alluvial, 141
Gordon, Dr. G. B., 182
Gossip, 123
Grace before meals, 136
Grain, 141
Grammar, 160
Graves, 144, 189; at Kish, 203;
    Sumerian, 172
Great Man, 7
Great Mountain, 83
Great Swamp, 4
Greek Theatre at Babylon, 55
Grotefend, G. F., 148
Grove of Life, 49
Gubaru, 44
Gudea, 22, 23, 87, 208; clay cylinders
    of, 22

Gugulanna, 87
Gula, 60, 83, 87, 126, 171
Gungunu, 196
Gunidu, 12
Gutians, 21

Hair, dressing of, 135
Hairpins, 184, 209
Halévy, J., 10
Hall, H. R., his discovery at Tall al-
    'Ubêd, 175 ff. Hall of Justice, 194
Hall of Pillars, 208
Hammawind, 12
Hands, cutting off of, 102
Harappa, 148
Harbouring of slaves, 129
Harps, large and small, 139
Harran, 85; Moon-god of, 43
Harût, 56
Hatchets, 209
Haynes the excavator, 175
Headcloth, 134
Healing, art of, 170; goddesses of,
    94
Heaven, 80; creation of the, 65
Heavens, the Three, 80; the Seven,
    80
Hells, the Seven, 81
Henmemt, chap. ix 222n[1]
Hennu Boat, 138
Herbs, decoctions of, 118; medici-
    nal, 173
Herodotus quoted, 53
Her-Tuati, 65
Hesketh, Mr., 203
Hiddekel, 3
High priestess, 140
Hillah, 57, 202
Hilprecht, H.V., 180
Hincks, E., 10, 149
Hindîyah Canal, 58

Hindu Kûsh, 177
History, Synchronous, 164
Hît, 2
Hittite Language, 163
Hittites, 32, 163, 169; capture
    Babylon, 30
Hoes, stone, 177
Horse, the, 31, 118, 141, 188; of the
    god's chariot, 135
Horus, 84; of Edfu, 85
House of Dust, 92
House of Life, 201
House of the Mountain, 42
House of Tablets, 158
House of Water, 65
Houses of mud and reeds, 133, 177
House-breaker, 101
House Spirit, 82
Humrah, 53
Hunter, 109
Hurricane, 117
Huts, daub and wattle, 188; of reed
    mats, 6, 134
Hydra, 87
Hydraulic machinery, 53
Hyksos, 31
Hymns, 106
Hystaspes, 148, 152

Ibex, 84
Ibi-Sin, 24, 183
Ibn Hawkal, 170
Ibni Martu, 28
Ibn Jubayr, 170
Id-dugal-la, 3
Idigna, 3
Idiklat, 3
Igigi, the, 88, 99, 106, 108
Igigi, king, 21
Il-abrat, 114
Ilbaba, 205

Ili, 15
Iltasadum, 204
Ilulu, 21
Imgig, 181
Imgur Bêl, 53, 60
Imgur Enlil, 43
Imi, 21
Immortality, 91, 114, 172
Incantations, 116, 145
Incense, 123; for houses, 135; Stand
    for, 137
India, 141
Infant mortality, 131
Inghara, 207
Inlay, 208; limestone and shell, 187
Innina, 86
Innini, 208
Innini Ishtar, 207
Insects, 135
Intimidation, 101
Irkalla, 91
Iron, 141
Irra, 88, 94; Legend of, 113; Song of,
    108
Irrigation, 1
Ishbi-irra, 25
Ishkhara, 73, 86
Ishkun-Sin, 22
Ishkur, 86
Ishme-Dagan, 26
Ishnunak, 20
Ishtar, 26, 56, 73, 76, 83, 86, 88, 92,
    93, 125, 136, 163, 205; descent of,
    into Hell, 111; maidens of, 123,
    140; palace of, 61
Ishtar Gate, 52
Ishum, 113
Isin, 25, 87, 196
Isis and Ra, 81
Israelites, 82
Itineraries, 170

Ivory, 141
Iyyar, 168

Jasper, 181
Jazirah, 9
Jerusalem, 40, 42
Jesus, son of Sirach, 122
Jews at Babylon, 56
Jones, Felix, 2, 58
Jones, Sir Harford, 62
Josiah, King of Judah, 40
Judah, tribute of, 40
Jupiter, 58, 84, 85, 168

Kadashman-Enlil, 32
Kadashman Kharbe, 32
Ka-Dingirra-ki, 99
Kâdîsîyah, 48
Kal'ah Sharkât, 3, 88
Kaldu, 38
Kara Su, 3
Karbala, 57, 202
Kar-Duniash, 32
Kashtiliash I and II, 32, 33
Kasr at Babylon, 50, 52, 56
Kassites, 31, 113, 124, 189
Khabban, 125
Khabûr, 3
Khallab, 26
Khammurabi, 9, 16, 49, 70, 160, 163,
    165, 172, 205; against magic, 116;
    Code of Laws of, 96 ff.; Conquests
    of, 32; letter of, 27
Khar-sag-kalamma, 205
Khashkhamer, 22
Khiklu, 113
Khimitu, 117
Khubur, 87, 91
Khumbaba, 73
Khumbanigash, 38
Khumuttabal, 91
Khushbisag, 87

Kidinnu the astronomer, 169
Kifl, 57, 202
Kigallu, 91
Kilulla-guzalal, 24
King, the, 6, 126 f.
King Lists, 30, 31
King, L. W., 28, 108, 121, 164
Kingu, 66–69, 95
Kish, 7, 10, 12, 17, 56, 87, 150, 165;
    excavations at, 203 ff.
Kishar, 65, 95
Kislev, 167
Kissing the feet, 137
Kisurra, 7, 86
Kizallu, 165
Knives, cutting the body with, 143
Koldewey, Dr., 50, 51, 55
Kubau, 205
Kudur-Mabug, 27, 183, 196
Kuechler, F., 173
Kûfah, 57, 202
Kuffah, 80
Kug-bau, 205
Kurds, 12
Kuri-galzu, 32, 193, 195, 196; III, 33
Kur-lil (?), 182
Kûrnah, 3, 203
Kurnugia, 81
Kutaean, 113
Kût al-'Amârah, 4
Kûthâh, 7, 87, 159
Kuti, 45
Kutasar, 87

Labartu, 89, 117, 131
Labâshi-Marduk, 42
Labasu, 117
Labbu, 83, 110
Lagamal, 87
Lagash, 7, 12, 21, 185; city wall of,
    13; Library of, 159
Lake of temple, 138

Lake Wân, 155
Lakhamu, 95
Lakhmu, 64, 95
Lamassu, 89
Lamps, 134; in temple, 138
Lancet, copper, 103, 173
Landmark, 124
Land measurement and measures,
    166
Land of No Return, 87
Land surveying, 158
Lane, Col., 203
Langdon, Prof. S., 10, 68, 122, 150;
    his excavations at Kish, 203 f.
    Lapis lazuli, 141, 185; paste of,
    141
Larsa, 7, 86, 175, 195; dynasty of, 26
Law, Laws, 158, 165; Codes of, 95 ff.,
    165
Law, the Civil, 90; the Commercial,
    165; Moral and Religious, 90
Layard, Sir A. H., 52, 203
Lead, 141
Lebanon, 60
Leedes, W., 51
Legends, 110
Legrain, Dr. L., 201
Leopard, 117
Letters and Dispatches, 165
Libations, 145
Libit Ishtar, 26
Librarian of Temple, 159
Libraries, 158
Library of Kish, 201
Library of Nabû at Nineveh, 72
Life after death, 142
Lil, 84
Lilith, 89
Lîlîtu, 89, 117
Lîlû, 117
Limb for a limb, 103
Limestone, 141

Line of flax, 198
Linen, 134
Lion, 86, 104; of Babylon, 52; of Irra,
    113
Lions, colossal, 137
Lists, bilingual and explanatory, 162;
    of kings, 163
Literature, Babylonian, 158; profane
    and sacred, 105
Liturgies, 207
Liver, sheep's, 120
Lockets, 184
Loftus, Sir W. K., 10, 175
Loin string, 134
Lower Sea, 16, 59
Lugal, 7
Lugal-anda, 15
Lugal-andanu-shuga, 15
Lugalbanda, 73, 86, 212
Lugal-dul-azuga, 63
Lugal-shag-engur, 12, 204
Lugaltarsi, 204
Lugal-ushum-gal, 21
Lugal-zaggisi, 16
Lullubaean, 113
Lullubi, 124
Lumashi, 67
Lydia, 44
Lyre, 139

Maat plant, 200
Mace-head, 12, 197
Mackay, E., 203
Magan, 20
Magic, 115; black, 106, 120; white,
    117
Magician, 147
Makan, 141
Makh, 84
Makhkhu priests, 139
Maklu Series, 116
Malachite, 185

Mama, 84
Mammitu, 87, 92
Man, creation of, 64, 65, 89; the first, 96
Manishtusu, 19
Manungal, 87
Map of the World, 170
Maps, 170
Mar, 85
Marble, 141
Marchesvan, 168
Marduk, 45, 47, 48, 49, 63, 80, 84, 88, 94, 124, 176; Chief of gods, 66 f.; the Fifty names of, 69; the god ONE, 81; Hymn to, 107; image of, 30; shrine of, 54; Temple of, 97
Marduk-balatsu-ikbi, 36
Marduk-nadin-akhê, 34
Marduk-shâpik-zêri, 33
Marduk-zakir-shumi, 36
Maria, F. V., 52
Marriage, 132; ceremony of, 127; rejoicings at, 136; contract of, 132
Mars, 58, 87, 168
Marshall, Sir J., 148
Marût, 56
Mashu, Mount, 74
Mason, 104
Mat-burial graves, 208
Materia medica, 172
Mathematics, 166
Mats, 141; burial, 177
Medes 40, 164
Median Wall, 2
Medicaments, 172
Medicine, 87, 158, 170; how mixed and taken, 172
Mediterranean Sea, 16, 18, 59, 97, 141
Mêdûm, Pyramid of, 192
Megiddo, 40

Meli-shipak, 32
Mer, 86
Merchants, 110
Mercury, 58, 85, 168
Merodach Baladan, 38, 205
Mes-anni-padda, 181, 185
Mesilim, 12, 204
Meskem-Nannar, 186
Mesopotamia, 2
Metals, debasing of, 169; working in, 5, 169
Midnight, 167
Mineralogy, 174
Minor, the estate of, 101
Miracle plays, 111, 139
Miscarriage, 103
Mitanians, 33
Moat of Babylon, 55, 60
Mohenjo-Daro. 148
Monkeys, 194
Monogamy, 133
Monotheism, 82
Monsters, fabulous, 110
Monstrosities, 121
Month, the intercalary, 167
Months of the year, 168
Moon, 58, 68; observations of, 168
Moon-god, 43, 94, 194; of Babylon and Harran, 43
Morgan, J. de, 20, 98, 148, 177, 182
Mosul, 202
Mother-of-pearl, 141, 187, 208
Mountains of Sunrise and Sunset, 83
Mourners, women, 143
Mukaddasî, 170
Mukayyar, 7, 201; excavations at by Taylor, Thompson, Hall and Woolley, 175 ff.
Mummu, 65, 84, 95
Murâd Su, 3
Murajib, 179

Murashu, 158
Museum at Ur, 196
Mushezib Marduk, 38
Mushkînu, 128
Music, 138
Musicians, 157
Musyân, Tepé, 177
Myths, Babylonian, 110

Nabonidus, 17, 36, 43–44, 47, 130, 158, 183, 189, 193
Nabopolassar, 36, 40, 53, 55, 60, 163, 164; canal of, 60
Nabû (Nebo), 35, 47, 54, 57, 85, 108, 158
Nabû-apal-iddina, 35
Nabû-mukinapli, 35
Nabû-nadin-zêri, 36
Nabû-rimannu, 169
Nahrawân Canal, 4
Nakedness, 134
Namar, 125
Name, giving of the, 132
Nammu, 84
Namtar, Namtaru, 87, 92, 111, 117
Namtartu, 92
Nanâ, 83, 126; Gate of, 60
Nannai, 163
Nannar, 85, 94, 153, 188, 194
Nanni, 83
Nanum, 21
Naplanum, 26
Naram Sin, 17, 20
Nâsirîyah, 176
Nazi-Maruttash, 32
Nebo, 35, 85, 94
Nebuchadnezzar I, 34, 124
Nebuchadnezzar II, 40, 52, 54, 137, 158, 165, 169, 183, 195, 206; his conquests, 58; image of, 183; prayer of, 60; his works at Ur, 44
Necho, 40

Nenu, 64
Neolithic Period, 49
Nergal, 87, 92, 93, 94, 108, 118, 126; visits Hell, 112; of Ur, 44
Nergal-Sharezer, 42
Neriglissar, 42
Nesi-Amsu, 64
Net, 67
Newberrie, J., 51
Newton, F. G., 183, 201
New Year's Day, 76; Festival, 35, 43, 44, 139
Nibiru, 68
Niebuhr, K., 52, 148
Night, phantoms of the, 118
Nikkal, 85
Nile, 2
Nimitti Bêl, 60
Nimrod, 58
Nimrûd, 3, 85; Library of, 160
Ninâ, 13
Ninazu, 87, 92, 172
Ninegal, 87
Nineveh, 3, 32; Fall of, 40, 164
Ningal, 85, 195, 196
Ningirda, 87
Ningirsu, 12, 15, 21, 87, 181, 204
Ningishzida, 87, 172
Ninkarrak, 87
Ninkharsag, 12, 171, 180, 187, 189, 207
Ninkhursagga, 84
Ninkigal, 95, 117
Ninlil, 83, 88, 95
Ninmakh, 84; Temple of, 52
Nin-Mar, 85
Ninmug, 88
Ninni, 86
Ninshakh, 15
Ninsun, 86
Nintinugga, 87
Nintu, 84

Nintud, 207
Ninursalla, 83
Ninurta, 83, 87, 171
Nin-uru, 87
Ninzalli, 83
Nippur (Niffar, Nuffar), 7, 20, 49, 63, 83, 88, 100, 113, 177; Library of, 158
Nisan, 168
Nisir, 76
Noah, 71
Nomads, 5
Norris, E., 149
Notation, musical, 139
Nubia, 141
Nudimmud, 84, 94
Nun-ki, 100
Nur-Adad, 178, 193
Nurimmer, 178
Nurse, 102, 131
Nusku, 84

Obedience, 123
Obelisk of Manishtusu, 19
Obelisks, 165
Obsidian, 177
Oefele, F. von, 173
Offerings, 90, 93, 107, 123, 136; to the dead, 145
Oil, 141, 144; medicated, 173
Olivier, M., 52
Omens, 120, 147
Opartes, 71
Operations, medical, 172
Opis, 9, 34, 44
Oppert, Dr. J., 203
Osiris, 65, 92, 199

Pabilsag, 87
Palestine, 40, 155
Palm, 198
Pamirs, 177

Panjab, 148
Papsukhal, 209
Papyrus, 149
Parchment, 149
Parents, honouring of, 123
Par-Sagale, 164
Parthians, 48, 177, 206
Pât, 129
Patesi, 7
Pausanias, 172
Pearls, 141
Pedestal, inscribed, 197
Pehlevi, 148
Perâth, 3
Perfumes, 135
Persepolis, 148
Persia, 48, 155, 182
Persian Gulf, 3, 16, 59, 84, 142; the, 38 peoples of, 20
Persians, 48, 206
Pestle and mortar, 209
Pictographs, 148, 150, 157
Pigs, 194
Pillar altar, 138
Pillars at Kish, 208
Pins, obsidian, 177
Pir Husên, 20
Plague-god, 87, 94, 112
Plain, the Great, 2
Planets, 168
Plant, the life restoring, 78
Plaque from Kish, 150
Pliny, 167
Pluralists, 139
Poebel, A., 70
Polyandry, 133
Polygamy, 133
Pomades, 135
Population, 9
Porphyry, 141
Porter, Sir R. Ker, 203
Pottery, 141; hand-made, 188;

painted, 207; pre-historic, 179, 182, 196; wheel-made, 189; from Kish, 209
Powers of the air, 66
Prayer, 90, 106, 123; prayer of Nebuchadnezzar II, 61
Precious stones, imitations of, 169
Preserved Tablet, 65
Priestesses, 140, 157
Priest Kings of Lagash, 15
Priests as physicians, 170; orders of the, 139
Procession Street, 54
Prophets, 121
Prose, rhythmic, 106
Prostrations, 123
Proto-Chaldean, 10
Psalms, Penitential, 106
Ptah-Tanen, 65
Ptolemy the Geographer, 2
Pûlu (Tiglath Pileser III), 38
Purattu, 3
Puzur Bêl, 76
Puzur-mama, 21
Pylons, 91

Quarries, 22
Quartzite, 141
Querns, 177

Ra, 116; and Isis, 83
Rabmag, 42
Rainbow, 77
Ra Khepera, 200
Rameses II, 12
Rammân, 86, 94
Rammân-apil-iddina, 35
Rammân-shum-nasir, 33
Rampart of Babylon, 61
Rape, 102
Rassam, H., 52, 58, 203
Rauwolf, 51

Raven, 77
Rawlinson, Sir H. C, 10, 19, 52, 57, 148, 175, 192, 203
Rebirth, 189
Record Office, 158
Red Sea, 141, 179
Reed-chests, 131; flute, 138; mats, 134, 141; measuring, 198
Reeds, 144
Rekhit, chap. ix 222n[1]
Repentance, 91
Reservoir, 16; and dam, 13
Resurrection, 189
Retribution, 123
Rice, D. T., 203
Rich, C. J., 52
Rimmon, 60, 86
Rim-Sin, 27
Rimush, 19, 165, 185
Ring-gold, 141
Rîsh-Adad, 20
Ritti Marduk, 124
River, the, 2, 3
Robber, highway, 101
Rock-salt, 141

Sâbum, 27
Sachan, 172
Sackcloth, 143
Sacrifice, 119, 124
Sacy, Silvestre de, 148
Sadaranunna, 84
Sagila, 49
St. Albert, E. de, 52
Sakkârah, Pyramids of, 192
Salt, 144
Salves, 135
Samsuditana, 30
Samsuiluna, 30
Samugan, 92
Sanctuary, 137
Sandals, 135, 141

Sandstone, 141

Sankarah, 7, 86; excavations at, 175

Sardonyx, 185

Sargon I of Agade, 17–18, 131, 171, 204

Sargon II of Assyria, 18, 38

Sarpânîtum, 30, 85

Sarzec, E. de, 208

Sassanians, 48, 148

Saturn, 58, 83, 168

Scaraboid, 188

Scheil, J. V., 53, 70, 98, 148, chap. x 223n[1]

Schnabel, P., 169

School children, teaching of, 157

School exercises, 196

Schools, 160

Scorpion men, 74

Scribes, 130, 157

Scythe, metal, 209

Scythians, 40, 164

Sea-Country, Kings of the, 30

Sea, the World, 88; serpent, 111

Seal of Life, 111

Sebat, 168

Seleucia, 48, 56

Seleucus I, 48, 56

Semiramis, Wall of, 2

Semites, 9, 24

Sennacherib, 36, 205

Serpent, two-headed, 172

Serpents, 61; and staff, 87

Serpent Gryphon, 84

Serpent River, 4

Seti I, 200

Settlement, prehistoric, 188

Seven devils of Irra, 113

Seven Evil Spirits, 117

Seven Gates, 111

Sexagesimal system, 167

Shakh, 13

Shala, 86

Shalash, 83

Shalmaneser III, 36

Shalmaneser V, 36

Shamash, 17, 60, 76, 85, 94, 99, 114, 118, 123, 136; Hymn to, 108; of Sippar, 34 ff.

Shamash-shum-ukin, 39

Shamshi-Adad VI, 36

Shangu priest, 139

Shaving, 135

Shawl, 134

Shar-gali-sharri, 21

Sharru-kin, 17

Shasu, 34

Shatrah, 7

Shatt al-'Arab, 3

Shatt al-Hayy, 4

Sheep, sacrificial, 137; model of liver of, 121

Shedu, 89

Shell, plaque in, 196

Shells, freshwater, 179

Shenirda, 86

Shinar, 4, 27

Shidlam-ta-uddua, 24

Shirpu Series, 116

Shirpurla (ki), 7, 159

Shirt, 134

Shoes, 134

Shu, 200

Shubula, 88

Shudurul, 21

Shulpa'e, 84

Shulgi, 23, 180, 181, 196

Shulmânu, 88

Shulmânitu, 88

Shumalia, 126

Shumer, chap. i 221n[1]

Shuqamuna, 84

Shuruppak, 7, 71, 74

Shûsh, 20, 97, 144, 148, 177, 182, 198

Shushan the Palace, 19, 177
Shu-Sin, 24
Shutruk-Nakhkhunte, 20, 33
Sickles, clay, 183
Sickness, 86 demons of, 112; the quaking, 117; the 62 kinds of, 111
Siduri-Sabitu, 74
Silli-Adad, 196
Silver, 141
Simmash-Shipak, 35
Sin, the Moon-god, 43, 60, 79, 85, 118
Sin against the gods, 90; loosed by prayer, 124
Sinai, 140, 179
Sin-balatsu-ikbi, 193, 196
Sind, 148
Singing in temples, 139
Sin-idinnam, 29, 196
Sin-muballit, 27
Sin-shar-ishkum, 40, 164
Sippar, 7, 33, 34, 44, 72, 86, 115, 169, 205; river of, 164; of Anunitum, 34
Sirdu, 86
Sirius, 83
Sirrush, 51
Sîru, 126
Sittace, 2
Siwan, 168
Skin, 149; skins, 141
Skull from Kish, 10, 208
Slave, the, 129; the runaway, 101, 129
Slave trade, 141
Slavery, domestic, 132
Slings, 177
Smith, George, 19, 53, 121, 149
Smith, Sidney, 43, 44, 53, 89, 148, 164, 183, 206
Snake and Etana, 115
Soane, Sir J., 200

Soap, 136, chap. ix 222n[2]
Sockets for doors, 188
Songs, 105
South wind, 114, 117
Spear-heads, 209
Speech, hasty, 122
Spells, 116, 147; illegality of, 100
Spindle-wheels, 179
Spirit of house or village, 81
Spirits of heaven and earth, 116
Square root, 167
Stag, bronze, 209
Standard Inscription, 62
Stars, study of the, 168
Statues of gods, 137
Stele of Vultures, 13
Stewards of the gods, 139
Stilus, 85, 206
Stone Age, 5
Stone, trade in, 179
Story, J., 51
Strabo, 2, 52, 55, 55
Stripe for stripe, 103
Subarian, 113
Sumer, 6; limits of, 6; and Akkad, 47; language of, 10, 160
Sumerians, 2, 5; origin of the, 9
Sumuabum, 27
Sumu-ilum, 196
Sumulaila, 27
Sun, 58
Sunburn, 135
Sun-clocks, 167
Sun-god, 94, 99; of Sippar, 17, 20; Tablet of the, 35, 158
Sunrise, 80
Sunset, 80
Surgeon, 172
Susa, 19, 40, 97, 144
Susian language, 149
Sutaean, 113
Sutû Semites, 34, 35

Swallow, 77
Syllabaries, 160
Synchronous History, the, 164
Syria, 40, 140; desert of, 1
Syrians, 22

Tâbisubûrshu, 61
Table, 134
Tablet of Destiny or Fate, 65, 66, 67, 83, 85, 111
Tablet of Wisdom, 113
Takht-i-Jamshîd, 148
Takrit, 2
Talbot, H. Fox, 10
Tales, 105
Tall Abû-Sakhâri, 7
Tall al-Amârnah tablets, 32, 165
Tall al-Bandar, 207
Tall al-Jabarah, 179; Tall al-Judêdah, 179
Tall al-Lahm, 7, 179; excavations at, 175
Tall al-'Ubêd, 7, 180 ff.
Tall Dalêm, 7
Tall Ibrâhîm, 7
Tall Lôh, 7, 22, 180, 208
Tall Sifr, 175
Tall Tawaiyil, 179
Tall Yôkha, 7
Tall Zurghul, 7
Tambourine, 139; players on, 157
Tammuz, 86, 92, 111, 112, 114
Tashmitu, 85, 108
Taurus, 141
Taylor, J. E., 175, 189
Tebet, 168
Teispes, 47
Têma, 43
Temenos, at Kish, 207; at Ur, 194
Temple of Enurta, 54
Temple of Ishtar, 55
Temple of Nabû, 55

Temples, 6; Sumerian, 137
Temple-tower, 176, 189
Temple women, 53, 101, 193
Tepé Musyân, 182
Terra-cotta, figures in, 185
Teshub, 86
Teumman, 39
Tharthar, 3
Theft, 101
Thief, burning of the, 101
Thompson, R. C, 119, 173
Thoth, 85
Thothmes III, 32
Throne-bearers, 118
Thunderbolt, 67
Thureau-Dangin, F., 107
Tiâmat, 65 ff., 80, 84, 94
Tidal, 28
Tiglath Pileser I, 34
Tiglath Pileser III, 38, 205
Tigris, 3, 20, 64
Til, 3
Tin, 141
Tinctures, 172
Tintira, 49
Tirigan, 21
Tishpak, 87
Tishritu, 168
Tisri, 168
Tools, building, 198
Toothache, 119
Tooth for tooth, 103
Tortoises, 194
Tower of Babel, 50, 51, 53; stages of, 50 ff.
Towers of Babylon, 50
Trade routes, 141
Tray for food, 136
Triads of devils, 117
Trowel (?), 198
Trumpet, 136
Truth, 201

Tuat, 201
Tube, the physician's, 173
Tukuls in Sûdân, 134
Tukulti-Enurta I, 33
Tunic, 134
Turanians, 9
Turbans, 134
Tutu, 85
Tyre, 42

Ubara-Tutu, 44
Ugme, 21
Ulâ, 125
Ukhêmar, 7, 201, 203
Ululai, 38
Umma, 7, 12
Ummu-Khubur, 66
Underworld, 81, 86, 91, 142
Unguents, 112, 135, 145, 173
Unir-kidur-makh, 205
Universe-Mother, 65
Upi, 9
Upper Sea, 16, 59
Upshukkinaku, 66, 81
Ur of the Chaldees, 7, 13, 53, 85,
    113, 175, 201; high priestess of,
    195; see Excavations.
Urartians, 155
Urash, 87
Ur-bau, 21
Ur-Engur, 23
Ur-Enurta, 26
Urigallu, 139
Ur-Ilbaba, 205
Urlumma, 14
Ur-mama, 21
Ur-Nammu, 22, 176, 177, 180, 183,
    189, 193; bricks of, 152, 153;
    canals of, 198; stele of, 194
Ur-Ninâ, 12, 182, 204
Ur-Ningirsu, 23
Ur-Shanabi, 74, 78

Uruk (Erech), 7, 83, 204
Urukagina, 15
Uru-Khegal, 21
Uta-Napishtim, 71, 74, 75, 76, 77, 78,
    134
Utu, 85
Utuhegal, 197
Utukku, 117, 146

Vampires, 145
Van (Wân), 155
Vaulted Building, the, 52
Vegetation, 1
Venus, 58, 86, 168
Verdict, 100
Village communities and gods, 6
Viper, 117
Virgins, 130
Virolleaud, C, 173
Vocabularies, 160

Wailers, 143
Wall from Kish to Babylon, 206
Warad-Sin, 27, 193, 196
Wardum, 128
Warka, 7, 83, 204; excavations at,
    175 f.
Warlocks, 119
Washing of hands, 136
Wâsit, 4
Water, medicated or "holy," 118
Water, trial by, 166
Water of life, 112
Water-clocks, 167
Water-pots, 134
Waters of Death, 74
Way of the God, 107
Weaning, time of, 131
Weapons, 5, 189
Weaving, 177
Wedge writing, 147
Weeping before God, 123

Weights and measures, 23
Weld, H., 203
Well of temple, 188
Well with 3 shafts, 52
Wells, sinking of, 13
Wheat, 200
Whip, 103
Whirlwind, 117
Whiskers, 135
Wife, the childless, 101
Wilson, Sir A. T., 180
Wind-god, 94
Winds, the Four, 67
Wine merchant, 101
Wine, palm, 136
Wine shop, 101, 130
Witchcraft, 56
Witches, 119
Witnesses, 100
Wives, purchase of, 132
Woman, the strange, 123
Woolley, C. L., 44, 182 ff.
Words of power, 116
World, duration and end of, 93
World-Mother, 83
World-Ocean, 169, 176
World-Year, 93
Worm, the toothache, 119
Worship, public, 136, 183

Writing, art of 10, 147; cuneiform,
    148; pictorial, 148; oldest
    Sumerian, 209
Writing on the wall, 53
Writing materials, 150

Xenophon, 2
Xerxes I, 48, 55, 148
Xisûthros, 71

Year, the, 167

Zâb, Zâbh, the Great, 3, 201; the
    Little, 3
Zababa, 87
Zababa-shum-iddin, 33
Zamana, 87
Zanki, 34
Zedekiah, 42
Zehnpfund, R., 173
Zêr-bânîtu, 85
Zikkurat, 44, 50, 53; of Babylon, 58;
    of Borsippa, 57, 60; of Eridu,
    176; of Ukhêmar, 206; of Ur, 180
    ff.; clearing of, 189 ff.
Zodiac, 66, 68, 168
Zoology, 174
Zû, 83, 111

SUGGESTED READING

BLACK, JEREMY. *Reading Summerian Poetry.* London: Athlone Press, 1998.

BUDGE, SIR E. A. WALLIS. *By Nile and Tigris: A Narrative of Journeys in Egypt and Mesopotamia on Behalf of the British Museum Between the Years 1886 and 1913., VOLS. I–II.* London: John Murray, 1920.

DALLEY, STEPHANIE. *Myths for Mesopotamia: Creation, the Flood, Gilgamesh, and Others.* Oxford: Oxford University Press, 1989.

FOSTER, BENJAMIN R. *Before the Muses. An Anthology of Akkadian Literature, Vols. I–II.* Bethesda, MD: CDL Press, 1996.

KUHRT, AMELIE. *The Ancient Near East: C. 3000–300 BC, Vols. I–II.* London: Routledge, 1995.

NEMEY-NEJET, KAREN RHEA. *Daily Life in Ancient Mesopotamia.* Peabody, MA: Hendrickson, 2002.

VAN DE MIEROOP, MARC. *A History of the Ancient Near East, ca. 3000–323 BC.* Oxford: Blackwell, 2004.